NATIONAL UNIVERSITY
LIBRARY

D0713200

Psychology of the Americas
(PGPS-126)

Pergamon Titles of Related Interest

Bochner CULTURES IN CONTACT: Studies in Cross-cultural Interaction

Brislin CROSS-CULTURAL ENCOUNTERS: Face-to-Face Interaction

Jenkins THE PSYCHOLOGY OF THE AFRO-AMERICAN: A Humanistic Approach

Landis/Brislin HANDBOOK OF INTERCULTURAL TRAINING (3 volumes)

Marsella/Pedersen CROSS-CULTURAL COUNSELING AND PSYCHOTHERAPY

Morris SAYING AND MEANING IN PUERTO RICO: Some Problems in the Ethnography of Discourse

Related Journals*

ANNALS OF TOURISM

HABITAT INTERNATIONAL

INTERNATIONAL JOURNAL OF INTERCULTURAL RELATIONS

WORLD DEVELOPMENT

***Free specimen copies available upon request.**

PERGAMON GENERAL PSYCHOLOGY SERIES
EDITORS
Arnold P. Goldstein, *Syracuse University*
Leonard Krasner, *SUNY at Stony Brook*

Psychology of the Americas
Mestizo Perspectives on Personality and Mental Health

Manuel Ramirez, III
The University of Texas at Austin

Pergamon Press

New York Oxford Toronto Sydney Paris Frankfurt

Pergamon Press Offices:

U.S.A.	Pergamon Press Inc., Maxwell House, Fairview Park, Elmsford, New York 10523, U.S.A.
U.K.	Pergamon Press Ltd., Headington Hill Hall, Oxford OX3 0BW, England
CANADA	Pergamon Press Canada Ltd., Suite 104, 150 Consumers Road, Willowdale, Ontario M2J 1P9, Canada
AUSTRALIA	Pergamon Press (Aust.) Pty. Ltd., P.O. Box 544, Potts Point, NSW 2011, Australia
FRANCE	Pergamon Press SARL, 24 rue des Ecoles, 75240 Paris, Cedex 05, France
FEDERAL REPUBLIC OF GERMANY	Pergamon Press GmbH, Hammerweg 6, D-6242 Kronberg-Taunus, Federal Republic of Germany

Copyright © 1983 Pergamon Press Inc.

Library of Congress Cataloging in Publication Data

Ramirez, Manuel, 1937-
Psychology of the Americas.

(Pergamon general psychology series ; 126)
Includes index.
1. Personality and culture--North America.
2. Personality and culture--South America. 3. Psychiatry, Transcultural--North America. 4. Psychiatry, Transcultural--South America. I. Title. II. Series.
[DNLM: 1. Ethnic groups--Psychology--America.
2. Cross-cultural comparison. WA 305 R173p]
BF698.9.C8R35 1983 155.8′404201812 83-8135
ISBN 0-08-026311-9

All Rights reserved. No part of this publication may be reproduced, stored in a retrieval system or transmitted in any form or by any means: electronic, electrostatic, magnetic tape, mechanical, photocopying, recording or otherwise, without permission in writing from the publishers.

Printed in the United States of America

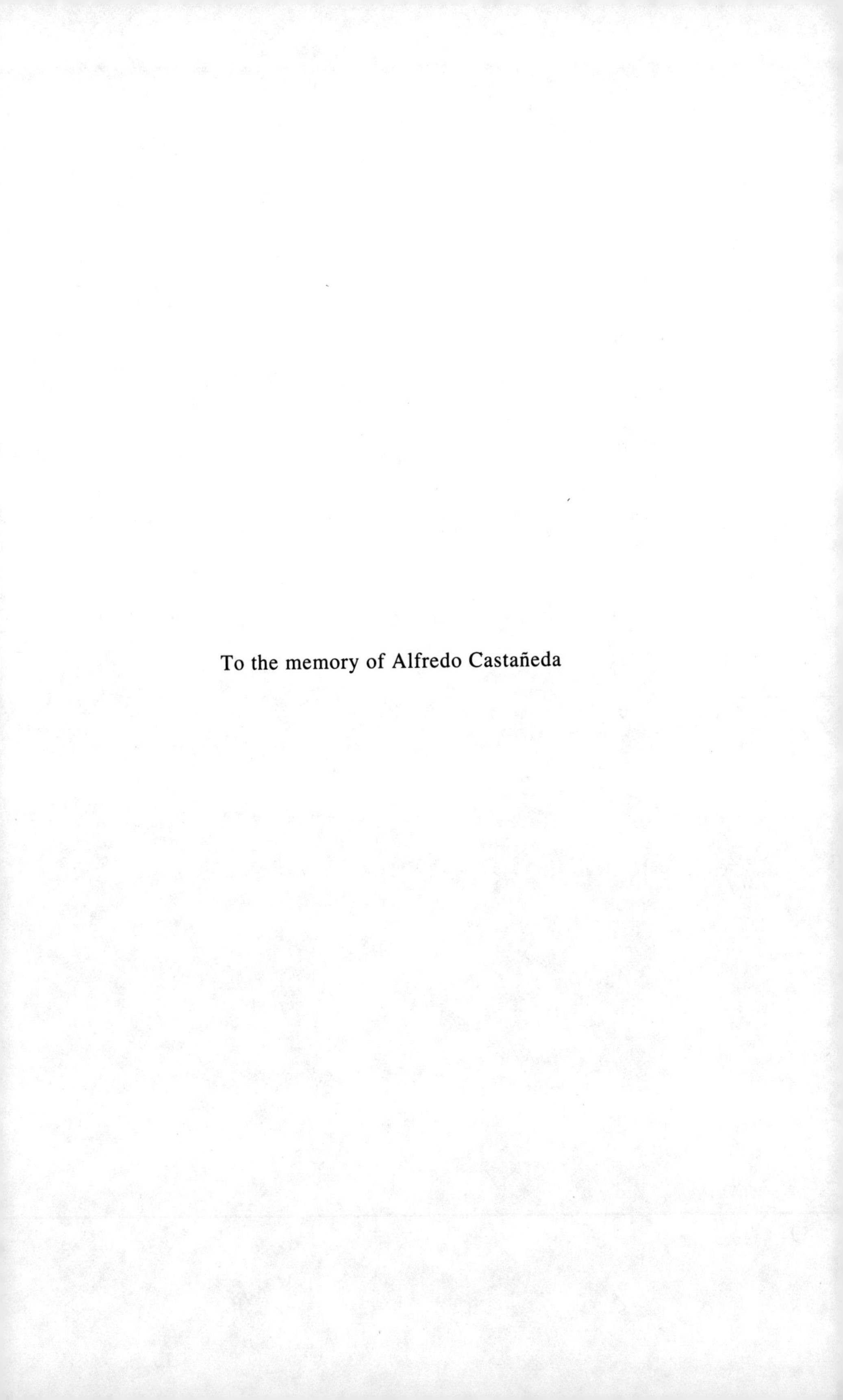

To the memory of Alfredo Castañeda

Contents

Acknowledgments

The idea for this book grew out of several conversations with Alfredo Castañeda before his untimely death in January 1981. Susanne Doell read parts of the manuscript and listened patiently as I attempted to put thoughts into words; many of her constructive criticisms and suggestions were incorporated in the text.

The financial support for the research on multiculturalism and leadership was provided by the Organizational Effectiveness Branch of the Office of Naval Research Contract No. N00014-79-C-0015. Support of the inter-American relations project was provided by the University of Texas at Austin. I am grateful to several persons who assisted me on the multiculturalism and leadership study, among them: Raymond T. Garza, Barbara Goffigon Cox, Alexander Gonzalez, P. Leslie Herold, Raymond Buriel, Camilo Chavez and Roque Mendez. I also owe a debt of gratitude to Robert Guthrie and Robert Hayles of the Office of Naval Research for their help and guidance on the multiculturalism and leadership study. Finally, I am indebted to Terry Foster for her help in editing and preparing the manuscript.

Preface

This book presents the framework for a personality psychology and psychiatry of the Americas. This framework is based on the mestizo world view, a perspective which emerged from sociopolitical events which were unique to the development of many of the nations of the Americas. The word "mestizo" refers to the synthesis or amalgamation of native American and European people, cultures, and life styles. In the context of an Americas/mestizo personality psychology and psychiatry, all people in the Americas (regardless of race, nationality, or ethnic group) are considered to be psychological mestizos because they have been socialized in mestizo environments. Although most of the impetus for the Americas/mestizo psychology and psychiatry has come from the cultures of Native Americans and research on Latino mestizos, the assumptions, models, concepts, methodologies, and approaches of this new psychology and psychiatry can be applied to all the people of the Americas.

What is the mestizo world view, vis-à-vis personality psychology and psychiatry? The answer can be found in what Julian Rappaport (1977) has referred to as the new paradigm in psychology—respect for human diversity, the right to be different, and the belief that human problems are those of person-environment fit, rather than of incompetent (inferior) people or inferior psychological and cultural environments. But it is much more than this; it is a belief in the importance of synthesizing and amalgamating diversity to arrive at multicultural identities, perspectives on life, and new approaches to solution of problems. In line with this view, this book offers some new models which are based on the paradigms of diversity and synthesis. Specifically, it presents a values/belief systems-cognitive styles framework based on research which has explored the relationship between traditionalism-modernism and cognitive styles. The specific models presented in the book are focused on individual development of pluralistic identities, the mental health of families coping with acculturation stress, person-environment fit of migrating individuals who are mismatched with institutions and agencies of the "new" community, and on intergroup and international relations in situations of conflict.

A review of research and development efforts of the last ten years in the Americas reveals that the new Americas/mestizo personality psychology and psychiatry is gradually emerging. This book provides guidelines for the continued development of these efforts. Furthermore, it argues that, without this new multicultural perspective on behavior, the Americas may be doomed to a future of divisionism and conflict. On the other hand, the success of the Americas/mestizo perspective, it is argued, will provide answers not only to the peoples and nations of the Americas but to peoples and nations elsewhere in the world who are struggling to come to terms with their diversity.

In conclusion, I wish to make it clear that I am not condemning Europe, or European psychology, or those psychologists who have employed European world view-based theories and methodologies in their work. I am, instead, criticizing a world view which developed out of sociopolitical events connected with the history of the European continent and which was imported to the Americas at a time when the European world view was very influential in the development of science. Similarly, the fact that I am proposing a psychology of the Americas should not be construed to imply that I believe all people and nations in the Americas are alike. I am arguing, however, that most people and nations of the Americas have had to develop a consciousness about their diversity; it is these perspectives which have provided the impetus and the base on which the new mestizo psychology and psychiatry are being developed.

References

Rappaport, J. *Community psychology: Values, research, and action.* New York: Holt, Rinehart, and Winston, 1977.

Psychology of the Americas
(PGPS-126)

CHAPTER 1

A Psychology of the Americas

In spite of our efforts to create a science that is universal, culture-free and beyond the boundaries of time and space, psychology is still very much culture bound. . . .

—Ruben Ardila (1982)

The concept of person-environment "fit" rather than inferior or superior people or cultures is beginning to take hold. Recognition and support for diversity is emerging.

—Julian Rappaport (1977)

Pursuit of imitation science, though a highly sophisticated skill, can only lead to the evasion and demeaning of subject matter, and a constriction of problematic interests. It is a deadly form of role-playing if one acknowledges that the psychological universe has something to do with people. This kind of spurious knowledge can result in a corrupt human technology and spew forth upon man's stream of ever more degrading images of himself.

—Sigmund Koch (1975)

Why propose a psychology specific to one area of the world, to one hemisphere? After all, psychology is a science and, as such, it should be applicable to everyone. These thoughts could easily occur to the readers of this chapter, for we have all been encouraged to believe that all scientific knowledge is universal. What I am proposing in this book, however, is that the definition of science represented in personality psychology and psychiatry is a product of the European world view. That is, for the most part, personality psychology and psychiatry have not represented the world view which emerged from the experience of the Americas—the mestizo world view. Observations made by Tocqueville (1835) regarding the uniqueness of life in the United States, vis-à-vis Europe, and those of Vasconcellos (1925) and Zea (1945), in Latin America, have not had an impact on the consciousness of psychologists and psychiatrists in the Americas. Americans throughout the hemisphere are, therefore, being viewed, evaluated, and treated by way of theories, assessment instruments, and research and intervention methodologies which are based on a European perspective of life and health. In the last few years, increasingly greater discontent has been expressed concerning assumptions in psychology and psychiatry that are based on the European world view (Cronbach, 1975; Osborne, 1982; Rappaport, 1977). Rappaport

(1977) traces the origins of professional psychology in the United States to Darwin's theory of evolution.

> Here in the study of individual differences was the perfect combination of laboratory measurement methods developed in the German physiological tradition and philosophical ideas concerning how man "ought" to be [p. 9].

Rappaport (1977) also observes that Reigel (1972) has succeeded in tracing some of the origins of developmental psychology in America to Darwin's theory:

> Darwin's notion of the "struggle for survival" was supportive of a reemergence of the philosopher Hobbes' argument that man is essentially competitive and established social order only as a means for protection of self and property [p. 39].

Ardila (1982) has observed that the development of psychology in Latin America has been unduly influenced by psychology in the United States (and, thus, indirectly by European world view). Diaz-Guerrero (1977) was one of the first Latino social scientists to criticize the European perspective as reflected in the research done by Fromm and Maccoby (1970) and also by Oscar Lewis (1961) in Mexico. Ramirez (1976) has also been critical of the use of European world view-based theories and approaches to studying people in Mexico and the United States.

This book, thus, urges psychologists and psychiatrists in the Americas to become cognizant of the fact that the theories, instruments, methodologies, and approaches they use in their work ignore the realities of the people of the Americas. The book also encourages psychologists and psychiatrists to recognize that, as long as the European world view bias exists in their professions, it will be difficult for the people of the Americas to understand themselves and their hemisphere, and we will continue to drift toward misunderstanding and conflict.

TWO HISTORICAL TRADITIONS, TWO WORLD VIEWS, AND TWO PERSPECTIVES IN PERSONALITY PSYCHOLOGY AND MENTAL HEALTH

The European World View in Psychology and Psychiatry

The world view which has had the greatest influence on the evolution of developmental, personality, and clinical psychology as well as psychiatry is the product of certain events which were significant in the development of countries on the European continent. Perhaps the most important of these events was the extensive colonization efforts by France, England, and Spain. In particular, it was the detribalization and accompanying enculturation programs which were so important to the evolution of the European world view vis-à-vis perspectives on pluralism, diversity, and individual differences.

The colonization programs reflected the colonizers' belief that their culture and life style and, most especially, their religious beliefs were superior to those of the colonized populations (Collis, 1954). The detribalization and enculturation efforts of the colonization programs, thus, were attempts to break up loyalties and allegiances of members of the colonized populations to families, tribes, religions, regional areas, and countries. The principal objectives of these efforts were to replace the old loyalties with total allegiance to the culture and religion of the colonizer. The enculturation program adopted by the British was particularly thorough—it involved sending members of the native populations to England, where they learned English, were trained in Christianity, and were taught about British history and culture. After several years, these people were returned to their native lands to assist in implementation of the enculturation programs.

Inherent in the belief that the colonized populations must replace their cultural identities, life styles, and religious beliefs with those of the colonizers was the assumption that the colonized cultures and peoples were somehow psychologically deficient and primitive. Mannoni (1960), a French psychoanalyst, published a paper on the psychology of colonization in which he concluded that colonization was made possible by an inherent need in the subject populations to be dependent. He believed that this need for dependency was satisfied by the high degree of individualism and self-dependency characteristic of Europeans. In fact, Mannoni made it appear as if the colonized populations were characterized by an unconscious desire for colonization:

> Wherever Europeans have founded colonies of the type we are considering, it can safely be said that their coming was unconsciously expected—even desired—by the future subject peoples [p. 644].

Mannoni recognized the need to prepare young men for a colonial career by giving them a "really modern psychology" which would allow them to better understand the natives and their relations to them. This emphasis on the use of knowledge of the social sciences to ensure the success of colonization programs provided some of the early impetus for the development of cross-cultural psychology in Europe. For example, Geza Roheim, a psychoanalytically trained ethnologist, did psychoanalytic field studies from 1928 to 1931 in central Australia, Somaliland and the Normanby Islands with the support of Marie Bonaparte. The first report based on Roheim's research was entitled "The Psychoanalysis of Primitive Culture Types" (1932).

In general, the colonization programs followed by the European countries and, in particular, the application of psychological concepts to understand the behavior of members of the colonized populations helped to shape a world view, vis-à-vis peoples whose cultures and life styles differed from those of the colonizers. In turn, this view had a significant impact on the development of personality and clinical psychology as well as psychiatry with respect to individual and cultural diversity.

Other sociopolitical events which helped to shape the European world view, vis-à-vis psychology and psychiatry, were the democratic and the industrial revolutions. The extensive psychological and sociological impact of these revolutions have been eloquently described by Robert Nisbet in his book, *Tradition and Revolt* (1970). Nisbet observed that the industrial and democratic revolutions led to the displacement of the traditional belief system in Europe and to its replacement with a modernistic system of values. That is, the modern beliefs of individualism, egalitarianism, and secularism replaced beliefs in the sacred origin of the universe, group identity, and respect for ritual and tradition. Nisbet further observed that traditional beliefs came to be perceived as being incompatible with technology and progress. Black (1972) observed that modernization eventually became identified with Europeanization or Westernization. Thus, from the perspective of the European world view, peoples and cultures identified with traditional values and belief systems are assumed to be psychologically underdeveloped and in need of Europeanization or Westernization. The reasons behind Mannoni's (1960) conclusion that colonized peoples "unconsciously desired" colonization and that they needed the "high degree of individualism and self-dependency characteristic of Europeans" becomes clear. In line with this, Nisbet (1953) has observed that the exaggerated emphasis of individualism in Western psychological theories of development of personality and functioning can be attributed to the impact of the Industrial Revolution on the social sciences. It is no accident, then, that concepts such as psychological differentiation have figured so importantly in theories of personality, psychiatry, and child development.

The third major series of sociopolitical events that helped to shape the European world view as reflected in psychology and psychiatry was the separation of the domains of science and religion. The origins of the separation are believed to be Galileo's confirmation of the fact that the earth is not the center of the universe. The introduction of Darwin's theory of evolution led to further separation between the domains of science and religion in Europe. In contrast to the European experience, science and religion remained conjoined in the cultures of the native peoples of the Americas. This one historical fact accounts for many of the crucial differences between the

European and mestizo world views as reflected in psychology and psychiatry. For example, with few exceptions such as Jungian theory, religion and spiritualism have not played a major role in the theories and intervention approaches of psychology and psychiatry.

The three sets of sociopolitical events discussed above have influenced the development of some of the tenets of the European world view, vis-à-vis personality and clinical psychology as well as psychiatry. These tenets are as follows:

1. The technological and economic development of a culture or society are synonymous with the degree of psychological development of its members. This belief states that countries which are technologically underdeveloped are populated by peoples who are not psychologically sophisticated and/or who are pathological. The writing of Mannoni (1960) concerning dependency complexes in colonized populations and McClelland's (1961) cross-cultural speculations regarding need achievement are examples of how psychological development has been equated with technological development. A more recent example is the conclusion by Witkin and Berry (1975) that members of non-Western cultures are undifferentiated psychologically; that is, they are field dependent in their cognitive style. Examples in the cross-cultural personality literature are numerous. In fact, a review of the culture-personality literature could easily lead to the conclusion that one of the primary goals of this area of study has been to prove that European cultures are superior to cultures of non-European origin.

2. The second tenet concerns the equation of psychological development with religious ideology—the greater the adherence to European-Christian beliefs by a culture or a nation, the more civilized, sophisticated, and well adjusted its inhabitants or members are assumed to be. Although science and religion officially separated in Europe, Christianization and modernization came to be seen as synonymous because early colonization efforts by Spain and England emphasized Christianization of native populations. People whose religious beliefs were not based on the European-Christian ideology were believed to be superstitious and underdeveloped; belief in European-Christian ideals was seen as synonymous with degree of psychological sophistication.

3. The third tenet concerns the belief in genetic superiority which was nurtured by the Darwinian theory of evolution. Certain people are believed to be genetically and/or biologically superior to others. Specifically, people of Northern and Western European stock are believed to be genetically superior to the native peoples of the Americas and to Blacks (Guthrie, 1976). The most recent expression of this belief is reflected in the writings of Jensen (1969) and Shockley (1965), but this belief has a long history in European science. Sir Francis Galton, a cousin of Charles Darwin, authored a book entitled *Hereditary Genius: Its Locus and Consequences*, published

in 1869. The book sought proof for the hypothesis that genius and greatness followed family lines. Galton, thus, introduced a science of heredity entitled eugenics, which proposed "a program of racial improvement through selective mating and the sterilization of the unfit." Galton established the Eugenics Society of Great Britain and published the *Eugenics Review*, a monthly journal that served as the chief medium of communication for eugenicists throughout the world. The works of Galton and other eugenicists eventually led to the recapitulation theory which held that an individual organism, in the process of growth and development, passes through a series of stages representing phases of development which had appeared in the evolution of the species. A principal proponent of the recapitulation theory in the United States was G. Stanley Hall, the famous psychologist and president of Clark University. In his book entitled *Adolescence*, published in 1904, Hall described Africans, Indians, and Chinese as members of "adolescent races." Hall argued that people who had not "recapitulated" beyond an inferior stage should be prevented from reproducing their kind. He believed that society should be ruled by the "innately superior."

4. The fourth tenet of the European world view holds that certain cultures and belief systems are superior to others. European cultures are believed to be superior to non-European cultures, which are usually described as primitive and underdeveloped. Cultures which are not of Northern and Western European origin are believed to interfere with the psychological development and adjustment of their members. This damaging culture view has pervaded many theories and conceptual frameworks in psychology and psychiatry. The writings of both Piaget (1966) and Bruner (1966) have implied that non-Western cultures interfere with intellectual development in children. McClelland (1961) concluded that certain characteristics of non-Western cultures interfere with development of need achievement, and Witkin and Berry (1975) viewed socialization practices of non-Western cultures as interfering with the development of psychological differentiation.

The Mestizo World View in Psychology and Psychiatry

In contrast to the European world view, the mestizo perspective reflected in the new psychology and psychiatry which is emerging in the Americas had its origins in events and experiences unique to living and surviving in the new world. One of the most important of these was the challenge of survival in a new environment. The history of the Americas abounds with stories of people who went in search of new environments to effect new beginnings. From the legend of the Aztecs, describing their search for a permanent home at a place where an eagle would be seen perched on a cactus eating a serpent, the long voyages made by the European settlers to the new world, the lonely voyages of trappers in Canada and the traders in the Southwest and Northwest, and the long treks by wagon train which carried settlers from East to West, the story of the Americas is one of struggling to survive in a new environment. There were many instances in which early settlements in America did not survive. The key to survival was cooperation—collaboration among peoples of different backgrounds in order to learn skills and life styles that ensured success in the new environment. This cooperative experience eventually provided the impetus for mestizoization.

Another important series of events which shaped the mestizo world view was the common practice of intermarriage between the European settlers and the native peoples of North and South America as well as the Caribbean. This resulted in the development of a new race and a new culture representing combinations of Eastern and Western traditions, an amalgamation of two different world views and orientations to life. This cultural synthesis ensured that most people in the Americas would come to view themselves as "psychological mestizos"; that is, the feeling that their life styles were the products of different cultures and ways of life. For most people in the Americas, even for those who were not genetic mestizos, involvement in a mestizo way of life was an inescapable reality which led them to the conclusion that multicultural orientations to life were both possible and desirable.

A third set of sociopolitical events that contributed to the development of the mestizo world view were those related to the amalgamation of Native American and European religious practices and ideologies. Some of the cultural products of the synthesis of Native American and European religions are the peyote religion (Native American Church) and the Catholic religion of Mexicans and Mexican Americans. Both of these mestizo religions are discussed in more detail in other chapters of this book.

A fourth cluster of sociopolitical experiences that helped to stimulate the development of the Americas' world view was revolution against European domination and subsequent struggles to prevent European nations from reestablishing their influence in the hemisphere. These sets of experiences led to strong feelings (among the peoples of the Americas) of independence from European ideologies and life styles. They also created a strong feeling of "Americanness"—making people in the Americas conscious of their differences from Europeans. Finally, the struggles for independence encouraged the tenacity to hold onto one's heritage. While Americans were proud of their independence from Europe, they also believed that some of the "old" value systems and life ways should be preserved in the "new" environment. They, thus, made an attempt to hold onto some of the old while adopting the new. This orientation, this consciousness about group and individual identity, eventually encouraged development of the melting pot and raza cosmica ideologies; and these, in turn, influenced pluralistic conceptualizations of the identity development process.

The following tenets of the mestizo world view are influencing the development of personality and psychiatry in the Americas:

1. Knowledge obtained from living and surviving the challenges of life makes every individual's philosophy of life valuable and makes every person a potential teacher. History, heroes, heroines, legends, individual psychohistories, and family and community psychohistories are all important to a psychology of the Americas. Every person, every family, and every community has learned valuable lessons about survival and adjustment. Perhaps the most distinctive feature of the Americas is that everyone has a right to tell his/her story because every individual is considered to be a unique observer of life. Every person is believed to have attained a unique life meaning from learning to confront certain challenges in life, from overcoming personal adversities, and from learning to adapt to certain life circumstances. It is also interesting to note that one of the most salient observations made by Tocqueville (1835) in *Democracy in America*, and one which he felt was in direct contrast to observations he had made in Europe, was the genuine concern that men had for one another in the United States. In fact, he equated this genuine interest in others with freedom. He believed that love of freedom by Americans was related to the genuine interest they had in each other and their willingness to learn from one another. He observed (Stone & Mennell, 1980), ". . . indeed, it is no exaggeration to say that a man's admiration of absolute government is proportionate to the contempt he feels for those around him." He also noted,

> In the United States the more opulent citizens take great care not to stand aloof from the people; on the contrary, they constantly keep on easy terms with the lower classes: they listen to them, they speak to them every day [p. 297].

2. The second tenet of the mestizo world view which had a major influence on psychology and psychiatry in the Americas stresses the importance of ecology in personality development and functioning. Community psychology, which had its origins in the Americas, has evolved out of an ecological perspective in the social sciences. This perspective had its origins in the philosophies and religions of the native peoples of the Americas (Lee, 1976). The Indian cultures view the person as an open system which both affects and is affected by his/her surroundings. Harmony with the environment, both physical and social, is thus of primary concern in psychological adjustment.

3. The third tenet of the mestizo world view concerning psychology and psychiatry speaks to the importance of openness to diversity; the ultimate criterion for achieving knowledge and sophistication in life is acceptance

and respect for the beliefs of all cultures and religions. Rappaport (1977) refers to respect for diversity and the right to be different as the new paradigm in psychology. Accordingly, the person considers that all cultures and religions represent important sources of knowledge about life which can be helpful to his/her own development. It is this acceptance of diversity which facilitated the development of the mestizoization process and which, in turn, resulted in the development of bicultural/multicultural identities and ways of life by many people in the Americas.

4. The fourth tenet of the mestizo world view as reflected in psychology and psychiatry concerns the advantages of pluralistic socialization—the more a person is willing to learn from the knowledge, life experiences, and life meanings of other peoples' religion and cultures, the more he/she has opportunity to incorporate these into his/her own personality and, in turn, make use of these additional resources to become more flexible and adaptable in meeting the diverse demands of life. The melting pot ideology which emerged in the United States in the late eighteenth and early nineteenth centuries was reflective of this belief (Crevecoeur, 1904). This tenet also mirrors the views of two Mexican scholars, José Vasconcellos and Leopoldo Zea. In his two major works, *La Raza Cosmica* (1925) and *Indologia* (1927), Vasconcellos extolled the advantages of diversity reflected in the mestizo race and observed that in the mestizo race lies the greatest hope for the future of the Americas:

> Our major hope for salvation is found in the fact that we are not a pure race, but an aggregation of races in formation, an aggregation that can produce a race more powerful than those who are products of only one race [1927, p. 1202].

Vasconcellos predicted that a race composed of synthesis, a "cosmic race," would emerge to fulfill "the divine mission of America." This new race will represent the "synthesis of the four races now existing—the black, the brown, the yellow, and the white." Each member of the new race, he predicted, would be a "whole human." Furthermore, he concluded that the mestizos were the beginning of this new cosmic race. Like Vasconcellos, the social historian, Leopoldo Zea (1945, 1974) also described the advantages of synthesis, but he referred to a synthesis of world views and life styles rather than to one of races.

CONTRASTING EUROPEAN AND MESTIZO PSYCHOLOGY AND PSYCHIATRY

I began this chapter by proposing that the European and Americas world views had influenced the development of opposing theories and orientations to psychology and psychiatry. What follows is a detailed description of some of those differences.

General Characteristics of the Fields of Study and of the People Who Work in Them

The European world view encourages development of orientations to personality and psychiatry which are characterized largely by specialization, compartmentalization, and intellectualization. Psychologists and psychiatrists are trained to become specialists in either psychosis or mental retardation, the intellectual or the affective aspects of personality, in either assessment or psychotherapy (and there are a myriad of specializations within psychotherapy itself). Differences between the various areas of specialization are usually highly intellectualized, and minor distinctions are viewed as major differences between the specialty areas. There is intellectual isolation fostered by each specialty area, with each developing its own terminology, research, and intervention approaches and methodologies; and there is little cooperation between specialists in the different areas.

Within the context of the European world view, psychologists and psychiatrists are selected for training primarily on the basis of their ability to think analytically, and they are trained to use inductive thinking approaches to theory construction. Training is based on the scientific model of physics and chemistry with considerable attention focused on the reductionistic approach; that is, analyzing complex behaviors by breaking them down into their component parts.

The mestizo world view is encouraging the development of a psychology which is interdisciplinary, synergistic, and unified. From the mestizo perspective, the person is viewed as intimately linked to the sociocultural and physical environments in which he/she interacts. The mestizo orientation is, therefore, interdisciplinary, bringing together such diverse fields as biology, medicine, economics, political science, history, folklore, sociology, anthropology, literature, and the arts. The generalist scholar/practitioner modeled after the Latin American "pensador" is seen as the ideal psychologist. The approaches to personality study and to community and individual intervention are global and holistic; there is no separation made between mind and body or between the intellectual and affective domains of behavior.

The Role of the Psychologist and the Psychiatrist

In the context of the European world view, psychologists and psychiatrists are encouraged to be "objective" and nonpolitical. Personal values and belief systems are supposed to be kept separate from the problems being studied or the client being treated. In fact, the values and belief systems of psychologists and psychiatrists rarely become a source of focus in training unless the candidate is experiencing difficulty in the training program.

Ideally, it is also expected that the roles of interventionist and researcher will be kept separate, since it is believed that a person who is involved in intervention is likely to "lose his scientific objectivity." Much of the role of the psychologist and psychiatrist is also determined by the fact that the professional is expected to be responsible primarily to him/herself (that is, his/her own goals and objectives in life) and to the academic/professional communities to which he/she belongs.

The mestizo world view encourages psychologists to adopt a participant/conceptualizer role. It is believed that, for a proper understanding of the problem and/or the people with which the psychologist is working, it is necessary for the psychologist to share the world view of his subject or client. It is also believed that the psychologist is primarily responsible to the community and/or people he/she is working with. The primary goal in execution of the psychologist's role is the well-being and betterment of the subject/client and of humanity as a whole.

Approaches to Research and Interpretation of Data

The European world view values approaches to psychological and psychiatric research which emulate the methods used by chemistry and physics. The assumption is that psychological reality is fixed in time and place, and methodology is characterized by maximum control and manipulation of variables. Tests and other techniques for data collection are believed to be equally valid for all peoples regardless of race, sex, personal background, and culture. Data interpretation is made by using existing personality theories and concepts with minimal concern for the values, life styles, and belief systems of the people from which the data were collected. Interpretation of data and of assessment information are usually done in the abstract; that is, independent of the sociocultural, economic, political, historical, and ecological variables in which the subjects or clients are embedded.

The mestizo world view encourages research which is historical, contextual, and ecological in its orientation. Research in naturalistic settings and the use of assessment techniques which are observational and unobtrusive as well as holistic and historical are thought to be ideal. Life, family, and community histories are used to understand the complex dynamics of individuals and groups. The person/environment and person/historical interaction are considered to be of central importance. In choosing assessment methods and instruments, the values, life styles, and belief systems of the subjects are given primary consideration. Data are interpreted by making use of conceptual frameworks and theories that are reflective of the reality of the persons being studied.

Goals of Applications and Interventions

In the context of the European world view, clients and research subjects are generally considered to be responsible for their problems and the circumstances of life in which they exist. Consequently, most intervention approaches based on the European world view are likely to focus on changing the client or the subject rather than the institutions and the society in which they live. Ryan (1971) has referred to this orientation as "blaming the victim" and describes its application in intervention programs as follows:

> The formula for action becomes extraordinarily simple: change the victim. All of this happens so smoothly that it seems downright rational. First identify a social problem. Second, study those affected by the problem and discover in what ways they are different from the rest of us as a consequence of deprivation and injustice. Third, define the differences as the cause of the social problem itself. Finally, of course, assign a government bureaucrat to invent a humanitarian action program to correct the difference [p. 8].

The basic assumption behind the "blaming the victim" philosophy is that the majority society is perfect because it reflects the "superior" European value system and life style—shades of the enculturation programs of the colonization period. Theories, concepts, and techniques for assessment and intervention are viewed as reflections of a superior culture which can help inferior and "culturally deprived" peoples to change for the better. It is, thus, not necessary to get to know the clients or subjects well, for according to the "blaming the victim" line of reasoning, what clients or subjects have to offer is not worth knowing. The interventionist, on the other hand, is the expert, because he/she knows the superior culture; has the credentials to prove it; and, as a member of that culture, can become a model for the "disadvantaged" subjects or clients. This leads us to still another characteristic of intervention according to the European world view—only those with the proper credentials can serve as models in intervention.

The mestizo world view encourages development of change in both the subject/client and in society and its institutions. As Ryan has observed, the client/subject needs to be helped to a higher level of morale and to develop more skills and knowledge to deal effectively with institutions and the society. Job skills, education, and knowledge of how to deal effectively with society and its institutions and how to keep from being victimized by them are the main goals of intervention done in the context of the mestizo world view. In turn, society and its institutions must be changed to become more responsive to diversity and to provide equality of opportunity for those whose life styles and value systems differ from those of the majority. Intervention techniques are tailored to reflect the value systems and life styles of the subject/client. In the mestizo context, the most important criterion for determining intervention expertise is first-hand knowledge by the psychologist or psychiatrist of the group he/she is working with and the degree to which he/she is accepted by that group. In this perspective indigenous healers such as curanderos and medicine men are placed in the category of expert; and intervention approaches used must, at the very least, emerge partially from the cultures, life styles, and belief systems of the people with whom the interventions are being carried out.

Models of Culture Change and Identity Development

The most important differences between European and mestizo world views are embodied in the conceptualizations which each encouraged, vis-à-vis culture change and identity development. Within the European world view perspective, diversity is perceived as being potentially negative and as interfering with psychological development and adjustment. In the European view, two or more cultures cannot co-exist in harmony and, thus, they create conflict for the individual which, in turn, results in an identity crisis. In this context, the only alternative is abandonment of minority identities and cultures and complete and total acceptance of identities and cultures associated with the European world view. The European-based cultures and life styles are viewed as being superior to others—all change is conceptualized as greater movement in the direction of accepting the European-based culture and life style with simultaneous abandonment of minority cultures and life styles. This view of acculturation and identity development could be properly entitled conflict replacement. The conflict replacement models consider that synthesis of different cultures and life styles is impossible. On the other hand, mestizo perspectives on culture change and diversity are characterized by a positive view of diversity and pluralism. Culture change is viewed as adoption of values, life styles, and perspectives of both European and non-European cultures. It is also believed that the characteristics of several cultures can merge together through synthesis. A pluralistic identity is viewed as ideal, representing a commitment to the person's original culture as well as to other cultures and life styles. The pluralistic identity represents a synthesis of different life styles, values, perceptual and thinking styles, and coping techniques. (An example of a pluralistic model of identity and culture change is presented in chapter 4.)

Table 1.1 summarizes the principal differences between European and mestizo psychology and psychiatry which were discussed in this chapter.

TABLE 1.1. Major Differences between European and Americas/Mestizo Psychology and Psychiatry

Areas of Difference	European	Americas/Mestizo
Characteristics of theories	Specialization and compartmentalization—example: separation of cognitive and affective development. Minor distinctions in areas of research and interventions are viewed as major—social, developmental, personality, clinical, and community have considerable overlap. Isolation and separatism are fostered by development of a specialized terminology and methodology with little intercommunication and cooperation with people outside one's own in-group.	Interdisciplinary and unified. Personality is viewed as holistic and interwoven with the physical and social environment. Emphasis is on communication and cooperation, not only with other psychologists and educators, but with representatives of other disciplines as well (Iscoe, 1982).
Characteristics of social scientists and psychiatrists	Minimizes importance of values, belief systems, and world views vis-à-vis the study of personality and psychotherapy; unquestioning acceptance of modern values/belief systems; minimal interest in understanding relationship of own values and belief systems to personal research interests and to preference for certain theories and methodologies (Gergin, 1973).	Ability to introspect with a high degree of awareness regarding relationship of own values and belief systems to personal interests in research and intervention; ability to synthesize and to integrate different disciplines, approaches, and world views. The ideal is the generalist, the Latin-American "pensador" (thinker-doer) who is knowledgeable about history, politics, economics, religion, art, and philosophy. Must have lived through some of the same life experiences as the client or subject. Effectiveness is assessed in terms of ability to help in the solution of real problems.

Characteristics of social scientists and psychiatrists (cont'd.)	Analytic thinking is emphasized as is individual competition. The ideal is the "real" scientist who has little interest in applications of knowledge to social problems.	
Role of psychologists and psychiatrists	Objective and non-political; personal values and belief systems kept separate from research and intervention activities (at least as an ideal); primarily responsible to self and to the academic community.	Participant/conceptualizer and change agent; deep personal commitment to finding solutions for problems being researched; primary responsibility is to members of group and to community he/she is working with.
Approaches to research and interpretation of data	Laboratory setting research with maximum control and manipulation of variables; the assumption that psychological reality is fixed in time (Cronbach, 1975); instruments and methods for data collection are believed to be equally valid for all subjects; data are interpreted using existing personality theories with no modifications made for differing experiences or world view of subjects; emphasis is on universalism.	Naturalistic setting with non-obtrusive approaches for data collection; use of observational and life history approaches with person-environment and person-socio/historical/political interactions given great importance; data are interpreted in the context of social and physical environment of the subject and with theoretical orientations consonant with world view of subjects; emphasis is on individual and cultural differences (Garza & Lipton, 1982).
	Clients and subjects are believed to be at least partially responsible for their problems (Ryan, 1971); the primary goal of intervention is to change the client; therapists and consultants view	Society is viewed as primarily responsible for problems of the client; the primary goal of intervention is to change both society and the client; client is instructed on how to best interact with institutions and how to be

(Table continued on p. 16.)

TABLE 1.1. *(continued)*

Areas of Difference	European	Americas/Mestizo
Approaches to research and interpretation of data (cont'd.)	themselves as representatives of a "super" culture and society.	a change agent—he/she is given conceptual frameworks and skills to deal effectively with society and to make society more responsive to diversity; intervention techniques and approaches reflect values and life styles of client; therapist or consultant shares the world view of client.
Models of identity development and culture change	Two or more cultures cannot co-exist in harmony; thus, they create conflict for the bicultural/multicultural person (identity crisis); conflict/replacement models of acculturation.	Two or more cultures can merge to create new and more flexible orientations toward life; a person can identify with two or more cultures and participate in them without conflict or maladjustment; flexibility, synthesis, and unity model of acculturation.

SUMMARY

Different sociopolitical events in the histories of Europe and the Americas have influenced the development of two different world views. These world views, in turn, have helped to shape development of theories and approaches in psychology and psychiatry which are vastly different from each other. Differences between European and mestizo psychology/psychiatry can be observed in different domains: (1) general characteristics of the fields and the persons who work in them; (2) roles; (3) approaches to research and interpretation of data; (4) applications and interventions; and (5) types of models used to conceptualize culture change and identity development.

REFERENCES

Ardila, R. International psychology. *American Psychologist*, 1982, *37*, 323–329.

Black, C. E. Dynamics of modernization. In R. A. Nisbet (Ed.), *Social change*. New York: Harper, 1972.

Bruner, J. S., Oliver, R. R., & Greenfield, P. M. *Studies in cognitive growth*. New York: Wiley, 1966.
Collis, M. *Cortes and Montezuma*. New York: Avon Books, 1954.
Crevecoeur, J. H. St. J. *Letters from an American farmer*. New York: Fox, Duffield, 1904.
Cronbach, L. J. Beyond the two disciplines of scientific psychology. *American Psychologist*, 1975, *30*, 116–127.
Diaz-Guerrero, R. Mexican psychology. *American Psychologist*, 1977, *33*, 934–944.
Fromm, E., & Maccoby, M. *Social character in a Mexican village: A socio-psychoanalytic study*. Englewood Cliffs, N.J.: Prentice-Hall, 1970.
Galton, F. Hereditary genius: An inquiry into its locus and consequences. London: Clay and Sons, 1869.
Galton, F. Annals of eugenics, Galton Laboratory for National Eugenics, October 1925, Vol. 1, Part 1.
Garza, R. T. & Lipton, J. P. Theoretical perspectives on Chicano personality development. *Hispanic Journal of Behavioral Sciences*, 1982, *4*(4), 407–432.
Gergin, K. J. Social psychology as history. *Journal of Personality and Social Psychology*, 1976, *26*, 309–320.
Guthrie, R. V. *Even the rat was white: A historical view of psychology*. New York: Harper & Row, 1976.
Hall, G. S. *Adolescence: Its psychology and its relations to physiology, anthropology, sociology, sex, crime, religion, and education* (2 volumes). New York: Appleton, 1904.
Iscoe, I. Toward a viable community health psychology. *American Psychologist*, 1982, *37*(8), 961–965.
Jensen, A. R. How much can we boost IQ and scholastic achievement? *Harvard Educational Review*, 1969, *39*, 1–123.
Koch, S. Psychology and the humanities. Unpublished manuscript, University of Texas at Austin, 1975.
Lee, D. *Valuing the self: What we can learn from other cultures*. Englewood Cliffs, N.J.: Prentice-Hall, 1976.
Lewis, O. *The children of Sanchez: Autobiography of a Mexican family*. New York: Random House, 1961.
Mannoni, O. Appel de la fédération de France du FLN, *El Moudjahid*, 1960, *59*, 644–645.
McClelland, D. C. *The achieving society*. Princeton, N. J.: Van Nostrand, 1961.
Nisbet, R. A. *Quest for community*. New York: Oxford University Press, 1953.
Nisbet, R. A. *Tradition and revolt*. New York: Vintage, 1970.
Osborne, J. W. The hegemony of natural scientific conceptions of learning. *American Psychologist*, 1982, *37*, 330–332.
Piaget, J. Necessité et signification des recherches comparatives en psychologie genetique. *International Journal of Psychology*, 1966, *1*, 3–13.
Ramirez, M. A mestizo world view and the psychodynamics of Mexican-American border populations. In S. R. Ross (Ed.), *Views across the border: The United States and Mexico*. Albuquerque, N. M.: University of New Mexico Press, 1978.
Rappaport, J. *Community psychology: Values, research, and action*. New York: Holt, Rinehart, and Winston, 1977.
Reigel, K. F. Influence of economic and political ideologies on the development of psychology. *Psychological Bulletin*, 1972, *78*, 129–141.
Roheim, G. Psychoanalysis of primitive cultural types. *International Journal of Psychoanalysis*, 1932, *13*, 1–224.
Ryan, W. *Blaming the victim*. New York: Random House, 1971.
Shockley, W. Population control or eugenics. *U.S. News and World Report*, 1965, November 22, 68–71.

Stone, J. & Mennell, S. *Alexis de Tocqueville on democracy, revolution, and society*. Chicago: The University of Chicago Press, 1980.

Tocqueville, A. *Democracy in America*. Paris: Michel-Levy Freres, 1835.

Vasconcellos, J. *La raza cosmica: Mision de la raza iberoamericana*. Barcelona: Agencia Mundial de Libreria, 1925.

Vasconcellos, J. *Indologia: Una interpretacion de la cultura iberoamericano*. Barcelona: Agencia Mundial de Libreria, 1927.

Witkin, H. A. & Berry, J. W. Psychological differentiation in cross-cultural perspective. *Journal of Cross-Cultural Psychology*, 1975, *6*, 4–87.

Zea, L. *En torno a una filosofia americana*. Mexico, D.F.: El Colegio de Mexico, 1945.

Zea, L. *Dependencia y liberacion en la cultura latinoamericana*. Mexico, D.F.: Editorial Joaquin Mortiz, S. A., 1974.

CHAPTER 2

The Cultural and Philosophical Foundations of Mestizo Psychology and Psychiatry

> The Sun Dancer believes that each person is a unique Living Medicine Wheel, powerful beyond imagination, that has been limited and placed upon the earth to Touch, Experience and Learn. . . . All the things of the Universe Wheel have spirit and life, including the rivers, rocks, earth, sky, plants and animals. But it is only man of all the Beings in the Wheel, who is a determiner. Our determining spirit can be made whole only through the learning of our harmony with all our brothers and sisters, and with all the other Spirits of the Universe. To do this we must learn to seek and to percieve. . . .
>
> —Hyemeyohsts Storm (1972)

> The wise men were firmly convinced of the importance of finding "true roots" for man in this life. This was not an easy task, for as one Nahuatl poet remarked:
>
> What does your mind seek?
> Where is your heart?
> If you give your heart to everything,
> You lead it nowhere; you destroy your heart.
> Can anything be found on earth?
>
> —Miguel Leon-Portilla (1963)

This chapter focuses on concepts and principles of developmental, personality, community, and clinical psychology/psychiatry which are reflected in the cultures of the indigenous peoples of North and South America as well as the Caribbean. These concepts are providing the basic framework on which mestizo psychology is being established; and they have also played an important role in the amalgamation of native American and European cultures, life styles, and world views. This chapter also describes the role which the syncretic process of mestizoization has played in the development of mestizo psychology. Finally, the chapter presents a short review of Mexican philosophy, a product of the mestizoization process in the Americas as well as the intellectual wellspring from which mestizo psychology is emerging.

PSYCHOLOGY REFLECTED IN THE CULTURES OF THE INDIGENOUS PEOPLE OF NORTH AMERICA

From the varied beliefs of the Indian nations of North America certain common psychological concepts have emerged to influence the development of mestizo psychology. The North American Indian psychological concepts which have had the greatest impact on mestizo personality psychology are the following:

The Person Is an Open System. The individual is viewed as an integral part of the environment and the universe and as being completely open to experience. What is learned from interactions with others and with the environment and the universe (both the natural and the supernatural) helps the person to achieve harmony with his/her surroundings and to arrive at understanding of the meaning of life. This concept is reflected in a passage from *Seven Arrows* (Storm, 1972):

> The Universe is the Mirror of the People and each person is a Mirror to every other person. . . . Any idea, person or object can be a Medicine Wheel, a Mirror for man. The tiniest flower can be such a Mirror, as can a wolf, a story, a touch, a religion or a mountain top [p. 5].

Much of the education of children is based on the notion of the person as an open system and focused on the teaching of sensitivity and openness to the environment. Lee (1976) has observed:

> The mother initiated her unborn baby into relatedness with nature and continued to do so in various ways through infancy. She took the very tiny baby out and merely pointed to natural manifestations without labeling. Only after the baby experienced directly, only later, did she offer him concepts. She sang songs referring to the animals as his brothers, his cousins, his grandparents. Early in life he was also helped to develop a sensitivity toward nature, so that he might be enabled to relate openly. . . . [p. 9].

The notion of interpenetration is an integral part of the view of the person as an open system. Specifically, information and knowledge coming from others and from the environment is seen as being modified, incorporated and as actively influencing the psychodynamics of the person. The individual modifies and affects others and the environment as he/she interacts with these. Lee (1976) explains this phenomenon as follows:

> In such societies, though the self and the other are differentiated, they are not mutually exclusive. The self contains some of the other, participates in the other and is in part contained within the other. By this I do not mean what usually goes in the name of empathy. I mean rather that where such a concept of the self is operative, self-interest and other-interest are not clearly distinguished. . . .
>
> It enables him to value himself as well as the other, to develop himself while developing the other and to relate himself in a transaction which enhances the value of both self and other [pp. 112, 14].

The spiritual world holds the key to destiny, personal identity, and life mission. The spiritual world is perceived to be a great source of power and knowledge. By achieving communication with the spritual world, it is believed that the person can have a vision or a dream which can provide him/her with an adult identity, a life mission, and a spirit helper which can facilitate the attainment of life goals. Communication with the spiritual world is encouraged through both individual contact with the supernatural in visions and group contact in organized ritual. Most of the Indian cultures of North America make use of the vision quest for making contact with the spiritual world. Driver (1969) provides the following description of the vision quest:

> A youth would travel to an isolated spot with a reputation as an abode of spirits, usually a mountain or a lake or an uninhabited wood. Here he remained for several days and nights, fasting from both food and water, naked in the cold, mutilating his body, and otherwise denying the desires of the flesh to the point that an hallucination was likely to occur. He prayed by asking a spirit to take pity on him in his condition of deprivation and want, the idea being that the more miserable his condition, the more likely was a spirit to come to his aid. Such "visions" usually took the form of both visual and auditory hallucinations. The neophyte would frequently see an animal spirit, which would speak to him, teach him a song or show him designs to paint on his body, clothing or weapons for protection against the enemy. On returning home, the youth would eventually describe his experience to his family or camp mates, sing the songs he had acquired, and paint the designs on his possessions. If his demonstration was convincing, he might later acquire a following on a future hunting or warring expedition. If the knowledge he acquired in the vision was efficacious in curing the sick, he could set himself up as a medicine man [p. 391].

It is also believed that the power and knowledge of the spiritual world can also be accessed by employing the help of a shaman or medicine man—someone who is seen as the mediator between the individual and the supernatural.

Community Identity and Responsibility to the Group Are of Central Importance. The individual is socialized to develop a strong sense of community identity and to feel a deep sense of responsibility for his/her group. The person then comes to feel that at all times he or she is the representative of the group. "I am the people" is a statement often made by members of North American Indian groups.

Two observations by Lee (1976) attest to the importance of community identity among the North American Indians:

> The individual was considered as a representative of his camp circle, his prayer to Waken Tanka, the Great Spirit, was: "Help me that my people may live. . . ."

> Concern and care for the community had to manifest themselves in behavior; a feeling of responsibility is not enough and this behavior predisposed development of all aspects of the self. So, the strengthening of character, of courage, of the capacity to endure; the development of powers of observation, of the ability to concentrate; the stretching of the span of attention; and everything we subsume under the name of education; all this the individual undertook as part of his responsibility to the community [pp. 12, 34].

Full Development of Abilities and Skills is Achieved Through Self-Challenge. Self-challenge and endurance of pain, hardship, hunger, and frustration were used to encourage the development of the individual's full potential. Children were encouraged to seek out competitive situations, and the goal of education was the full development of capacity. Lee (1976) has observed:

> They were taught to engage themselves in the elements—to meet them with an answering strength. If a torrential rain fell, they learned to strip and run out in it, however cool the weather. Little boys were trained to walk with men for miles through heavy snow drifts in the face of biting winds, and to take pride in the hardship endured [p. 53].

PSYCHOLOGY REFLECTED IN THE CULTURES OF THE INDIGENOUS PEOPLE OF CENTRAL AND SOUTH AMERICA AND THE CARIBBEAN

The following psychological concepts which have emerged from the cultures of Indian nations of Central and South America and the Caribbean have influenced the development of mestizo psychology.

The Search for Self-Knowledge, Individual Identity, and Life Meaning Is a Primary Life Goal. Both the Mayas as well as the Nahuatl-speaking peoples of the Valley of Mexico believed that man came to earth without a face, without an identity. An individual identity was achieved through socialization and education. In order to develop identity, it was believed that a person had to learn self-control. Achievement of identity through self-control and personal strength was believed to lead to development of free will. Much of education had as its major goal what the Nahuas referred to as self-admonishment, which meant to know for oneself what one should be. Leon-Portilla (1963) observed that the Nahuas even more than the Greeks had arrived at the relationship between identity and change of self-image; they conceived of the self as being in constant motion and change.

The individual is embedded in history and time. Knowledge of the history of one's group and accurate measurement of time were used to predict the destiny of both the individual and his/her group. The Nahuas had a book which they used to make calendaric diagnoses at the time of the infant's birth. To predict the destiny of a child, the Nahuas used the *Tonalamatl* (Book of Fortunes) in conjunction with the *Tonalpohualli* or Count of Days (the divine calendar of twenty groups of thirteen days). Leon-Portilla (1963) describes this process as follows:

> First you had to attend to the character of the year in question (whose function depended on the particular century and spatial region of orientation). Also the character of each Trecena of both years and days, then the twenty signs of Tonalamatl, and lastly the day, all had to be coordinated sign with number in order to show the various influences in the "Calendaric diagnosis" [p. 116].

A birth under a bad sign could be overcome both by baptizing the child on a day of a favorable sign and by ensuring that through education and socialization a child would develop a free will. Thus, knowledge was seen as the key to destiny to some degree of control over one's life.

For the Mayas, time was even more important than for the Nahuas; the accurate measurement of time and the association of time with important events in the history of the group resulted in the development of an elaborate psychological system for prediction of the individual's future. As with the Nahuas, the Mayas sought favorable signs to overcome a bad fate. Leon-Portilla (1963) describes this complex psychological time theory as follows:

> The ancient concern in finding through the calendar the norms of the agricultural cycles and the moments to propitiate the gods, thus attains a fuller meaning. To ascertain the units of measurement of kinh, to know the order of its alternations, to investigate its past burdens, leads to the prediction of its future recurrences. Thusly, religious thought, supported by observations and calculations, unites its peculiar form of cosmic history with an astrological knowledge so vitally important throughout the life of the Maya. . . .
>
> Those who recognized the presences of the different moment-deities would find "remedies for their ills." They would be able to seek, thanks to the rites and sacrifices, and with the aid of computations, the favorable deities, those which confronted with adverse fates, would neutralize contrary influences. *In this way it was possible to escape absolute fatalism and open the door to knowledge leading man to better acting and thinking at prescribed moments* [Emphasis added] [pp. 104, 106].

The Duality of Origin and Life in the Universe. Polar opposites—male and female, religion and war, poetry and math—were often fused in the cultures of the Nahuas and the Mayas. In the religion of the Nahuas, the god Ometeotl represents the dual nature of the culture. Ometeotl is androgynous—it has both masculine and feminine features; it is both father and mother of the gods. The duality for the culture is also reflected in the many male/female deities contained in the religion of the Nahuas. Duality was also present in other aspects of the Nahua and Mayan cultures; for example, the association of science with mysticism reflected in the time theory of the Mayas and the calendaric diagnoses of the Nahuas.

Education Plays a Central Role in Personality Development. It is almost impossible to exaggerate the magnitude of the role which education played in the Mayan and Nahuatl cultures. It was important because it was seen as the key to the proper development of the personality and of a free will. Education was believed to be the responsibility of both the parents and the philosophers (*tlamatinime*). The parents educated the child up to about age fifteen, at which time he or she entered a school and was taught by the *tlamatinime*. Education was formalized and mandatory.

One of the rituals following the birth of a child was initiation of the infant into the school he or she would attend at adolescence. There were also specific scripts which parents had to follow in giving their children advice when they reached a certain prescribed age. For example, the script used by a father counseling his son on greed and vanity was as follows:

> Receive this word, listen to this word.
> I hope that for a little time you will live with Our Lord,
> He who is Master of the Close Vicinity.
> Live on earth;
> I hope you will last for a little time.
> Do you know much?
> With good judgment, look at things, observe them wisely.
> It is said that this is a place of hardship, of filth, of troubles.
> It is a place without pleasure, dreadful, which brings desolation.
> There is nothing true here . . .
> Here is how you must work and act;
> Safely kept, in a locked place,
> The elders left us these words
> At the time of their departure.
> Those of the white hair and the wrinkled faces, our ancestors. . . .
> [Leon-Portilla, 1963, p. 149].

At a certain age, the child would attend a formal school. With respect to the education given at these schools, Duran (1964) wrote:

> They had masters and teachers who would teach and instruct them in all kinds of art—military, ecclesiastical, and mechanical—and in astrology based on the knowledge of the stars. About all these things they had large and lovely books of paintings and characters [p. 140].

The schools taught the culture and history of the group and sought to identify the proper life mission which each individual should adopt. Instruction consisted primarily of history, poetry, and mathematics. The goal of education was to humanize the passions, to make the students wise, and to give them a firmness of purpose. The ultimate goal was to develop a free will which was not subject to the passions of the individual, but which could serve the individual and his/her people. With a free will, the person could overcome a negative fate or keep from straying from the path of a positive fate.

The most important personality characteristics in Nahuatl culture are reflected in the following passage contained in one of the codices: "The mature man is a heart solid as a rock, is a wise face. Possessor of a face, possessor of a heart, he is able and understanding [Leon-Portilla, 1963, p. 141]."

THE MESTIZOIZATION OF PEOPLES AND CULTURES IN THE AMERICAS

The psychological concepts discussed above have played a central role in encouraging the development of the synergistic process which evolved in the Americas. Mestizoization involved the confluence and amalgamation of peoples and cultures from two continents as well as the bringing together of cultures, life styles, and world views based on Eastern and Western thought.

Of all the psychological/philosophical concepts which emerged from the cultures of the native peoples of the Americas, man as an open system was probably most influential in encouraging the mestizoization process. Their openness to experience and diversity, and sensitivity to the environment and the universe, made the indigenous Americans recipient to other ways of life and other philosophies. The concept of duality, combining opposites, also encouraged the incorporation of other peoples and ways of life in the cultures of the native peoples of the Americas. But it was the perpetual search for self-knowledge and for life mission which was most influential in stimulating the development of the mestizoization process in the Americas. Every person, every culture, every world view was believed to reflect knowledge necessary to understand the mysteries of life and the self. Diversity was accepted and incorporated into the self through both genetic and cultural amalgamation.

The Emergence of Genetic Mestizos

Genetic mestizos were a necessary precursor to the development of mestizo cultures and life styles. Persons who were the genetic products of European and native American peoples facilitated the integration of European and native American cultures and ideologies. These mestizos could play the roles of cultural "ambassadors" and "brokers" because they spoke two or

VISTA LIBRARY

more languages, and they were familiar with the two sociocultural systems which were being amalgamated.

Genetic mestizoization was more common in some areas of the Americas than in others. This determined that cultural and religious mestizoization would be more evident in some regions of the hemisphere than in others. For example, genetic mestizoization was less common in those areas settled by the English on the east coast of North America because these areas were settled mainly by families and not single men as was the case in many parts of Canada, the southwestern United States, Central and South America, and the Caribbean. The religious philosophies of the European settlers also played a major role in the development of the mestizoization process. Driver (1969) noted:

> The presence of English women in the colonies and the strict Protestant moral codes prevented the creation of a mestizo class from large numbers of mixed concubinages and marriages, [and] the Puritans were too narrow-minded on the whole to have devoted much effort to Christianizing the Indians, who they regarded as agents of Satan [p. 480].

The situation on the east coast of the United States, thus, contrasts with that in Canada, the southwestern region of North America, Latin America, and the Caribbean. In these latter regions, genetic mestizoization was more common and, with it, cultural mestizoization flourished.

Cultural Mestizoization

In North America, peyote religion is a product of the cultural mestizoization process. In all areas of the hemisphere, cultural mestizoization has influenced psychology and psychiatry through healing and religion. Driver (1969) offered the following description of the peyote religion of the Native American Church:

> The doctrine includes the belief in supernatural power, in spirits, and in incarnation of power in human beings. Spirits consist of the Christian Trinity (the Father, the Son and the Holy Ghost); other Christian spirits such as the devil and the angels; and still other spirits derived exclusively from Indian religion. The Christian spirits tend to be equated with comparable Indian spirits: God is the Great Spirit, Jesus is the culture hero; the devil is the evil spirit [p. 524].

Driver goes on to describe the rituals of the religion:

> Peyote ritual is heavily weighted in favor of Indian elements, such as the eagle-bone whistle, cedar incense, the fan of bird tail feathers, the bundle of sage

> sprigs, the gourd rattle, and the water drum. Eating peyote induces rapport with the supernatural and brings various spirits of departed ones, sometimes with aid in solving personal problems and with warning to abandon evil thoughts and deeds [p. 525].

One of the best examples of cultural mestizoization in Latin America and in the Caribbean is folk healing. *Curanderos(as)* (folkhealers) and *espiritistas* (spiritists) use a combination of rituals and paraphernalia common to both Indian and European religions. In the case of Puerto Rican *espiritistas*, African beliefs and practices are also combined with the Indian and European (see chapter 7 for a more extensive description of folk medicine).

From the point of view of mestizo psychology and psychiatry, the most important product of the mestizoization process is Mexican philosophy. The writings of Mexican philosophers have provided most of the philosophical base on which mestizo psychology and psychiatry is being developed. Mexican philosophy succeeded in integrating the psychological concepts of the native American cultures with important contributions by European philosophers. What follows is a short history of the development of those aspects of Mexican philosophy that have had the greatest influence on the development of mestizo philosophy and psychiatry.

Philosophical Roots of Mestizo Psychology and Psychiatry

The young philosophers who were active in the period of Mexican history which preceded the Revolution of 1910 were described by Romanell (1971) as the "intellectual forerunners of the Mexican revolution." These scholars were members of a group which became known as the *Ateneo de le Juventud* or the Athenaeum of Youth. Romanell observed:

> The Ateneo de la Juventud was founded in Mexico City on October 28, 1909. Its first president was Antonio Caso. The membership came to fifty or so, a few of whom lived in the provinces, like Diego Rivera, the famous mural painter. The members came from all walks of life and the majority of them were lawyers by profession. Though the group was heterogeneous in composition, the members had a common goal: to contribute to the spiritualization of a demoralized country [p. 57].

In 1910 the Ateneo organized a series of lectures on the personality and work of Spanish-American thinkers and men-of-letters. The focus on Spanish-American culture was a reflection of the interest of the group in expressing themselves and not merely in imitating European thought. The Ateneo was also a reaction against the positivistic school which had been the dominant theme in Mexican philosophy during the presidency of Porfirio Diaz. The positivists had adapted concepts from European science and philosophy and applied them to Mexico. They were organized into a political party known as the Party of Scientists, and they used Darwinian arguments to justify the dishonest and oppressive government of Diaz. Romanell observed:

> They had the audacity to affirm that the very survival of the powers that be signified that they were the fittest to govern the country. Along with the doctrine of "honest tyranny" for home consumption, they urged Saxonization of the Latin soul to compete with the "great nation" growing by leaps and bounds across the border [p. 53].

The focus of philosophy which the members of the Ateneo adopted could be identified as perspectivistic, and it was based on the writings of Jose Ortega y Gasset (1946). According to this perspectivistic view, philosophy is not a quest for certainty but the search for *a point of view on human life*. This was in every sense a cross-cultural philosophy since every point of view on human life reflects a particular sociocultural system.

Romanell (1971) observed that the contributions made by the members of the Ateneo succeeded in "initiating the rehabilitation of thought of a mestizo peoples." Thus, it provided the initial philosophical base on which psychology of the Americas could be established. In fact, the writings of the Ateneo members were based on a concept of central importance to cross-cultural psychology in general and to mestizo psychology and psychiatry in particular—the emic point of view. That is, the belief that peoples and cultures must be studied and understood on their own terms.

The adoption of the emic perspective was initiated by the writings and works of Jose Vasconcellos, one of the members of the Ateneo, and the person who became known as the intellectual of the Mexican revolution. The two works by Vasconcellos which have the greatest implications for a mestizo psychology of personality are *La Raza Cosmica* (1925) and *Indologia* (1927). Although Vasconcellos engaged in much speculation in these two books and also contradicted himself on various points, he nevertheless consistently argued for the synthesis of diversity through the process of mestizoization and multiculturalism. He asserted his belief that genetic and cultural amalgamation of different races and cultures could contribute to greater knowledge of life for all. Vasconcellos saw the mestizo race as the greatest hope for the future of Latin America. He stated (1927)

> Our major hope for salvation is found in the fact that we are not a pure race, but an aggregation of races in formation, an aggregation that can produce a race more powerful than those which are the products of only one race [p. 1202].

Although Vasconcellos argued for the development of a new Latin race, his was, above all, a philosophy of synthesis; that is, it was not exclusivistic.

He specifically stated that the new race should not exclude white peoples. Latin America, he observed, owed much of what it was to the European whites and to North Americans.

A general theme that ran through much of Vasconcellos' writings was his strong conviction regarding the value of indigenous culture in the Americas. This argument was also very prevalent in the writings of another famous Mexican philosopher who was also the first president of the Ateneo, Antonio Caso. Caso emphasized the importance of understanding Mexico's roots in order to properly understand Mexico. He felt that the most serious and immediate problem facing Mexico was the establishment of a Mexican collective consciousness. Caso's philosophy was instrumental in the rejection of the ideology of European science in Mexico and also in the rejection of Nietzsches' ideal of the "superman." He accepted the premises of traditional Darwinism as true in biology but false in ethics. Romanell (1971) observed:

> For Caso science is only a part of the truth, the rest must be found in metaphysics; because man is more than reason, he is sentiment and will. Science cannot penetrate to the depths of life. This world is only accessible to intuition. Intuition unites the metaphysics of the mystic and the laws of the scientist by obtaining concrete reality, like the mystic wanted and the universal knowledge, like the intellectualists demanded [p. 91].

Caso also emphasized the importance of personalism—the fact that the person is a unique element in the universe and, thus, the central part of reality (Klor de Alva, 1972). Caso's writings provided two central concepts for the philosophical base on which mestizo psychology and psychiatry are being established: (1) a methodology which is an amalgamation of phenomenology with the best of the European scientific approach, and (2) the uniqueness of the individual. Thus, Caso provided a very important concept for the philosophical base on which mestizo psychology was to be founded, a mestizo methodology.

The work of Vasconcellos and Caso was continued by Samuel Ramos, who had studied under Caso and worked with Vasconcellos at the Secretariat of Public Instruction. Ramos, like Caso, believed that Mexico needed to develop a national consciousness. To help in the achievement of this goal, he applied historicism and perspectivism. These two approaches were evident in his major work, *Profile of Man and Culture in Mexico*, published in 1934. His principal arguments in this book were that Mexicans were suffering from an inferiority complex which had its origins in the Spanish conquest, and which had been reinforced by the Spanish colonization period as well as by the interventions of France and the United States. He argued that this inferiority complex had forced Mexicans to look to Europe for guidance and direction. He wrote:

> Throughout its history Mexico has fed on European traditions and expressed much interest and appreciation for their value. . . . No one can deny that interest in foreign culture has signified for many Mexicans a spiritual flight from their own land. In this case, "culture" is a cloister in which men who disdain native realities take refuge in order to ignore them. From this erroneous attitude Mexican "self-denegration" was born more than a century ago, and its effects have been crucial in our historical orientation [1975, p. 17].

He concluded his analysis by providing an antidote to the poison of self-denegration and inferiority feelings—an education which was established on the Mexican experience. The basis of all educational reform in the country, he argued, should be the study of the culture and the people of Mexico. He called for the establishment of a new philosophical anthropology which could free the people of Mexico from their psychological maladjustment:

> When these depressive complexes vanish, our false character will automatically disappear. Like a disguise it has covered the Mexican's authentic way of being as a compensation for painful feelings of inferiority. That day will be the beginning of our second War of Independence, which may turn out to be more transcendental than the first, because it will free the spirit for the fulfillment of its own destiny. . . .
>
> The concepts of Mexico that appear in the textbooks must be revised, for they have been distorted by self-denegration and an inferiority complex. There must be enthusiasm and respect for Mexican things. Observing our circumstances objectively, one discovers surprising values, the knowledge of which will undoubtedly contribute to uplifting the Mexican spirit [1975, pp. 114–15, 131–32).

Ramos' principal contributions to mestizo psychology and psychiatry were his focus on the psychodynamics of self-rejection characteristic of Mexicans who were denying their original culture and his arguments that Mexico, a nation which is a product of the mestizo experience, should develop a philosophy and a national conscience based on its mestizo culture. It is unfortunate that Ramos employed a European theory of personality, that of Alfred Adler, to explain some of the observations he made of Mexican psychodynamics. The use of Adlerian theory forced him into conclusions that were extremely pessimistic and negative (a more detailed discussion is presented in chapter 3).

Ramos' detailed descriptions of the psychodynamics of self-denial did, nevertheless, lay the groundwork for mestizo psychology and psychiatry, vis-à-vis their focus on identity development in bicultural/multicultural settings. However, his most important contribution regarding the philosophical base of mestizo psychology/psychiatry was his insistence that Mexico develop a culture and a consciousness based on its mestizo experience. It was this idea that influenced the work of the Mexican philosopher/social historian Leopoldo Zea.

Zea focused on the experience of the individual in the Americas, indicating that his/her feelings of inferiority and anomie were the result of not having a native philosophy—a philosophy of the Americas— for guidance. Zea (1945), thus, proceeded to argue for an American philosophy, a framework for an American culture which could help people in the nations of the hemisphere to solve the major problems which they face and to avoid the failures of Europe. Zea pointed out that, if we are to succeed in creating an American philosophy and culture, we need to accept the diversity which is evident in all areas of the hemisphere. In addition, he emphasized the nations and peoples of the Americas' need to put notions of cultural and individual superiority aside. He stated that a necessary prerequisite to the development of an American culture and philosophy is the meetings of the peoples of North and South America on an equal basis, recognizing the value of the unique experience which each individual, each nation has to offer. In the following passage, he provided the basic tenets of the philosophical base on which mestizo psychology and psychiatry are being developed:

> The objective should be to incorporate the culture of the White man, the European culture, Western culture, the same holds for all cultural expression from all human beings, without having to sacrifice who we are as Blacks and Latin Americans. Being Black or Latin American should be enriched, expanded, but not negated or rejected. In turn, the White man, the Western man, all men can enrich their cultural expressions by incorporating the culture of the Black and Latin American. What Blacks and Latin Americans have to offer is cultural experience in other life circumstances, other settings, in another context of life challenges. These experiences need to be known by other human beings in other parts of the world so that the diversity of the human race will be more familiar to all of its members [p. 71].

SUMMARY

Some of the basic components of the philosophical framework for the mestizo theory of personality psychology and psychiatry and the primary impetus for the mestizoization of peoples and culture are reflected in the psychological concepts which have emerged from the cultures and philosophies of the indigenous peoples of North and South America. The most important contributions to the philosophical base of mestizo personality psychology, however, have been made by Mexican philosophy—a product of the mestizoization process. The contributions of Mexican philosophers such as

Vasconcellos, Caso, Ramos, and Zea along with the ideas of the melting pot ideology of the United States set the stage for contributions by mestizo social scientists and psychiatrists of the Americas.

REFERENCES

Caso, A. *El problema de Mexico y la ideologia nacional*. Mexico, D.F.: Cultura, 1924.

Caso, A. *Nuevos discurosos a la nacion Mexicana*. Mexico, D.F.: P. Robredo, 1934.

Caso, A. *Mexico: Apuntamientos de cultura patria*. Mexico, D.F.: Imprenta Universitaria, 1943.(a)

Caso, A. *La existencia como economia y como caridad: Ensayo sobre la esencia del cristianismo*. Mexico, D.F.: Secretaria de Educacion Publica, 1943.(b)

Driver, H. E. *Indians of North America*. Chicago: The University of Chicago Press, 1969.

Duran, D. *Historia de las indias de nueva espana y islas de tierra firme*. New York: Orion Press, 1964.

Klor de Alva, J. J. *Introduction to Mexican philosophy*. San Jose, Ca: San Jose State College, 1972.

Lee, D. *Valuing the self: What we can learn from other cultures*. Englewood Cliffs, N.J.: Prentice-Hall, 1976.

Leon-Portilla, M. *Aztec thought and culture: A study of the ancient Nahuatl mind*. Norman, Okla.: University of Oklahoma Press, 1963.

Leon-Portilla, M. *Time and reality in the thought of the Maya*. Boston: Beacon Press, 1973.

Ramos, S. *Profile of man and culture in Mexico*. Austin, Tex.: The University of Texas Press, 1975.

Romanell, P. *Making of the Mexican mind*. Notre Dame, Ind.: University of Notre Dame Press, 1971.

Storm, H. *Seven arrows*. New York: Ballantine Books, 1972.

Vasconcellos, J. *La raza cosmica: Mision de la raza iberoamericana*. Barcelona: Agencia Mundial de Libreria, 1925.

Vasconcellos, J. *Indologia: Una interpretacion de la cultura iberoamericana*. Barcelona: Agencia Mundial de Libreria, 1927.

Zea, L. *En torno a una filosofia americana*. Mexico, D.F.: El Colegio de Mexico, 1945.

Zea, L. *Dependencia y liberacion en la cultura latinoamericana*. Mexico, D.F.: Editorial Joaquin Mortiz, 1974.

CHAPTER 3
Social Science Foundations of a Mestizo Theory of Personality and Psychiatry

> The discovery of America meant not only the geographical exploration of new lands, but also the unveiling of a spiritual new world . . . the life cycle of Spanish America gravitates around behavioral patterns indelibly established in pre-Columbian times, some of which are still alien to traditional European standards.
>
> —Francisco Guerra (1971)

> Contemporary man has rationalized the myths, but he has not been able to destroy them. Many of our scientific truths, like the majority of our moral, political, and philosophical conceptions, are only new ways of expressing tendencies that were embodied earlier in mythical forms.
>
> —Octavio Paz (1961)

The social science knowledge base upon which a mestizo psychology of personality is being established has emerged primarily from research with mestizo peoples in Latin America. Most of the work has been done in Mexico and with people of Hispanic descent in the United States, but in the last ten years data important to the development of mestizo psychology have also emerged from research done in other countries of Central and South America and in the Caribbean.

This chapter does not attempt to provide a comprehensive review of the social science literature on Latinos; rather, it is an effort to examine the research which has had the greatest impact, by either negative or positive influence, on the development of a mestizo perspective in personality psychology. Discussion begins with the early anthropological and psychological research in Latin America; it proceeds to a review of the philosophical works of the Mexican national character; it then continues with the psychoanalytically oriented psychological research in Mexico. The chapter concludes with a review of the more contemporary research on some of the mestizo peoples in the Americas.

EARLY ANTHROPOLOGICAL CULTURE—PERSONALITY RESEARCH

Although the earliest research on culture and personality in Mexico had been done by Gamio (1922), it was the research by Redfield (1930), Lewis

(1951), and Foster (1952) in Mexico and that of La Farge (1947) and Gillin (1952) in Guatemala that attracted the attention of most social scientists in the Americas. Most of these studies focused on the effects of culture change, and, in particular, on the effects of modernization on the life and psychological adjustments of the person and his/her community. In general, these early researchers adopted one of two perspectives: they either idealized the life of Latino peasants (happy, noble savages à la Rousseau) or they presented a negative picture of their psychodynamics and their life styles. The perspective of these early researchers was heavily influenced by the European world view. The following description of the behavior of Guatemalan peasants which was provided by LaFarge (1947) gives a good example of the European world view-based approach of interpreting behavior independent of the historical, political, social, economic, and ecological context in which it occurs:

> Like the Hopis, these Indians are at once peaceful and quarrelsome; dreading open warfare and overt action, they bicker endlessly. One feels that living too close together plus the effects of a religion of fear and much belief in black magic, has produced a condition of exasperation expressed in gossip, fear and ill-will [p. 305].

Foster (1948) described Mexican peasants in a similar negative vein:

> Self-criticism is an unknown virtue—if such it is—and failure is always due to elements beyond one's control: the weather, bad luck and the unscrupulousness of other persons, but never is it the fault of the individual himself [p. 305].

Gillin (1952) also provided a pathological picture of his *Ladino* (mestizo) subjects in Guatemala. The following conclusions were drawn from observations and data he collected with the Rorschach Inkblot Test:

> In contrast to the manifested personality characteristics of Indians, the Ladinos show much more emotionalism, not only are likes and dislikes more demonstratively expressed, but the average Ladino is characterized by mood swings which range from depression and helplessness to feelings of high euphoria. Consistent with this is the impression that the typical Ladino is basically much less secure than the typical Indian. He has no feeling of certainty that any of his available culture patterns will produce satisfactions which he expects and he is uncertain about their effectiveness when practiced outside the community. The result is that may Ladinos tend to withdraw from or be hesitant about interaction in the larger world outside, but since they wish to adjust to the larger world, this produces feelings of frustration and inadequacy. Ladinos are much more aggressive, at least on the overt level, both toward themselves and toward members of the other caste. This aggressiveness can be interpreted in

the light of frustration which Ladinos face. Furthermore, the Ladinos show a higher percentage of hypochondriasis, psychosomatic ailments, neurotic twitches, and the like [p. 209].

Redfield's writings present a positive view of the Latino peasant, but his use of simple dichotomies to explain complex processes resulted in a misleading picture of the people and their culture. Redfield's (1930) conceptual framework categorized societies as either folk or urban. Members of folk societies were described in idyllic terms. For example, he described the people of Tepoztlan, in Mexico, as a relatively homogeneous, isolated, smoothly functioning, and well integrated society made up of a contented and well-adjusted people. However, he also saw these people as vulnerable to the evils of modernization. Because of his fears of the destructive influences of modernization, he predicted a sad destiny for the people of Chan Kom, another community he studied:

> The people of Chan Kom are then a people who have no choice, but to go forward with technology, with a declining religious faith and moral conviction, into a dangerous world. They are a people who must and will come to identify their interests with those people far away, outside the traditional circle of loyalties and political responsibilities. As such they should have the sympathies of the readers of these pages [p. 178].

Using a perspective reflective of the mestizo world view, Herskovitz (1947) criticized Redfield's folk/urban model. He based his criticisms on observations he had made in Africa regarding the bicultural nature (combination of urban and folk characteristics) of villages there:

> In West Africa, however, many urban communities are to be found that range from one hundred thousand inhabitants [the approximate size of Merida, Redfield's Yucatan city] to over three hundred and fifty thousand. These populations have complex specialized economies exhibiting, as we have seen, the use of money and presence of profit motivation. Yet in these cities relationships are as personal as in any "folk society" and religion is the focal aspect of the culture. In short here we have an anomaly, that is, in terms of the concept of the folk society—of urban sacred communities [p. 606].

This is an important observation because it provides an analogy for conceptualizing the pluralistic or bicultural/multicultural identity of individuals—one of the most important differences between mestizo and European world view-based psychologies.

The writings of another anthropologist, Oscar Lewis (1951, 1961, 1965), have had considerable influence on the development of a mestizo psychiatry and psychology of personality. On the negative side, Lewis (like Redfield,

Foster, and LaFarge) made extensive use of European world view-based perspectives; he also introduced the notion of the culture of poverty which is closely tied to a European world view perspective. On the other hand, Lewis introduced a research methodology which is consonant with mestizo values and life styles and, more importantly, a methodology which has produced data that clearly contradicted the negative, simplistic picture of mestizos presented by previous research. Unfortunately, Lewis himself largely ignored the complex and positive picture of psychodynamics reflected in the verbalizations of his subjects. He relied too heavily on data from the Rorschach Inkblot Test to draw conclusions about personality and about psychological development in general. It was his reliance on psychoanalytic theory and its techniques for personality assessment that led him to make statements such as the following: "The Rios family is closer to the expression of the unbridled id than any other people I have studied [*La Vida*, p. XXVI]."

Despite the questionable nature of his psychoanalytic interpretations of Latino behavior and culture, Lewis made a significant positive contribution to the development of mestizo psychology through the introduction of the technique which he referred to as the multiple autobiography of the family. This approach involved the use of the life history interview with different members of a single family; it presents the life history of the family as seen through the eyes of each of its members. This approach to data collection is both consonant with the world view and value system of mestizo populations and also represents a significant departure from approaches which had been used by social scientists in the past—projective tests and participant observation. The method afforded an opportunity to examine how the subject views himself/herself and also those people in his/her environment. The most important advantage of this approach is that the material does not have to pass through the researcher's interpretive filters. Thus, in the words of Lewis' subjects, we can see the complex interrelationships which exist between the person, family, and society in the world of the Latino. Many of his subjects emerge as articulate, introspective, historically and politically sophisticated people who are struggling with enormous challenges and demands in life. The following excerpts from *Pedro Martinez*, *The Children of Sanchez* and *La Vida* reflect the psychological sophistication of the Mexican and Puerto Rican who is poor, and who has had little or no formal education. The picture given to the reader by the words of Lewis' subjects contrasts sharply with the psychoanalytic interpretations he made and with views reflected in his culture of poverty model.

The following is from the prologue to *Pedro Martinez*:

> Anyone who is a man of ideas is that way from birth. Such a man is aware of what goes on. Others die just as they are born, still children. Some study, yet they are nothing—no better than the rest. At dawn, when God awakes, off they

> go to the fields, and from the fields, back home to supper, and from supper to bed . . . and that is all. These men are like dead ideas. . . .
>
> I always want to be poor. My thought has been to improve the village not myself. No! The Lord came to struggle for the people, not for Himself! I fought with Zapata in the Revolution and since then I have been struggling for justice. That's why I have nothing and my family has suffered. To be a hero, a man cannot think of how his home or his children or parents will suffer. They must suffer! There is no other way. A man who thinks first of his family is not a hero or a patriot. He is nothing.

Consuelo from *The Children of Sanchez*, describing her brother Roberto:

> Even though Roberto was a man, he walked along the highway of life like a child of eight or nine, in knee pants, short-sleeved shirt and heavy boots. He was a frightened child whose intelligence had been sidetracked by the broken road. His way was full of accidents and he had fallen countless times, leaving him deeply scarred. He walked with his right hand stretched out trying to reach something. . . . In contrast to Manuel, Roberto had a fixed goal—to find the security he needed. When he has finally found it, the sobbing will end and he will smile as he looks back over the whole course he covered [p. 273]."

Cruz from *La Vida*:

> I don't ever want to live in New York again. I'm better off in my own country because I went to the States twice and suffered a lot. I have suffered in Puerto Rico, but not as much. To me La Esmeralda is wonderful, better than New York or any other place. For me it's home. When I arrived here from New York, I felt happiness rise up in me again. I kept telling everybody that La Esmeralda was like a magnet who drew me back [p. 653].

These quotations stand in sharp contrast with some of the characteristics of the "culture of poverty" as described by Lewis (1965):

1. a lack of effective participation of the poor in the major institutions of the larger society (feelings of powerlessness);
2. a minimum of organization beyond the level of the nuclear and extended families;
3. an absence of childhood as a specially prolonged and protected stage in the life cycle (female- or mother-centered families);
4. a feeling of *marginality*, *helplessness*, *of dependence and inferiority* [emphasis added].

The above characteristics, according to Lewis (1965), were the result of "maternal deprivation of orality, weak ego structures, lack of impulse control, present-time orientation, and a sense of resignation and fatalism [p. xlviii]."

The influence of the European world view on Lewis' thinking is obvious. He took a "blaming the victim" perspective—because people were poor and powerless, he assumed that they had a non-culture or, worse yet, a negative culture which interfered with their psychological development (the damaging culture view).

The culture of poverty and the European world view were also very much in evidence in much of the early social science research done with Mexican Americans in the southwestern United States. The writings of Ruth Tuck (1946), Lyle Saunders (1954), Celia Heller (1968), and also William Madsen (1964) presented a uniform picture of a passive people who are held back bacause of the limitations of their culture. Mexican Americans were viewed as a people with a way of life that interfered with their assimilation into mainstream American culture, thus, preventing them from reaping the educational and economic opportunities offered by mainstream American society. The anthropologist Octavio Romano (1973) criticized the "culture is damaging, blaming the victim" perspective used by William Madsen (1964) in his research with Mexican Americans of South Texas and equated this model with that used by Oscar Lewis:

> To summarize Madsen's views, due to their own culture, Mexican Americans are the generators of their own problems. This impedes their material advancement. Therefore, today they are just as they have always been, and they will not progress until they change completely. Thus, Madsen has equated economic determinism with cultural determinism, just as Oscar Lewis has done. Finally, Madsen has made Mexican-American culture the final cause of all of the problems that Mexican Americans have encountered throughout history [p. 50].

Philosophical-Psychological Works

The influence of the European world view is also reflected in the writings of the philosophers/psychologists in Mexico and in the early psychological research done by Mexican psychologists and psychiatrists. One of the most influential of the early works was Ramos' *Profile of Man and Culture in Mexico* (1934). As was stated in chapter 2, Ramos argued that excessive reliance on European culture and ideology has interfered with the development of a true Mexican culture and consciousness. The following excerpts from his book are reflective of his arguments:

> Whoever aspires to a serious study of "Mexican culture" will find himself in a realm of vagueness. He will be struck by an abundance of Mexican works lacking qualities that could be said to proclaim the existence of an original vernacular style. But the existence of unoriginal works does not mean that the nation in which they appear lacks a culture of her own. . . . So it is that in the absence of objectivity, culture may still exist in another form; in subjectivity. . . .

> No one can deny that interest in foreign culture has signified for many Mexicans a spiritual flight from their own land. In this case, culture is a cloister in which men who disdain native realities take refuge in order to ignore them. From this erroneous attitude Mexican "self denegration" was born more than a century ago and its effects have been crucial in our historical orientation [pp. 15–16, 17].

Unfortunately, Ramos used a European world view-based theory of personality psychology—that of Alfred Adler—to explain the psychodynamics of the Mexican people. Ramos explained that the Mexicans' tendency to rely on European culture was based on unconscious feelings of inferiority which resulted from historical events such as the Spanish conquest, the reign of Maximillian and the various invasions by France and the United States. Thus, we have an example of the pervasiveness of the European world view; even in the process of making the argument that Mexico should develop its own culture independent of European influences, a European world view-based theory of personality is used to explain Mexican behavior.

The observations of still another Mexican psychologist-philosopher, Octavio Paz (1961), also reflect the belief that Mexicans have an inferiority complex which is linked to their historical past. Paz used this argument to explain the behavior of Mexicans who had migrated to the United States, concluding that an inferiority complex was interfering with the assimiliation of Mexican Americans into mainstream American culture. In one of the chapters ("The Pachuco and Other Extremes") in his book *The Labyrinth of Solitude*, he employs the European-based conflict/replacement model of identity and acculturation to describe the behavior of the Mexican American zoot suiters in the 1940s. He faults these young adults for not identifying completely with mainstream American culture, picturing them as people in identity crisis. Paz failed to recognize that the zoot suiters' unique life style and dress may have represented an attempt to develop new coping styles in a hostile environment. He failed to take into account the fact that the urban Mexican American male of the 1940s was straddling two cultures and evolving new life styles and coping patterns by integrating aspects of the two sociocultural systems—a bicultural/multicultural identity. Thus, by adopting the European world view, Paz ignored the possibility that these young people may have been developing pluralistic orientations to life.

PSYCHOANALYTICALLY ORIENTED WORKS

Although Ramos and Paz have both been influenced substantially by psychoanalytic theories, the best examples of the use of these theories to explain Mexican behavior and culture can be found in the works of Rogelio Diaz-

Guerrero (1955) and Aniceto Aramoni (1972). Diaz-Guerrero was trained as both a psychologist and a psychiatrist, and he has been doing research in Mexico since the 1940s. Although his most recent work (1977) (to be discussed later in this chapter) is supportive of the mestizo world view, his earlier writings were greatly influenced by European world view-based theories and perspectives in psychology and psychiatry. In an article entitled "Neurosis and the Mexican Family Structure," Diaz-Guerréro (1955) concluded that Mexicans have a disproportionately high incidence of neurosis because they suffer from conflicts fostered by the dynamics of the family and the separation of sex roles in the culture. He concluded:

> At a more specific level we can easily deduce that in the male there should be: (1) problems of submission, conflict, and rebellion in the area of authority; (2) preoccupation and anxiety regarding sexual potency; (3) conflict and ambivalence regarding his double role. He must at times love and act maternally and tenderly, and at other times sexually and virilly; (4) difficulties in superseding the maternal stage: dependent-feminine individuals; (5) problems before and during marriage: mother's love interferes with the love to another woman (Here one should expect an important area of stress where the husband, the wife, and the husband's mother play the dynamics of jealousy); (6) *the Oedipus Complex, as Freud described it: almost every aspect of the ideal setting for its development is provided by the premises of the culture and the role playing* (Emphasis added) [p. 415].

Aniceto Aramoni (1972) also relied extensively on psychoanalytic theory to explain the behavior of adult males in Mexico. For example, in an attempt to explain the phenomenon of machismo (i.e., the belief in super masculinity which is often attributed to Mexican males), Aramoni used a psychoanalytic perspective. The following excerpts from his writings represent his attempt to explain what he considered to be the disordered development of the male role in the Mexican family and culture:

> From the outsider's perspective, machismo represents an essentially pointless and destructive struggle by the man to overcome the humiliation of being an ineffectual little boy, especially in his mother's eyes. It is an ill-fated drama wherein the man, painfully attached to his mother, his sisters, and the Virgin, seeks their exclusive admiration and worship. . . . Further, there is reason to assume that the man unconsciously hates and fears the woman. This is why she must be disarmed, subdued, made impotent and harmless. But the woman subjugated and regarded as an object then resorts to her children to justify her existence, reflecting in them all of her hopes and frustrations, hatred and vindictiveness [pp. 69, 72].

In the works reviewed above, both Aramoni and Diaz-Guerrero used the European world view-based approach of taking observations and data out of the context of culture, history, and economics. The writings of both men also present an incomplete definition of machismo, ignoring that the concept is also used to refer to persons who live up to their social commitments and who are true to their word. The works by these two men also seem to imply that machismo is unique to Mexican culture, ignoring the fact that similar behavior was also characteristic of the knights of medieval Europe.

Other examples of the misapplication of the European-based personality theories and research methodologies to Mexican people can be found in the work of Fromm and Maccoby (1971). These researchers made use of psychoanalytic theory to interpret data they had collected on social character types in a Mexican village. Using a questionnaire, the Rorschach, Thematic Apperception Test, and Children's Apperception Test, they identified three main types of social characters: the productive-hoarding, the unproductive-receptive, and the productive-exploitative. The authors concluded that these three character types represented adaptations to distinct socioeconomic conditions in the country. Although the majority of the correlations reported were in the .2 to .4 range, the authors nevertheless concluded that the productive-hoarding type was the most adaptable and psychologically sophisticated of the three. As could be expected, it was the characteristics of people in this productive-exploitative type which were those most valued by the European Protestant ethic, and those which were characteristic of the "new merchant" class which evolved in Europe and America in the seventeenth and eighteenth centuries, e.g., practical, economical, patient, orderly, devoted, optimistic, etc. The authors employed a social Darwinistic perspective to explain how this entreprenurial type developed in the village they studied. That is, the productive-hoarding type evolved and flourished because of the social and economic conditions which were evident in Mexico at that time. They argued that, in a climate of developing capitalism, the obsessional hoarding type person was the most successful—shades of Darwinian natural selection.

RECENT PSYCHOLOGICAL RESEARCH IN LATIN AMERICA

The influence of the European world view is still very pervasive in psychology as it is being taught and practiced in Mexico and other countries in Latin America. In a recent article in the *American Psychologist*, Ardila (1982) observed that psychology in Latin America has been heavily influenced by psychology in the United States. What Ardila failed to point out, however, was that in the areas of personality, developmental, and clinical psychology, European world view masquerades as American ideology. The dominance of European psychology in Latin America was also evident in a special issue on clinical psychology in Latin America published in 1981 by the *Revista Latinoamericana de Psicologia*. European influence can also be seen in the majority of papers and symposia which are presented at the meetings of the Interamerican Society of Psychology and the publications which have appeared in the *Revista Interamericana de Psicologia*. However, in the past five years there has been some evidence that psychologists in Latin America are beginning to turn to their own cultures and to the experience of their own countries and peoples to evolve new approaches to psychological research and intervention as well as new conceptual frameworks for interpreting their data. For example, in his most recent work in Mexico, Rogelio Diaz-Guerrero (1977) has begun to give greater emphasis to the mestizo world view. His most recent work on the sociocultural premises of Mexican culture is a case in point. Diaz-Guerrero started with the assumption that culture is the result of historical processes typical of each country, and he asserted that it is imperative that the study of personality be an interdisciplinary effort. He defined the sociocultural premises of a culture as the sayings, proverbs, laws, and philosophy of life—philosophy of coping with life's problems, social roles, and social relationships. To assess the sociocultural premises of Mexican culture, Diaz-Guerrero developed two instruments: (1) one which assesses the sociocultural premises of the Mexican family and (2) another which assesses Mexican views of life. This work takes a step in a positive direction when examined from the perspective of mestizo psychology and psychiatry; it looks to the native culture for the definitions of personality and adjustment, and it also focuses on intracultural variability, highlighting differences which exist between people of the different regions in Mexico. Another Mexican psychologist whose work is reflective of the mestizo world view is Eduardo Almeida (personal communication from Diaz-Guerrero). Almeida is heading up a team of researcher-interventionist social scientists which includes economists, sociologists, and psychologists. The team is working in three rural communities in the state of Puebla. The team's objective is to provide assistance in community development without producing radical changes in the native culture of the region. The economists are developing a marketing program whereby local artisans and farmers can sell their products without losing profits to mid-level entrepreneurs. Psychologists and sociologists are assisting school personnel in upgrading curriculum and instructional techniques. They are also implementing a program of active parent participation in education.

In the last few years, the writings and also the research and development work of psychologists of other countries in Latin America and the Caribbean have also pointed to a trend toward the tenets of mestizo psychology and psychiatry. The Uruguayan psychologist Jose Varela (1975) has applied a mestizo perspective to social psychology in Latin America. He has employed a "social technology" orientation which is focused on intervention into social problems. The Venezuelan psychologist Jose Miguel Salazar (1981) has been advocating development of a social psychology which reflects the historical and political realities of the cultures in Latin America.

Another Venezuelan psychologist, Maritza Montero (1979), has argued for the development of a community psychology which has as its primary goal assisting people in the development of their communities. This same point of view has also been advocated by an American psychologist of Panamanian descent, Luis Escovar. Escovar (1980) observed that, since the formation of the Asociacion Latinoamericana de Psicologia Social (Latin American Association of Social Psychology) in 1973, psychology in Latin America has begun to follow a unique developmental trend which is related to the fact that most professors in Latin American universities were educated in the United States during the 1960s, a period of great social upheaval and change and a period in which U.S. psychologists were expressing disenchantment with the existing paradigms of psychology.

An overview of social psychology in Latin America by Gerardo Marin (1975) indicates that recent developments represent a good amalgamation of scientific objectivity with a definite commitment to the solution of social problems. He goes on to conclude that applied social psychology is the most important area of concentration in Latin American psychology.

Although recent developments in Latin American psychology and psychiatry have made a significant contribution to the development of mestizo psychology of personality, Ardila (1982) has correctly observed that European-based theories and methodologies (as reflected in U.S. psychology) are still very much in evidence in the work of many of the social scientists in Latin America. Thus, the majority of the impetus for a mestizo world view in psychology and psychiatry in the United States has emerged from research with Hispanics.

In a way, it seems incongruous that the philosophical base for a mestizo psychology/psychiatry has not been provided by Latin American scholarship, but that most of the social science base has emerged from work by social scientists in the United States. Perhaps this is testament to the fact that, although some domains of United States society have been described as racist (Report of the National Advisory Commission on Civil Disorder, 1968), the sociopolitical-intellectual climate unique to the United States has provided the necessary atmosphere for development of bicultural/multicultural orientations to life.

RESEARCH AND DEVELOPMENT WITH HISPANICS IN THE UNITED STATES: THE CALL FOR A MESTIZO PSYCHOLOGY

One of the earliest critics of European world view-based psychology was the Hispanic-American scholar George I. Sanchez, a professor at the University of Texas at Austin from 1940 to 1972. In an article published in 1934, Sanchez criticized the use of intelligence tests with culturally diverse children. The views presented reinforced arguments he had made in an earlier article (1932) to show that Spanish-speaking children are not inherently intellectually inferior to English-speaking children. He argued strongly for consideration of bilingual and cultural factors in interpreting results of intelligence tests. He identified one of the critical tenets of the European world view in the intelligence testing movement: he posited that the facts of genetics and heredity were being "garbled" in order to champion the superiority of one "race" over another. In many of his writings, Sanchez lamented the fact that the schools were not responsive to the cultures of Hispanic and Indian children and, thus, failed to serve them adequately. He continued to be a strong advocate for diversity in American society all his life. In testimony he gave before a congressional committee during the hearings held prior to the passage of the Bilingual Education Act in 1968, he likened the preservation of native languages in the United States to the preservation of natural resources. This testimony reiterated a view he had expressed in 1934, "The progress of our country is dependent on the most efficient utilization of the heterogeneous masses which constitute its population [p. 13]."

A major contribution to research methodology of mestizo psychology was made by a Mexican anthropologist doing research with Mexican immigrants and with second generation Mexican Americans in the United States. Manuel Gamio (1931) and his colleagues employed an open-ended life history-type interview to study the adjustment process of Mexicans and Mexican Americans in the United States. Gamio's results (like those of Oscar Lewis, which were to follow years later) showed that the poor mestizos with little formal education were articulate, introspective, perceptive, philosophical, and cognizant of historical, social, economic, and political factors affecting their lives.

Another major contribution to mestizo research methodology was the study done by the anthropologist Octavio Romano (1964) concerning the life and works of the famous Mexican-American *curandero* (folkhealer) Don Pedrito Jaramillo. Romano's study succeeded in placing his subject in cultural, social, and historical context, thereby allowing social scientists to better understand the relationship of folk medicine to Latino culture in South Texas.

One of the first psychologically oriented studies with Mexican Americans in the United States focused on adolescents living in urban centers in the states of California and Texas (Ramirez, 1967, 1969). The first of these studies identified family values with which Mexican-American adolescents and young adults were identified. The second study identified adolescent patterns of adjustment to acculturation stress. The focus of this latter study was on stress experienced by students as a consequence of conflicts between the values of Mexican-American culture and those represented by the schools they attended. The findings of a subsequent study (Ramirez & Castaneda, 1974) indicated that children and adolescents who had developed bicultural orientations to life were the most successful in academic and social activities and were less likely to drop out of school even when they encountered severe frustration.

The Bilingual/Bicultural Movement

With the passage of the Bilingual Education Act in 1968, researchers began to focus more intensively on the development of bilingualism and biculturalism in Mexican-American children and adolescents. Specifically, these studies sought to identify any advantages or disadvantages related to the learning of two languages and simultaneous participation in more than one culture. The early work on bilingualism was done by Amado Padilla (1977) and his colleagues at the University of California at Los Angeles and by Eugene Garcia (1977) and his students at the University of Utah. In general, the results of both these research programs led to the conclusion that learning two languages did not have an adverse effect on the intellectual development of Mexican-American children, and there was little interference between English and Spanish experienced by children who were being exposed to both languages simultaneously. Research by Mike Lopez and Robert Young (Lopez, Hicks & Young, 1974) at the University of Texas on bilingual memory also served to dispel some of the myths concerning language switching by bilinguals. Thus, the findings on bilingualism with Mexican Americans seemed to support the observations made by Sanchez in the 1930s and also tended to corroborate the findings of Lambert and his colleagues with French-English bilinguals in Canada (Peal and Lambert 1962).

The findings of research on dual culture participation were also heavily weighted on the side of advantages accruing to participation in more than one culture (Ramirez, 1969; Ramirez, Taylor, & Petersen, 1971). Ramirez and Castaneda (1974) conceptualized biculturalism in Mexican Americans in terms of a culture-cognitive styles conceptual framework. They postulated that traditional Mexican-American culture primarily (but not exclusively) encouraged development of a personality style characterized by global-deductive thinking, a personal style of relating to others, an orientation toward social rewards, and a cooperative orientation to achievement (a field-sensitive cognitive style); whereas mainstream American culture primarily (but not exclusively) encouraged the development of a personality style characterized by parts specific-inductive thinking, an impersonal style of relating to others, an orientation toward non-social rewards, and a competitive orientation to achievement (a field-independent cognitive style).

Through their observations of children (both Mexican-American and non-Mexican American) in schools, Ramirez and Castaneda identified subjects who could use both cognitive styles interchangeably and who could combine elements of both styles to arrive at new coping and problem-solving behaviors. Additionally, the investigators noted that those children who were cognitively flexible or bicognitive were also bicultural; that is, they had been socialized in both Mexican-American and Anglo cultures, and they participated actively in both.

Ramirez and Castaneda (1974) also discovered that the tests of cognitive style used by Witkin, Dyk, Faterson and Karp (1962) had a definite field-independent and European world view-bias. That is, these tests valued behavior associated with the European world view—analytical thinking, individual identity, and individual competition. As an alternative to the Rod and Frame and Embedded Figures Tests, Ramirez and Castaneda introduced two behavior observation instruments: one to assess cognitive style in children and another to assess the cognitive style of teachers. Basing their procedures on a mestizo world view in psychology, they arrived at the following conclusions:

1. the behavior of teachers and children must be observed in the context in which it occurs;
2. cognitive styles must be viewed as multidimensional and not unidimensional variables;
3. cultural and cognitive style changes in individuals can occur in both the directions of Anglo and Mexican-American cultures as well as in the directions of field sensitivity or field independence;
4. it is possible for children and adults to be bicognitive and bicultural; and
5. to encourage development of greater flexibility (greater bicognition and biculturalism), children, teachers, and schools must change to reflect pluralistic perspectives.

In addition, Ramirez and Castaneda presented the framework for an instructional program which could encourage development of cognitive flexibility in children and teachers in the context of bicognitive/bicultural education. More recently, Cox, Macaulay, and Ramirez (1982) have developed a complete interdisciplinary instructional program for encouraging bicognitive and multicultural development in preschool and elementary school children. The effectiveness of these bicognitive programs has been documented by other researchers (Kagan & Buriel, 1977).

Research on dual and multiple cultural participation (Ramirez, 1969, 1977, and 1980) by adolescent and young adult Mexican Americans has shown that active involvement in two or more cultures (biculturalism/multiculturalism) does not result in severe value conflicts and in identity crises;

but, in fact, tends to foster flexibility of personality functioning and development of skills as a cultural facilitator and a leader in mixed ethnic group situations. Thus, active involvement in different cultures seems to make the person more adaptable by virtue of introducing him/her to different coping techniques, different problem-solving strategies, and different ways of perceiving life problems and challenges.

Research with Cuban-American adolescents (Szapocznik, Scopetta, Kurtines, & Arnalde, 1978) has also shown that those adolescents who are bicultural tend to be better adjusted psychologically than those who are more likely to participate in either Cuban or Anglo culture exclusively. As is the case with Mexican Americans, identification with two cultures in Cuban Americans leads to a healthier adjustment than does a monocultural orientation to life. The authors concluded:

> The mounting evidence concerning the nature of the acculturation process and its implications for adjustment . . . suggests that in bicultural communities such as Dade County, exaggerated acculturation or exaggerated maintenance of ethnic identity, one to the exclusion of the other, is detrimental to the mental health of immigrant groups [p. 24].

Upon reviewing much of the social science research with mestizos in the Americas, Ramirez called for development of a mestizo psychology which could guide research, intervention, and theoretical development in all the Americas (1976 and 1977). He observed that theories of personality based on the European world view are misleading when applied to mestizos. Particularly misleading are those models of acculturation and culture change derived from European perspectives. Ramirez argued that findings of research throughout the Americas show that multicultural development and functioning are a reality—a reality which must be reflected in theories of personality and approaches to intervention and research.

SUMMARY

A review of the social science research done with mestizos in the Americas showed that the European world view contributed to a perspective of these people as pathological and as psychologically underdeveloped. Current research and thinking in Latin America as well as in the United States has produced a definite shift toward a mestizo world view. Recent findings of positive effects of bilingualism and biculturalism/multiculturalism have resulted in a call for development of a mestizo psychology in the Americas.

REFERENCES

Aramoni, A. Machismo. *Psychology Today*, 1972 (January) 69–72.

Ardila, R. International psychology. *American Psychologist*, 1982, *37*, 323–329.

Cox, B., Macaulay, J., & Ramirez, M. *New frontiers: A bilingual early learning program*. New York: Pergamon Press, 1982.

Diaz-Guerrero, R. Neurosis and the Mexican family structure. *American Journal of Psychiatry*, 1955, *112*, 411–417.

Diaz-Guerrero, R. Una escala factorial de premisis historico-socioculturales de la familia Mexicana. *Revista interamericana de psicologia*, 1972, *6*, 3–4.

Diaz-Guerrero, R. Mexican psychology. *American Psychologist*, 1977, *33*, 934–944.

Escovar, L. Design for a course on social psychology in Latin America. Miami, Fla: Latin American and Caribbean Center, Florida International University, 1980.

Foster, G. M. *Empire's children: The people of Tzintzuntzan*. Mexico, D.F.: Imprenta Nuevo Mundo, 1948.

Foster, G. M. The significance of anthropological studies of the places of origin of Spanish immigrants to the New World. In S. Tax (Ed.), *Acculturation in the Americas*. Chicago: The University of Chicago Press, 1952.

Fromm, E. & Maccoby, M. *Social character in a Mexican village: A socio-psychoanalytic study*. Englewood Cliffs: Prentice-Hall, 1970.

Gamio, M. *Introduction, sintesis y conclusiones de la obra: La poblacion del valle de teotihuacan*. Mexcio, D.F.: Secretaria de Educacion Publica, 1922.

Gamio, M. *The life story of the Mexican immigrant*. New York: Dover Publications, 1931.

Garcia, E. E. The study of early childhood bilingualism: Strategies for linguistic transfer research. In J. L. Martinez (Ed.), *Chicano psychology*. New York: Academic Press, 1977.

Gillin, J. Ethos and cultural aspects of personality. In S. Tax (Ed.), *Heritage of conquest*. Glencoe, Ill.: The Free Press, 1952.

Guerra, F. *The pre-Columbian mind*. New York: Seminar Press, 1971.

Heller, C. S. *Mexican-American youth: Forgotten youth at the crossroads*. New York: Random House, 1968.

Herskovitz, M. J. *Man and his works*. New York: Alfred A. Knopf, 1947.

Kagan, S., & Buriel, R. Field dependence-independence and Mexican-American culture and education. In J. L. Martinez (Ed.), *Chicano psychology*. New York: Academic Press, 1977.

La Farge, O. *Santa Eulalia, the religion of a Cuchumatan Indian town*. Chicago: The University of Chicago Press, 1947.

Lewis, O. *Life in a Mexican village: Tepoztlan restudied*. Champaign-Urbana: The University of Illinois Press, 1951.

Lewis, O. *The children of Sanchez*. New York: Random House, 1961.

Lewis, O. *Pedro Martinez*. New York: Random House, 1964.

Lewis, O. *La vida: A Puerto Rican family of the culture of poverty—San Juan and New York*. New York: Random House, 1965.

Lopez, M., Hicks, R. E., & Young, R. K. The linguistic interdependence of bilinguals. *Journal of Experimental Psychology*, 1974, *102*, 981–983.

Madsen, W. *Mexican Americans of South Texas: Studies in cultural anthropology*. New York: Holt, Rinehart, and Winston, 1964.

Marin, G. *La psicologia social en latinoamerica*. Mexico, D.F.: Editorial Trillas, 1975.

Montero, M. Aportes methodologicos de la psicologia social al desarrollo de comunidades. Paper presented at the XVII Congress of the Interamerican Society of Psychology, Lima, Peru, July 1979.

Padilla, A. Child bilingualism: Insights to issues. In J. L. Martinez (Ed.), *Chicano psychology*. New York: Academic Press, 1977.

Paz, O. *The labyrinth of solitude*. New York: Grove Press, 1961.
Peal, E., & Lambert, W. E. The relation of bilingualism to intelligence. *Psychological Monographs*, 1962, *76* (27, Whole No. 546).
Ramirez, M. Identification with Mexican family values and authoritarianism in Mexican Americans. *The Journal of Social Psychology*, 1967, *73*, 3–11.
Ramirez, M. Identification with Mexican-American values and psychological adjustment in Mexican-American adolescents. *International Journal of Social Psychiatry*, 1969, *15*, 151–156.
Ramirez, M. A mestizo world view and the psychodynamics of Mexican-American border populations. In S. R. Ross (Ed.), *Views across the border: The United States and Mexico*. Albuquerque, N.M.: University of New Mexico Press, 1978.
Ramirez, M. Recognizing and understanding diversity: Multiculturalism and the Chicano movement in psychology. In J. L. Martinez (Ed.), *Chicano psychology*, New York: Academic Press, 1977.
Ramirez, M., & Castaneda, A. *Cultural democracy, bicognitive development and education*. New York: Academic Press, 1974.
Ramirez, M., & Price-Williams, D. R. Achievement motivation in Mexican-American children. *Journal of Cross-Cultural Psychology*, 1974, *7*, 49–60.
Ramirez, M., Taylor, C., & Petersen, B. Mexican-American cultural membership and adjustment to school. *Developmental Psychology*, 1971, *4*, 141–148.
Ramirez, M., Garza, R. T., & Cox, B. G. Multicultural leader behaviors in ethnically mixed task groups. Unpublished technical report to Office of Naval Research, Arlington, Virginia, 1980.
Ramos, S. *Profile of man and culture in Mexico*. Austin, Tex.: The University of Texas Press, 1975.
Redfield, R. *Tepoztlan—a Mexican Village*. Chicago: University of Chicago Press, 1930.
Redfield, R. *The folk culture of Yucatan*. Chicago: The University of Chicago Press, 1941.
Redfield, R. *A village that chose progress: Chan Kom revisited*. Chicago: The University of Chicago Press, 1950.
Revista latinoamericana de psicologia, *13*, 1981.
Romano, O. Don Pedrito Jaramillo: The emergence of a Mexican-American folk saint. Unpublished doctoral dissertation, University of California at Berkeley, 1964.
Romano, O. The anthropology and sociology of the Mexican-Americans. In O. Romano (Ed.), *Voices*. Berkeley, Calif.: Quinto Sol Publications, 1973.
Salazar, J. M. Research on applied psychology in Venezuela. Paper presented at XVIII Interamerican Congress of Psychology, Dominican Republic, June 1981.
Sanchez, G. I. Group differences and Spanish-speaking children—A critical review. *Journal of Applied Psychology*, 1932, *16*, 549–558.
Sanchez, G. I. Bilingualism and mental measures: A word of caution. *Journal of Applied Psychology*, 1934, *18*, 756–772.
Saunders, L. *Cultural difference and medical care: The case of the Spanish-speaking people of the Southwest*. New York: Russell Sage Foundation, 1954.
Szapocznik, J., Scopetta, M. A., Kurtines, W., & Arnalde, M. A. Theory and measurement of acculturation. *Interamerican Journal of Psychology*, 1978, *12*, 113–130.
Tuck, R. *Not with the fist*. New York: Harcourt Brace, 1946.
Varela, J. Psicologia social aplicada. In G. Martin (Ed.) *La psicologia social en latinoamerica*. Mexico, D.F.: Editorial Trillas, 1975.
Witkin, H. A., Dyk, R. B., Faterson, D. R. & Karp, S. A. *Psychological differentiation*. New York: Wiley, 1962.

CHAPTER 4
A Mestizo Theory of Personality Psychology and Psychiatry

> The concept of person-environment "fit" rather than inferior or superior people or cultures is beginning to take hold. Recognition of and support for diversity is emerging. A major political-social question for the rest of this century will involve the ability of diverse groups to "live and let live," and this will mean understanding that there are neither sick persons (in the social-psychological sense) nor inferior cultures.
>
> —Julian Rappaport (1977)

> American psychology in general, and community psychology in particular, have been uncomfortable with the concept of culture and its implications for theory and application.
>
> —Seymour Sarason (1974)

> Man is always situated in a circumstance which offers its own solutions to the problems it creates. (The history of culture is the history of man struggling with his circumstances.) Every man has his own point of view, circumstances, and personality from which he must solve his own problems of life.
>
> —Leopoldo Zea (1943)

This chapter presents the framework for a theory of personality based on the mestizo world view. The intention is not to present a complete, polished theory but, rather, to outline the major assumptions and some of the components of such a theory. This chapter also introduces a model (which has been derived from the mestizo theory of personality) for understanding the development of pluralistic identities—a model which is based on research data obtained with members of one of the mestizo groups of the Americas.

GENERAL DESCRIPTION OF THE THEORY

In 1972, the Mexican psychologist-psychiatrist Rogelio Diaz-Guerrero published a book entitled *Towards a Historico-Bio-Psycho-Socio-Cultural Theory of Human Behavior*. The complexity of the title of this book reflects the interdisciplinary nature of the mestizo world view vis-à-vis personality psychology and psychiatry. In fact, the title of Diaz-Guerrero's book falls somewhat short of representing the global nature of the mestizo world view. A mestizo theory of personality should include knowledge from psychology, physiology, anthropology, sociology, and history; but, in addition, it should also include genetics, philosophy, folklore, economics, and politics. Finally, a mestizo theory of personality should reflect ecological and survivalistic perspectives of adjustment.

PRINCIPAL ASSUMPTIONS OF THE THEORY

Ecology shapes personality, affecting development and functioning through both the physical and social environments. The person is an open system inseparable from the physical and social environments in which he/she lives. Traits, characteristics, skills, ways of perceiving the world, and philosophies of life are developed by meeting the specific challenges presented by the environments in which the person interacts. In this ecological context, person-environment-fit is the primary criterion for determining the quality of human adaptation. Also important is the concept of circumstantialism as described in the philosophy of the Americas proposed by Leopoldo Zea (1943). That is, each set of life circumstances represents certain problems and challenges of life through which each individual finds solutions and adaptations, thus, developing his/her unique personality and philosophy of life. From the circumstantialist point of view, diversity is important because it reflects the different adaptations which individuals and groups have made to the diverse physical, social, and political environments in the Americas; each pattern of adaptation represents an important lesson on overcoming the challenges of life from which everyone can learn.

The ecological psychology of Barker (1968) and the social ecology approach (Kelly, 1971), both important developments in community psychology, provide conceptual frameworks and research and intervention methodologies which are consonant with the mestizo theory of personality psychology. For example, Garza and Lipton (1982) have recently proposed a socio-ecological model for understanding the behavior of mestizos.

Personality is shaped by history and culture. The history and culture of the group or groups to which a person belongs are major determinants of his/her personality. This assumption is the cornerstone of culture-and-personality psychology, a branch of psychology which had its origins in the Americas. The influence of the culture-personality perspective has been felt very strongly in both North and South America as well as in the Caribbean. The approach had its birth at the Institute of Human Relations at Yale in the 1930s where an interdisciplinary group of anthropologists, sociologists, and psychologists approached the study of human behavior from a global perspective. Psychologists focused on principles which concentrated on how an organism interacts with the environment and anthropologists and sociologists contributed information about the nature of those environments.

An important product of the work at the Institute of Human Relations was the establishment of the Human Relations Area Files, a compilation of ethnographic reports arranged in such a manner that quantitative cross-cultural testing of hypotheses became a real possibility. Prior to the establishment of the Institute of Human Relations at Yale, several Mexican philosophers (see chapter 2) emphasized the important role which history and culture play in personality development. Vasconcellos (1927) argued for the identification of the unique Mexican culture and personality (the mestizo) which had evolved as a result of the amalgamation of the Hispanic-European and native American cultures. Ramos (1975) showed how culture and history had affected the development of personality in Mexico and urged his countrymen to adopt a "living culture." More recently, the philosopher Paz (1961, 1972) and the psychologist-psychiatrist Rogelio Diaz-Guerrero have followed along the path pioneered by Vasconcellos and Ramos. The influence of history and culture on personality development is prominently represented in the theory of personality which has been proposed by Diaz-Guerrero (1972) mentioned at the beginning of this chapter. Ramirez (1978) has also emphasized the important role of history and culture in the development of pluralistic identities in the United States. That is, for individuals being socialized in a multicultural environment, the history and culture of the different sociocultural groups in which he/she is participating must be taken into consideration in explaining and predicting behavior.

Genetics and physiology figure importantly in personality development and functioning. Mind and body function in an integrated manner, and they are inseparable. To achieve good adjustment, it is necessary to have synchrony between mind and body. Approaches to treatment of adjustment disorders are holistic and synergistic. The predisposition to adjust effectively to certain life circumstances can be inherited. Certain personality traits, skills, and characteristics are linked to specific geographic regions, communities, and families.

Genetic Influences on Development

In the context of the mestizo world view, adaptive traits, coping techniques, and skills which have been developed by individuals can be transmitted to offspring. That is, certain traits, coping styles, and skills have been developed by individuals in specific geographic regions, communities, and families to solve the specific problems of human experience associated with their life circumstances and these are heritable. But in the mestizo perspective, there is more to genetic transmission of personality than is reflected in the German notion of Volksgeist (Herbart, 1816) which was based on the assumption that the characteristic traits of a people are biologically transmitted. Mestizo psychology views inheritance of traits in much the same way as proposed by the American sociologist William Graham Sumner (1906). Sumner's position was that folkways are habits of the individual and customs of the society that arise from efforts to satisfy certain needs. They become regulating for succeeding generations and take on the character of a social force. In the mestizo view, then, what is inherited is the predisposition to develop certain traits, skills, and characteristics in specific cultural, social, and geographic settings. From this perspective, Sumner describes the initial development of the mestizoization process in North America: "In the early days of the settlement of North America many whites Indianized; they took to the mode of life of Indians [p. 84]."

Psychopharmacological Influences on Development and Functioning

Herbs and plants are believed to play an important role in healing, self-understanding, and in achieving unity with the supernatural. Lopez-Austin (1975) and Guerra (1971) have documented the extensive use of herbs and plants in the medicine practiced by both the Nahuas and the Mayas in Mexico. Benitez (1975) and Spindler (1952) have described the use of peyote in the religious practices of contemporary native peoples in the Americas.

Spiritualism with its specific focus on identity development plays a major role in personality development. In the context of mestizo world view of psychology and psychiatry, spiritualism is centrally important in the individual's search for identity and life mission. As stated in chapter 2, spiritualism serves to link the individual with supernatural forces in the cosmos which can influence individual and group destiny. The emphasis on development is both on achieving control over the supernatural by attaining self-control and self-knowledge and also on enlisting the help of a person or spirit who can mediate between the supernatural and the individual. A strong identity with the group to whom the individual belongs is also important, because the group can provide access to knowledge concerning the maintenance of a proper balance between the individual and the supernatural. A good example of this is the astro-magical predictive models which both the Nahuas and the Mayas had developed to achieve control over the destiny of their group as well as that of their individual members (see chapter 2).

Those persons which are believed to have special knowledge, that is, access to supernatural powers, or to possess such powers play an important role in personality development and functioning. *Curanderos*, *espiritistas*, *shamans* and the clergy all play important roles both in helping individuals in their search for self-knowledge and identity and also in treating and advising those who are experiencing problems of adjustment. The specific roles played by *curanderos*, *espiritistas*, and *shamans* will be discussed in greater detail in chapter 7.

Religion is also perceived as playing an important role in achieving harmony with and protection from negative supernatural forces. Not only does religion provide models to identify with and codes of conduct in order to facilitate the achievement of meaning of life and death, but it also provides confession as a means of achieving reconciliation with the self and the supernatural. With respect to this latter point, Guerra (1971) observed,

> The distress of the pre-Columbian mind at not being at one with oneself was resolved by the mechanism of confession and the individual reached internal harmony at the moment of the interplay of time, place, attitude, and the sanctioned ritual converged. The patient at the moment of the pre-Columbia confession was also demanding immediate answers to questions and problems that had been taking shape for the better part of his lifetime within the pattern of behavior of the American civilizations [pp. 280—281].

Economic and political variables affect personality development and functioning. The history of the Americas is a history of struggle against political and economic repression, and the stories surrounding these struggles are important in the education and socialization of children. The heroes of these struggles are held up as models for young children and adolescents. In Mexico, countless novels, movies, radio and television programs, as well as school books have been written about the war of independence from Spain, the overthrow of the reign of Emperor Maximilian by Benito Juarez, and the revolution of 1930. Similarly, in the United States, holidays, school curriculum, and the media have placed considerable concentration on the War of Independence from England, on Lincoln and the freedom of the slaves, and, in particular, on the struggle to free the world from fascism in World War II.

Poverty, human misery, racism, repression of individual rights and equality of opportunity are all visible realities throughout the Americas. These realities also affect the socialization of individuals in the Americas, and they are the principal reason for the pragmatic orientation of American psychology. This is particularly true for the social sciences in Latin America (see chapter 5).

The process of confronting life's problems and challenges and, in particular, the process of coping with change lead to development of a unique individual identity and determine the person's orientation toward diversity. In the mestizo view, the personality is the sum total of the experiences of coping with life's challenges and problems. In addition, the personality is also reflective of the several changes—environmental and social as well as personal—which have been encountered in life. The life history of every person is a series of lessons resulting from both successes and failures in meeting the diverse challenges in life. The nature and quality of experiences with life challenges and change determine the degree to which the person is open to and accepting of pluralism and diversity in his/her environment. The person is either open to and accepting of diversity, viewing it as the key to surviving rapid and radical change, or he/she is protective, self-centered, and easily threatened by diversity and change.

In summary, the mestizo theory of personality is circumstantialistic, holistic, synergistic, and unified. It focuses on person-environment-fit and places the person in the context of cultural, social, political, historical, and economic forces. The theory views openness to diversity and flexibility of functioning as the principal goals of development.

The thread common to most of the assumptions of mestizo psychology is identity development. It is in the identity development process that the principal drama of personality development in the Americas unfolds. Thus, the mestizo theory of personality focuses on identity development.

STAGES OF IDENTITY DEVELOPMENT IN TRADITIONAL MESTIZO CULTURES

Early Childhood Years

In the earliest years of development, the child is encouraged to develop strong family ties and a strong sense of family identity. Family history is discussed frequently by parents and grandparents as well as by other relatives. Family members (both living and deceased) who are admired for their accomplishments are discussed often and held up as models for young children and adolescents.

Children are expected to inherit talents, abilities, learning problems, personality traits, and characteristics from both the mother's and the father's families. Through their personalities and life histories, children are expected to recapitulate part of the history of the families of both their parents.

Development of a sex-appropriate identity is emphasized during the early childhood years. Traditionally, in many mestizo families, there has been considerable separation of sex roles, and young children are frequently discouraged from engaging in play activities or from participating in family roles which are not considered to be appropriate to their sex. In recent years, there have been major changes in definition of sex roles in the family, with the most extensive changes taking place in families residing in urban areas.

Identification with ethnic or national culture is given great importance by both the family and the community. National and/or ethnic cultural heroines and heroes are held up as models, and celebrations of national holidays are taken as opportunities to teach history and cultural and/or national pride. Very early in development, the child is given the clear picture that rejection of national and/or cultural identities is tantamount to rejecting the self.

Middle Years of Childhood

About the age of six or seven, the peer group begins to play a major role in shaping the identity of children from mestizo cultures. In Latin American countries and in mestizo communities in the United States, Canada, and the Caribbean, peer groups play a central role in pre-adolescent and adolescent development. In fact, the peer group becomes the extension of the family in the community and neighborhoods. In some cases, the peer groups represent coalitions of families who reside in certain neighborhoods or sections of the city. Often, the child is given a nickname by the peer group which reflects either a physical characteristic, a personality characteristic, or a particular role which the child is expected to play in the group.

Competition between peer groups of different neighborhoods in the same city or between those of different cities or towns encourages and reinforces group identity. In most cases, the competition is in sports, such as soccer or baseball; but, in some cases (in large urban centers in particular), peer group competition takes the form of gang fights. The peer group exercises considerable influence on the life of the pre-adolescent and adolescent, and in situations where its values differ considerably from those of the family, the individual child could experience identity conflicts which are serious. The influence of the peer group often continues into adulthood and even into late adulthood if the person settles in the community in which he/she lived during pre-adolescence and adolescence.

Adulthood

In general, peer group relationships tend to move into the background once the young adult enters into marriage or a serious sexual commitment. At this stage in life, identification with the family assumes a prominent role once again. Having children and forming an alliance with another family through marriage renews the person's ties to the nuclear and extended family. The focus on family identity is also renewed through the socialization of children and the practice of encouraging children to identify with the family. Grandparents, aunts, uncles, cousins, and siblings play an important role in encouraging the young child to feel closely identified with the nuclear and extended family. This effort also serves to renew the adult parent's relationship with family and community as well as with the national and ethnic group to which he/she belongs.

Maturity

As the person moves into late middle age, he/she usually assumes the role of historian. As historian, the person plays an important part in encouraging children and adolescents, in some cases adults as well, to identify with family, community, and/or cultural and national group. The older person may also play the role of counselor or folk healer because adults usually develop strong spiritualistic orientations in the later stages of life.

PROBLEMS OF IDENTITY DEVELOPMENT

Most problems of identity development in mestizo communities and culture are related to the rapid and extensive changes which are taking place in the countries of Latin America, the Caribbean, and North America. Industrialization, urbanization, as well as economic and political problems in rural communities are causing severe tensions in families and neighborhoods. In many rural regions, people are having to leave their extended, and in some cases their nuclear, families to look for better opportunities in urban areas of their own country or in other countries in the Americas. In urban areas, extensive changes are taking place in family structures because both men and women are having to find employment outside the home. Patterns of family structure and sex- and age-related roles are changing rapidly. Parents also find it more difficult to pass on family and community histories to their children because it is not uncommon for the nuclear family to live at a considerable distance from the extended family and the community of origin.

Other major sources of identity problems in many mestizo communities are the generational disparities in life style, values, and world view which are developing between parents and children in many families. Effects of biculturation stress are being experienced by both parents and children. That is, they experience the marginalization effects of having to live between two cultures or between traditionalistic and modernistic belief systems in the same culture (Castaneda, 1977; Nisbet, 1970). Although these problems are common to most mestizo cultures in the Americas, they are more in evidence in the United States, where generational differences may be linguistic as well as cultural and generational. Most of the research on biculturation stress in the Americas has been focused on Mexican Americans, Cuban Americans, and Indians. Several researchers (Madsen, 1964; Padilla & Ruiz, 1973; Ramirez, 1969; Sommers, 1964) have documented the particular types of identity conflicts exhibited by Mexican-American adolescents and young adults who are experiencing biculturation stress. Ramirez (1969) identified two patterns of negative adjustment: (1) rejection of mainstream American culture—adolescents who exhibited this pattern rejected American culture and expressed bitterness and resentment toward its belief systems and institutions. These adolescents were frequently alienated from school personnel, from peers who were members of the mainstream American culture, and they experienced frequent difficulties with police, truant officers, and teachers; (2) rejection of Mexican and Mexican-American culture with accompanying efforts to become totally assimilated into Anglo society—adolescents and young adults who had adopted this pattern of adjustment became alienated from their parents, their Mexican-American peers and from authority figures. They functioned effectively within mainstream culture, but they seemed somewhat confused and ambivalent about their feelings toward Mexican and Mexican-American culture. Madsen (1964) found that young adults who exhibited this latter pattern of behavior experienced severe feelings of guilt and often turned to alcohol for relief. He labeled these individuals as "alcoholic agringados."

Two other patterns of adjustment to biculturation stress have been described more recently. One of these patterns has been identified among adolescents from families who have recently moved to the United States from Mexico. The behavior of these adolescents is characterized by confusion. They are closely identified with Mexican rural culture, and they find both Mexican-American and Anglo cultures alien and baffling. They, thus, have a tendency to reject both the principal groups and to interact exclusively with other individuals like themselves. A fourth type of adjustment pattern is evident in the behavior of those adolescents and young adults who were born in the United States, but who tend to participate minimally in both the Mexican-American and mainstream cultures of their communities. These young people maintain a marginal existence with respect to both cultures. They are minimally fluent in either English or Spanish; they know little about the history of either cultural group; and they have little or no commitment to the goals of either group. The individuals characterized by this pattern of adjustment also tend to isolate themselves from members of other groups in their communities.

Biculturation stress is also experienced by parents. The most common reaction experienced by parents in biculturation stress is the feeling that they are becoming alienated from their children. They fear that their children will reject the cultural and familial patterns and roles with which they themselves feel most comfortable. These concerns and fears are exacerbated by the fact that the children's dominant language may be English, whereas their own may be Spanish. The inability to communicate effectively is in itself a major problem and contributes to greater distance between children and parents and between children and grandparents. Parents also become concerned over the fact that, in many urban areas of the United States, middle class mainstream culture encourages adolescents to develop values and life styles which differ from those of adults. Parents become especially defensive when it appears that their children are losing respect for them and for other adults. It is not uncommon, then, for parents to become repressive in their socialization and to use techniques of behavioral control which lead to increased conflict and distance between themselves and their children.

OPPORTUNITIES FOR MUTLICULTURAL DEVELOPMENT

Growing up in mestizo communities and cultures of the Americas poses some dangers and difficulties in identity development, but it also affords some important opportunities for development of flexibility and diversity in orientations to life and for development of pluralistic identities. Many mestizo communities emphasize the advantages of being open to heterogeneity and also accepting of different values and ways of life. Since the mestizo perspective views survival of life challenges and acceptance of change as important to adjustment, adaptability and flexibility of coping are seen as the most important criterion of psychological health and competent functioning. The ability to relate to people who are of different origins and backgrounds—the rich and the poor, the rural and the urban, the young and the old—is considered to be one of the person's most important assets. The individual is expected to be able to empathize, to step into the other person's shoes and look at life through his/her eyes. The person is also encouraged to learn from other cultures and peoples in order to learn how to better the condition of his own people and community and family. Mestizo cultures and communities, thus, value pluralistic-transcendent identities. Peter Adler (1974) of the East-West Center at the University of Hawaii has provided one of the most thorough descriptions of multicultural personality:

> What is considered uniquely new about this emerging human being is a psychocultural style of self process that transcends the structured image a given culture may impress upon the individual in his or her youth. The navigating image at the core of the multicultural image is premised upon the assumption of many cultural realities. The multicultural person, therefore, is not simply the person who is sensitive to many different cultures. Rather, he is a person who is always in the process of becoming *a part of* and *apart from* a given cultural context. He is very much a formative being, resilient, changing and evolutionary. He has no permanent cultural character but neither is he free from

> the influences of culture. In the shifts and movements of his identity process, multicultural man is constantly recreating the symbols of himself [p. 31].

Our research (Ramirez, Garza, & Cox, 1980) with adults who are multicultural has led us to certain conclusions regarding the process by which individuals develop multicultural orientations to life and pluralistic-transcendent identities. Data from intensive life histories we have done with multicultural people of different ethnic backgrounds in the Americas led to the identification of several socialization-life experiences which were common to most of these people: (1) exposure to socialization practices which provided positive attitudes toward diversity and also positive experiences with diverse peoples and cultures—parents and significant others served as models and provided opportunities for positive experiences with diversity; (2) positive experiences with diversity in the school and neighborhood—beginning in early childhood, the person had opportunities to participate in several sociocultural environments and to shuttle back and forth between different sociocultural contexts; (3) experiences with situations in which previous patterns of behavior and problem-solving styles did not work (learning dilemmas)—in preadolescence, adolescence, and early adulthood, the person was challenged to develop multicultural coping skills, perceptual styles, attitudes, values, and world views needed to function effectively in multicultural settings. To cope with multicultural settings, the person combined personality resources acquired from experience with two or more sociocultural systems. This new combination of resources provided the building blocks for development of a multicultural orientation to life; and (4) experience with continual reformulation of identity and self-image—beginning in adolescence and early adulthood, the person made frequent and extensive changes in identity and self-image as he/she participated in different sociocultural and multicultural contexts (see fig. 4.1).

These data led us to specific conclusions concerning the dynamics which are characteristic of the development of multiculturalism (multicultural orientations to life and pluralistic-transcendent identities): socialization and life experiences which reflect the tenets of the mestizo world view tend to encourage an interest in diversity and a desire to participate in multicultural activities. This interest and desire are reflected in the philosophy that there is a potential lesson in living in every person, culture, and environmental setting. Socialization which is reflective of the mestizo world view also encourages development of respect for different life styles, philosophies of life, cultures, values, and belief systems. Thus, through socialization and life experiences, the mestizo world view encourages the individual to be open to and receptive of diversity. The individual is willing to learn from others and from experiences with diverse physical and social environments. What is learned from experience with diversity is stored in a reservoir of

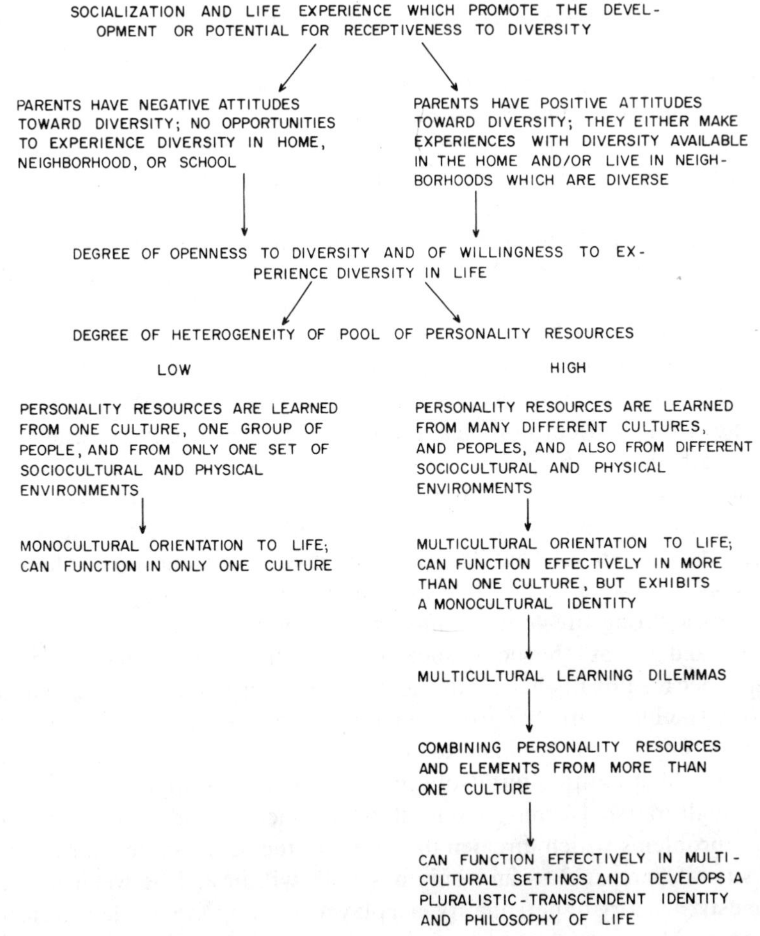

SOCIALIZATION AND LIFE EXPERIENCE WHICH PROMOTE THE DEVEL-OPMENT OR POTENTIAL FOR RECEPTIVENESS TO DIVERSITY
PARENTS HAVE NEGATIVE ATTITUDES TOWARD DIVERSITY; NO OPPORTUNITIES TO EXPERIENCE DIVERSITY IN HOME, NEIGHBORHOOD, OR SCHOOL
PARENTS HAVE POSITIVE ATTITUDES TOWARD DIVERSITY; THEY EITHER MAKE EXPERIENCES WITH DIVERSITY AVAILABLE IN THE HOME AND/OR LIVE IN NEIGH-BORHOODS WHICH ARE DIVERSE
DEGREE OF OPENNESS TO DIVERSITY AND OF WILLINGNESS TO EX-PERIENCE DIVERSITY IN LIFE
DEGREE OF HETEROGENEITY OF POOL OF PERSONALITY RESOURCES
LOW
HIGH
PERSONALITY RESOURCES ARE LEARNED FROM ONE CULTURE, ONE GROUP OF PEOPLE, AND FROM ONLY ONE SET OF SOCIOCULTURAL AND PHYSICAL ENVIRONMENTS
PERSONALITY RESOURCES ARE LEARNED FROM MANY DIFFERENT CULTURES, AND PEOPLES, AND ALSO FROM DIFFERENT SOCIOCULTURAL AND PHYSICAL ENVIRONMENTS
MONOCULTURAL ORIENTATION TO LIFE; CAN FUNCTION IN ONLY ONE CULTURE
MULTICULTURAL ORIENTATION TO LIFE; CAN FUNCTION EFFECTIVELY IN MORE THAN ONE CULTURE, BUT EXHIBITS A MONOCULTURAL IDENTITY
MULTICULTURAL LEARNING DILEMMAS
COMBINING PERSONALITY RESOURCES AND ELEMENTS FROM MORE THAN ONE CULTURE
CAN FUNCTION EFFECTIVELY IN MULTI-CULTURAL SETTINGS AND DEVELOPS A PLURALISTIC-TRANSCENDENT IDENTITY AND PHILOSOPHY OF LIFE

Fig. 4.1. Steps in multicultural development.

personality building resources or elements. The more learning experiences the individual has had with diversity, the more heterogeneous is this pool, and, thus, the more he/she can participate effectively in different sociocultural systems and environments. Also, there is more likelihood that he/she will achieve a pluralistic-transcendent identity.

In the early phases of development, personality building elements and resources in the individual's repertoire are exclusively linked to the cultural, socioeconomic, sexual, racial, religious, political, and geographic contexts in which they were learned; therefore, challenges to adapt to multicultural environments and situations are an important precursor to development of multicultural life styles and pluralistic-transcendent identities. These challenges encourage the individual to reorganize and synthesize the resources and elements in his/her repertoire so that efforts to adapt involve forming combinations of resources and elements learned from different cultures, environments, and peoples. The resultant coping techniques and orientations toward life are pluralistic. For example, in order to achieve consensus in a group in which members are diverse, the leader must arrive at a pluralistic leadership style and pluralistic perspectives on problems which are representative of the diversity which exists in the group he/she is leading. (This will be explained in greater detail in chapter 6.)

Also important to development of multiculturalism are continual reformulations of self-picture and philosophy of life throughout the life span of the individual. As the person is exposed to more diversity and to more challenges for multicultural adaptations, he/she continually modifies both his/her self-picture and philosophy of life. Eventually, the person makes a definite commitment to growth by continually seeking multicultural challenges. (It is at this point that the person begins to develop a pluralistic-transcendent identity.) That is, the person no longer comes to see himself/herself as a product of any one particular culture or group but, instead, expresses a strong life-long commitment to the well-being of all peoples, cultures, and groups. He/she is especially well suited to work in multicultural settings because of his/her ability to evaluate every culture and group objectively (including his/her group or culture of origin), becoming cognizant of their strengths and weaknesses. In this way, the multicultural person is able to arrive at multicultural solutions to problems of diversity.

Multiculturalism is, thus, essential to the Americas, because many of the serious problems which threaten the future of the hemisphere are related to diversity of perspectives and opinions both within and between nations. The mestizo theory of personality can play a very important role in assuring harmony and peace in the Americas; this idea will be discussed in more detail in chapters 6, 7, and 8.

SUMMARY

Theories of personality development and functioning based on the mestizo world view should be multidisciplinary. Included in a mestizo theory of personality is knowledge contributed by psychology, physiology, anthropology, sociology, and history. Additionally, knowledge from genetics, philosophy, folklore, economics, and politics also contributes to a mestizo theory of personality. The principal focus of the mestizo theory is on identity development. The diversity characteristic of many regions of the Americas and the rapid and extensive changes being experienced by people in most countries of the Americas pose major challenges to identity development. This situation can create problems of biculturalism/multiculturalism stress, but they can also offer the opportunity to develop a pluralistic/transcendent identity and multicultural orientations to life.

REFERENCES

Adler, P. S. Beyond cultural identity: Reflections on cultural and multicultural man. In R. Brislin (Ed.), *Topics in culture learning*. Vol. 2. University of Hawaii, East-West Culture Learning Institute, 1974.

Barker, R. *Ecological psychology*. Stanford, Calif.: Stanford University Press, 1968.

Benitez, F. *In the magic land of peyote*. Austin, Tex.: The University of Texas Press, 1975.

Castaneda, A. Traditionalism, modernism, and ethnicity. In J. L. Martinez (Ed.), *Chicano psychology*. New York: Academic Press, 1977.

Diaz-Guerrero, R. *Hacia una teoria historica-bio-psico-socio-cultural del comportamiento humano*. Mexico, D.F.: Editorial Trillas, 1972.

Guerra, F. *The pre-Columbian mind*. New York: Seminar Press, 1971.

Herbart, J. F. *Lehrfuch zur psychologie*, 1816 (Translated by Margaret K. Smith, New York: Appleton, 1897).

Kelly, J. G. Toward an ecological conception of preventive interventions. In J. Carter, Jr. (Ed.), *Research contributions from psychology to community mental health*. New York: Behavioral Publications, 1971.

Lopez-Austin, A. *Textos de medicina nahuatl*. Mexico, D.F.: Universidad Nacional Autonoma de Mexico, 1975.

Madsen, W. The alcoholic agringado. *American Anthropologist*, 1964, *66*, 355–361.

Nisbet, R. A. *Tradition and revolt*. New York: Vintage, 1970.

Padilla, A. M., & Ruiz, R. A. *Latino mental health: A review of the literature*. Washington, D. C.: U.S. Government Printing Office, 1973.

Paz, O. *The labyrinth of solitude*. New York: Grove Press, 1961.

Paz, O. *The other Mexico: Critique of the pyramid*. New York: Grove Press, 1972.

Ramirez, M. Identification with Mexican-American values and psychological adjustment in Mexican-American adolescents. *International Journal of Social Psychiatry*, 1969, *15*, 151–156.

Ramirez, M. A mestizo world view and the psychodynamics of Mexican-American border populations. In S. Ross (Ed.) *Views across the border: The United States and Mexico*. Albuquerque, N.M.: University of New Mexico Press, 1978.

Ramirez, M. A neighborhood-based, culture-responsive mental health model for Mexican-American children and adolescents. Unpublished manuscript, 1980.

Ramirez, M., Cox, B., Garza, R. T., & Castaneda, A. Dimensions of biculturalism in Mexican-American college students. Unpublished technical report to Organizational Effectiveness Research Programs, Office of Naval Research, Arlington, Virginia, 1978.

Ramirez, M., Garza, R. T., & Cox, B. G. Multicultural leader behaviors in ethnically mixed task groups. Unpublished technical report to Organizational Effectiveness Research Programs, Office of Naval Research, Arlington, Virginia, 1980.

Ramos, S. *Profile of man and culture in Mexico*. Austin, Tex.: The University of Texas Press, 1975.

Rappaport, J. *Community psychology: Values, research and action*. New York: Holt, Rinehart and Winston, 1977.

Sarrason, S. B. *The psychological sense of community: Prospects for a community psychology*. San Francisco, Calif.: Josey Bass, 1974.

Sommers, V. S. The impact of dual cultural membership on identity. *Psychiatry*, 1964, *27*, 332–344.

Spindler, G. D. Personality and peyotism in Menomini Indian acculturation. *Psychiatry*, 1952, *15*, 151–159.

Sumner, W. G. *Folkways*. Boston: Gin, 1906.

Vasconcellos, J. *Indologia: Una interpretacion de la cultura iberoamericana*. Barcelona: Agencia Mundial de Libreria, 1927.

Zea, L. *En torno a una filosofia americana*. Mexico, D.F.: El Colegio de Mexico, 1943.

CHAPTER 5
Research Methods and the Mestizo World View

I was very dissatisfied with Oscar Lewis's portrayal of the people of Tepoztlan (Lewis, 1951) and the Mexican family (Lewis, 1959) and first depressed and then angry with the application of Frommian characterology to Mexican villagers.

—Rogelio Diaz-Guerrero (1977)

A life historian, sophisticated in the above sense, can see his life history subject as a link in a chain of social transmission; there were links before him from which he acquired his present culture; other links will follow him to which he will pass on the current tradition. The life history attempts to describe a unit in that process; it is a study of one of the strands of a complicated collective life which has historical continuity.

—John Dollard (1935)

The future of mestizo psychology is closely linked to the research methodologies and the instruments for data collection which are used with mestizo populations and communities. As we have seen from the brief review of the social science literature on mestizos presented in chapter 3, the use of research methodologies and instruments which are reflective of the European world view have, for the most part, resulted in a distorted picture of the psychodynamics of mestizo people, their communities and cultures. This chapter takes a closer look at the European world view-based research methodologies and instruments which have been used with mestizo subjects. The chapter then proceeds to identify new instruments and intervention approaches that are based on specific components of the psychodynamics of mestizo subjects. The chapter concludes with the presentation of a procedure which can be used to assess the degree to which research and intervention projects are consonant with the tenets of the mestizo world view in psychology and pyschiatry.

METHODOLOGIES AND INSTRUMENTS REFLECTING THE EUROPEAN WORLD VIEW

Some of the distorted perceptions that social scientists and psychiatrists have developed of mestizo subjects and their cultures have emerged from research done with instruments and methodologies based on psychoanalytic theory. The notion of culture of poverty introduced by Oscar Lewis (1965) is a good example of the erroneous picture created by reliance on psychoanalytic methodologies and concepts. In his research in Tepoztlan, Mexico, as well as his studies in New York and Puerto Rico, Lewis used the Rorschach, Thematic Apperception, and Sentence Completion tests (all instruments based on the tenets of psychoanalytic theory) to collect data. The influences of psychoanalytic theory are apparent in his description of how the culture of poverty affects the behavior of individuals. Lewis (1965) concluded,

> On the level of the individual the major characteristics are a strong feeling of marginality, of helplessness, of dependence and of inferiority . . . other traits include a high incidence of maternal deprivation, of orality, of weak ego structure, confusion of sexual identification, a lack of impulse control, a strong present time orientation with relatively little ability to defer gratification and to plan for the future, a sense of resignation and fatalism, a widespread belief in male superiority and a high tolerance for psychological pathology of all sorts [pp. xlvii and xlviii].

The concept of culture of poverty led social scientists and psychiatrists to conclude that mestizos did not possess an authentic culture, a world view which was legitimately different from the European perspective. Furthermore, it led to the conclusion that the only culture mestizos possessed was negative—that it interfered with psychological development and mental health. It was no accident, then, that the "war on poverty" of the late 1960s and the early 1970s in the United States was based on some of the assumptions of the culture of poverty (Lewis, 1965). As a consequence of the influence of culture of poverty ideology, one of the principal goals of that effort was to encourage mestizos to assimilate to values and life styles which were reflective of the European world view. Ramirez and Castaneda (1974), writing about Mexican Americans, observed that the concept of culture of poverty was supportive of a damaging-culture perspective which had been evident in the social sciences since the 1920s:

> The theory that the culture and values of Mexican Americans are the ultimate and final cause of their low economic status and low academic achievement—the damaging-culture view—has been almost exclusively the framework within which social scientists have written about Mexican Americans [p. 14].

The link between culture of poverty and damaging-culture is also evident in Fromm and Maccoby's work in Mexico (1970). These researchers also relied on a psychoanalytic methodology to collect their data. While Oscar Lewis relied only partially on psychoanaltyic techniques, Fromm and Maccoby relied exclusively on these methods. They studied a small village of

800 inhabitants in the state of Morelos, located about 50 miles from Mexico City. To collect their data, they used questionnaires, the Rorschach, the Thematic Apperception Test, and the Children's Apperception Test. The questionnaire they developed for the study—the "interpretative questionnaire"—was clearly psychoanalytically based. The authors observed that the most important element of the interpretative questionnaire was the "interpretation of the answers with regard to their unconscious or unintended meaning." They continue,

> The task of interpretation is, like any other psychoanalytic interpretation, difficult and takes a great deal of time. It requires knowledge of psychoanalytic theory and therapy (including the experience of one's own analysis), a clinical psychoanalytic experience, and, as in everything else, skill and talent. Psychoanalytic interpretation—of associations and dreams as well as of answers to a questionnaire—is an art like the practice of medicine, in which certain theoretical principles are applied to empirical data [p 26].

Fromm and Maccoby's methodological orientation also led to a negative picture of mestizos and of their traditional culture. Their conclusion was that the passive-receptive character type—the pathological type which was prone to alcoholism and the tendency to avoid change—was the type most closely associated with the traditional culture of the village. However, the productive-hoarding type—that most closely associated with European values and beliefs—was seen as the most sophisticated in terms of psychological development. With respect to this latter type, they observed,

> The adventurous, individualistic entrepreneur has become a symbol of progress, of the better and glamorous life which the villager sees only on the screen. But the entrepreneurs are by no means only symbols. They take the lead in promoting those changes in village life and its institutions which destroy traditional culture and replace it by the modern principle of rational purposefulness [p. 231].

Culture of poverty and the theory of "social selection" of character types are both products of the European world view and both contribute to unfavorable assumptions regarding mestizos and their culture. From these assumptions, social scientists concluded that to better the lot of mestizos it was necessary to modernize, or rather Westernize, their culture and life styles. The Fromm and Maccoby study also supported the damaging-culture perspective among social scientists and reinforced the beliefs that only those mestizos who exhibited European characteristics in their behavior and psychodynamics were achievement oriented and well adjusted psychologically.

While psychoanalytically-based methodologies have contributed to a negative picture of mestizo adults, those methodologies based on the conceptual framework of psychological differentiation (Witkin, Dyk, Faterson, Goodenough, & Karp, 1962) have contributed to a negative picture of mestizo children and adolescents. Psychological differentiation is based on the ideas of the British philosopher Herbert Spencer. Spencer proposed that, as something develops, it becomes increasingly differentiated in parts and function, better integrated in the way the parts work together, and more segregated. By segregation, Spencer meant that each part attained more individualized qualities that distinguished it from other parts as time passed. The differentiation concept was applied to psychological development by Witkin and his colleagues (Witkin et al., 1962). Cognitive styles were defined as the characteristic self-consistent modes of functioning found pervasively throughout an individual's perceptual and intellectual activities. These modes of functioning are believed to lie along a dimension from global to articulated or from undifferentiated to differentiated. It is believed that at birth and in the early stages of development the individual exhibits a global mode or is undifferentiated (field dependent cognitive style); but, if proper socialization experiences are provided in the home and society in general, then the child becomes gradually more differentiated with age (more field independent in cognitive style).

To assess degree of field independence in children and adults, Witkin and his colleagues used several "cognitive" tests such as the Embedded Figures Test, the Portable Rod and Frame Test, and the Draw-a-Person Test. Culture and cognitive styles were believed to be linked through the socialization practices characteristic of certain sociocultural groups. For example, Dershowitz (1971) tested three groups (two Jewish and one Anglo-Saxon) of 10-year-old boys in New York City. His findings showed that the Anglo-Saxon group had achieved the highest scores on the "cognitive" tests (more field independent); they were followed by the more assimilated and Orthodox Jewish groups, in that order. Dershowitz concluded that the values and patterns of traditional living characteristic of the Orthodox Jewish group inhibited the development of a sense of separate identity, thereby resulting in less psychological differentiation.

This same "traditional values-inhibition of sense of separate identity" hypothesis was used to interpret the findings of a study (Holtzman, Diaz-Guerrero, and Swartz, 1975) which compared Anglo-Saxon children in Austin, Texas, with children in Mexico City. The two groups of children were compared on several instruments and tests including the Embedded Figures Test, the Wechsler Intelligence Scale for Children (WISC), and the Holtzman Inkblot Technique. The findings showed that the Mexican children had scored lower (in a more field-dependent direction) on the Embedded Figures Test than did the Anglo children although, interestingly enough, the first grade group of Mexican children performed better than their Anglo counterparts on the arithmetic and block design subtests of the Wechsler—

two tasks which are usually correlated with field independence. Nevertheless, a European world view perspective was used in interpreting those findings (Holtzman, 1979) which indicated that there were differences between the two cultures:

> From differences noted in the two cultures, *one would expect that in the traditional, passive, affiliative hierarchy of Mexico, there would be more value placed on affective rather than cognitive aspects of life, coupled with a preference for a static rather than a dynamic approach.* The Mexican should be family-centered rather than individual-centered; should prefer external controls to self-directed impulsiveness. At the same time the Mexican should be more pessimistic about the hardships of life and passive-obedient rather than active-rebelling in style of coping with stresses in the environment. For the U.S., on the other hand, the opposite of each of these statements should tend to be true. The many significant differences found between Mexican and North American children led to the above generalizations (emphasis added) [pp. 40–41].

In considering the results of the Austin-Mexico City study, together with those of other investigators who had worked with Mexican and U.S. populations, Holtzman (1979) proposed six major hypotheses concerning personality differences between Mexicans and North Americans. Again, the influences of the European world view are obvious:

> (1) North Americans tend to be more active than Mexicans in their style of coping with life's problems and challenges; (2) North Americans tend to be more technological, dynamic, and external than Mexicans in the meaning of activity within subjective culture; (3) North Americans tend to be more complex and differentiated in cognitive structure than Mexicans; (4) Mexicans tend to be more family-centered, while North Americans are more individual-centered; (5) Mexicans tend to be more cooperative in interpersonal activities, while North Americans are more competitive; and (6) Mexicans tend to be more fatalistic and pessimistic in outlook on life than North Americans (pp. 41–43).

The general conclusion reached by Holtzman et al. (1975) was that Anglo-American children are more field independent because American culture places a greater emphasis on autonomy in childrearing and because American society is more loosely structured. Mexican children, on the other hand, are more field dependent because of the emphasis Mexican culture places on conformity to adult authority and because Mexican society is characterized by a strict hierarchical social organization. However, no explanation was given for the fact that in the first grade (an age when children are most influenced by their families) Mexican children performed better than Anglo children on the math and block design subtests of the WISC, two indicators of field independence.

Research with Anglo-American and Mexican-American children in Houston, Texas (Ramirez & Price-Williams, 1974) showed that Anglos had scored in a more field independent direction than Mexican Americans. However, when a different research methodology was employed (one more consonant with the mestizo world view) in subsequent studies with children of the same two cultural groups, different findings were obtained (Ramirez & Castaneda, 1974). In the latter study, the researchers administered the Portable Rod and Frame and Children's Embedded Figures Tests to Anglo and Mexican American elementary school children and, in addition, did intensive observations of the behavior of their subjects in school settings. The results obtained indicated that Witkin's cognitive tests do not do justice to the richness of behavior exhibited by the children. It was also obvious that the Embedded Figures and Portable Rod and Frame Tests were biased toward field independence and did not reflect the flexibility of behavior which was being observed. The flexibility of behavior observed by Ramirez and Castaneda explains the contradictory findings obtained by Holtzman et al. (1975) discussed above. More intensive studies of these children and their families revealed that most of them could shift back and forth between field independent and field dependent behaviors. It was also observed that the field dependent behaviors, which Ramirez and Castaneda labeled "field sensitive," were not as negative and unadaptive as Witkin and his colleagues had assumed them to be. That is, when performing in a field-sensitive mode, children tended to be more cooperative, more attentive to the global features of a task, and more motivated to work for social rewards. Most important, however, was the observation that the most flexible children tended to have been socialized in bilingual/bicultural families. That is, both Anglo and Mexican-American children who had been socialized in mainstream American middle class and Mexican-American and/or Mexican culture, and who had learned both English and Spanish demonstrated that they were the most bicognitive. That is, they could function in both the field sensitive and field independent cognitive styles, and they could use elements of both styles to arrive at new problem solving and coping styles. Figure 5.1 describes the relationship between culture, language, and cognitive style.

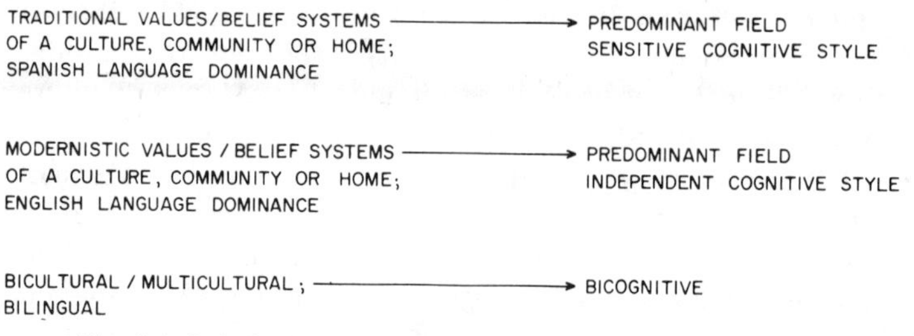

Fig. 5.1. Relation between culture, language and cognitive styles.

From the perspective of the bicognitive model proposed by Ramirez and Castaneda (1974), European world view-based research methodologies and instruments produce a fragmented and incomplete picture of individual psychodynamics. That is, if exposure to pluralistic values and life styles and to different languages encourages bicognitive development, then use of cognitive tests will, at best, provide researchers with only half the picture of the individual's psychodynamics. This distorted picture, thus, can lead social scientists and psychiatrists to arrive at inaccurate and unfavorable conclusions regarding the psychodynamics of mestizo subjects and the value systems and life styles of their cultures.

EUROPEAN VS. MESTIZO WORLD VIEWS AND THE EMIC-ETIC CONTROVERSY IN CROSS-CULTURAL PSYCHOLOGY

The European world view/mestizo world view controversy in psychiatry and social science research is analogous to the emic-etic controversy in cross-cultural psychology. The emic/etic distinction was first employed in anthropology by Pike (1954), who made an analogy with the usage of the term's components in linguistics—phonetics involves application of a universal coding system for sounds employed in any language, and phonemics involved study of meaning-bearing units in a particular language. Pike argued that social scientists should try to enter a culture and to see it as its own members do. Thus, the emic approach which he suggested is designed to show how a particular people classify their experiences in life. One of the best arguments for the use of the emic approach in cross-cultural research can be found in the book by Cole and Scribner entitled *Culture and Thought* (1974). However, most cross-cultural psychologists have been reluctant to reject universalistic perspectives. Even Cole and Scribner refused to take a definite position on this issue:

> The key problem . . . is that any fact, or small set of facts, is open to a wide variety of interpretations. So long as we are only concerned with demonstrating that human cultural groups differ enormously in their beliefs and theories about the world and in their art products and technological accomplishments, there can be no question: there are marked and multitudinous cultural differences. But are these differences the result of differences in basic cognitive processes, or are they merely the expressions of the many products that a universal human mind can manufacture, given wide variations of conditions of life and culturally valued activities? Our review has not answered this question [p. 172].

Nevertheless, Cole and Scribner issue a stern warning against the use of influential psychological theories (such as Piaget's theory) in other cultures.

> But carrying such theories overseas without some awareness of their cultural roots and their real limitations, even in cultures in which they arose, carries with it the risk of experimental egocentrism—mistaking as universals the particular organizations of cognitive skills that have arisen in the historical circumstances of our own society, and interpreting their absence in other cultures as "deficiency" [p. 200].

Although Price-Willams (1975) has taken a strong stand in support of the emic point of view, other influential cross-cultural psychologists have proposed combining the etic and emic perspectives. Koivukari (1977) has criticized these proposals:

> From my most critical viewpoint, all strategies that take an "assumed etic" or "what appears to be a universal construct" as a starting point latently involve a flaw in two respects: 1) the "assumed etic" is, at any rate in several cases and at least partly, Euroamerican emic. How shall we obliterate the cultural bias of our concepts *before* entering the field of observations? 2) the correctional method, while striving at minimizing bias, still entails a danger, common to any deductive strategy. When we approach a field of observations with preformed conceptualizations, we run the risk of selecting what we observe and of categorizing and interpreting what we have observed as a function of those preformed concepts, thus losing and distorting the information we would otherwise obtain. Our best intentions of testing the constructs against our observations will not ensure that such bias will be eliminated. The "emic" measurements may have construct validity because the construct directed our choice of the operationalizations to be measured and the "emic definitions" of "etic constructs" are influenced by the fact that we had the construct in mind when we started exploring the field of possible emic operationalizations. [p. 27].

Koivukari is right is asserting that, as long as European world view-based methodologies and constructs are used in cross-cultural research, it will be impossible to obtain an unbiased view of the subjects and cultures being studied. For example, research by Garza (1977) has shown that the items of internal-external locus of control instruments have different meanings for Mexican Americans than they do for Anglos. Garza administered Rotter's (1966) Internal-External scale to 203 Anglo and 244 Mexican-American university undergraduates. The data from both groups of subjects were factor analyzed separately. The findings showed that out of five conceptually based factors that emerged from the data the cultural equivalence of three of these factors was questionable. The content of the items which loaded on some of the factors for Anglos and Mexican Americans indicated that the concepts themselves did not appear to carry the same meanings for the members of the two groups. Garza concluded,

> The problem of cultural equivalence is extremely complex and entails more than merely controlling for such obvious factors as readability and language

> usage. As clearly indicated by the data presented in the present paper, even simple statements regarding beliefs in internal as opposed to external control may evoke totally different meanings for Chicanos in comparison with Anglos. It is conceivable that a great deal of research literature comparing Chicanos and Anglos may be based on equivocal measurements of a given psychological construct, casting serious doubt on the validity of the findings [pp. 106–107].

The pervasiveness of the etic perspective has also resulted in administration of instruments and techniques to mestizo subjects which are no more than translations of instruments reflecting the European world view. Researchers committed to the etic point of view have not been cognizant of the fact that translating an instrument into another language does not alter its culturally biased content and structure. That is, translating the semantic differential does not alter the fact that it encourages a segmented, fragmented view of psychodynamics which is not in keeping with the mestizo world view.

One of the best examples of the fallacy of the etic-quasi-emic approach is Triandis' model of subjective culture (1972). Triandis defined subjective culture as a cultural group's characteristic way of perceiving the man-made part of its environment—the perception of the rules and the group's norms, roles, and values. Athough the conceptualization of the subjective culture notion is reflective of both the emic and mestizo perspectives, the methodology which Triandis and his colleagues have used to collect most of their data is not—they rely heavily on the semantic differential technique.

Thus, from the perspective of the mestizo world view, priority must be given to development of research methodologies and instruments which are consonant with the psychodynamics of mestizos. What follows is a review of methodologies and instruments whose development has been inspired by specific characteristics of the psychodynamics of the mestizo peoples.

RESEARCH METHODOLOGIES AND INSTRUMENTS INSPIRED BY THE MESTIZO WORLD VIEW

Importance of Individual Uniqueness

"*Cada cabeza un mundo*" (every person is a world unto himself/herself). This saying, used so often in Hispanic cultures, attests to the importance of the belief that every individual is unique because he/she has a perspective on life which no other person can duplicate. This assertion is reflected in the philosophy of the Americas proposed by Leopoldo Zea which was discussed in chapter 2—the unique life circumstances of the individual have shaped the person's life style and his/her view of life.

The Life History. The life history approach can capture the uniqueness of the individual and the unqiue nature of the life circumstances which shaped his/her personality. The most important work on the use of this approach in social science research was written by John Dollard, a sociologist and social psychologist, in 1935. In contrasting the perspective of the person which could be obtained through the life history with that afforded by the "conventional cultural view" (used most often by social scientists studying other cultures), he identified the advantages of the life history method:

> In the long-section or life history view the individual remains organically present as an object of study; he must be accounted for in his full, immediate, personal reality. The eye remains on the details of his behavior and these we must research on and explain. Here culture is bedded down in a specific organic locus. The culture forms a continuous and connected wrap for the organic life. From the standpoint of the life history the person is viewed as an organic center of feeling moving through a culture and drawing magnetically to him the main strands of the culture. In the end the individual appears as a person, as a microcosm of the group features of his culture. It is possible that detailed studies of the lives of individuals will reveal new perspectives on the culture as a whole which are not accessible when one remains on the formal cross-sectional plane of observation. In pure cultural studies, on the other hand, the organic man has disappeared and only that abstracted portion of him remains that is isolated and identified by the culture pattern. If, in the "pure" cultural study, the organic reality of the person is lost, then we should expect that cultural studies would tell us little about individual experience and meaning [pp. 4–5].

The quotation above not only reflects some of the major tenets of the mestizo world view in psychology, but it also provides guidelines for research which would have helped us to avoid many etic-emic methodological problems in cross-cultural research. If we were to substitute "European world view" for "pure cultural studies" in the quotation presented above, Dollard, 48 years ago, would have foreseen the methodological problems which we are currently experiencing in cross-cultural research.

In recent work with the life history approach, Ramirez and his colleagues (Ramirez, Cox & Castaneda, 1977; Ramirez, Cox, Garza, & Castaneda, 1978) have developed a life history interview for young adults with a special focus on development of pluralistic identities. The interview follows five different periods in the person's life: early childhood, elementary school, middle school, high school, and college. The length of the interview varies from an hour and fifteen minutes to an hour and thirty minutes. Questions asked center around the following themes: language learning and usage; family and community life; school experiences; academic achievement; peer relations; relationships with authority figures; political activities; religious beliefs; life crises; identity crises; perceived advantages and disadvantages of mainstream American, Mexican, and Mexican-American cultures; degree of comfort and acceptance experienced while participating in different cultures; contemporary sociocultural identity; preference for ethnic background of marriage partners; philosophy of life; and career goals. Information obtained from the Psychohistory Schedule for Assessing Multiculturalism (PSAM) is scored on variables relating to four major areas of functioning: sociocultural competencies, multicultural participation, interethnic facilitation, and leadership experience in pluralistic situations. With respect to sociocultural competencies, the interviewee is assessed according to successful experiential history in three general domains or settings (the home, the community, and the school) in each of Mexican-American and mainstream American cultures. Three areas of functioning were assessed in this manner: language, peer relations, and relations with authority figures. Scoring was done by using a five-point scale for each of these variables. Scores for interethnic facilitation, multicultural participation, and leadership experience in pluralistic situations were assigned on a three-point scale in each of the domains of school, home, and community. Use of the PSAM to study multicultural subjects is described in chapter 6.

Importance of Family Identity

From the perspective of the mestizo world view, the individual is seen as embedded in the context of his/her family group. Recognition of the important role played by the family in individual psychodynamics has been one of the major contributions of the native cultures of the Americas to the fields of psychology, psychiatry, and sociology.

The Multiple Autobiography in a Single Family. Oscar Lewis' (1961) multiple autobiography in a single family is a major contribution to mestizo research methodology, because it identifies the nature of the familial context in which the individual has been reared and in which he/she presently finds himself/herself. This technique is not only reflective of the important and central role which the family plays in the psychodynamics of the individual, but it also affords a view of the unique perception which each member has of his/her family. This latter point permits us to see that families can be viewed as both positive and negative by individuals in terms of different life events and stages of development. Another advantage of the technique is that it permits a view of the same family from the individual perspectives of different members. Thus, the multiple autobiography in a single family can assess the quality and the degree of the individual's identity with the family and the true nature of that identity; that is, what identification with the family really means to the individual. The advantages offered by the multiple autobiography in a single family are best described by Lewis himself:

> . . . Each member of the family tells his own life story in his own words. This approach gives us a cumulative, multifaced, panoramic view of each individual, of the family as a whole, and of many aspects of lower-class Mexican life. The independent versions of the same incidents given by the various members provide a built-in check upon the reliability and validity of much of the data and thereby partially offset the subjectivity inherent in a single autobiography. At the same time it reveals the discrepancies in the way events are recalled by each member of the family. . . . The tape recorder used in taking down the life stories . . . has made possible the beginning of a new kind of literature of social realism. With the aid of the tape recorder, unskilled, uneducated, and even illiterate persons can talk about themselves and relate their observations and experiences in an uninhibited, spontaneous, and natural manner. . . . This method of multiple autobiographies also tends to reduce the element of investigator bias because the accounts are not put through the sieve of a middle-class North American mind but are given in the words of the subjects themselves. . . . While I use a directive approach in the interviews, I encouraged free association, and I was a good listener. I attempted to cover systematically a wide range of subjects: their earliest memories, their dreams, their hopes, fears, joys and sufferings; sex life, their concepts of justice, religion, and politics; their knowledge of geography and history; in short, their total view of the world. Many of my questions stimulated them to express themselves on subjects which they might otherwise never have thought of or volunteered information about. However, the answers were their own [pp. xi, xii, and xxi].

The Family History Questionnaire. As an outgrowth of his work with the Psychohistory Schedule for Assessing Multiculturalism, described above, Ramirez (1982) has developed a "Family History Questionnaire." The approach involves holding separate interviews with both husband and wife concerning the good and bad times experienced by the family. The interviewer also focuses on how individual and family problems were resolved and on the particular people, agencies, and institutions which husband and wife view as sources of support in times of crisis. Questions asked in the interview focus on the following topics: degree to which the husband's and wife's families approved of the marriage, recollection of the best times experienced by the family, recollection of the greatest family crisis endured and how the family coped with the situation, perceived sources of support in times of crisis (both hypothetical and actual), and the perceived ability of the family to confront a crisis in the past, in the present, and in the future. The results of a recent study (Ramirez, Diaz-Guerrero, Hernandez, & Iscoe, 1982) in which the Family History Questionnaire was used with mothers in San Antonio, Texas, and Monterrey, Mexico, revealed that the technique was very useful in assessing the degree of effectiveness with which families cope with life stress. In addition, data collected with the instrument indicated the degree to which families rely on members of the extended family and on institutions outside the family such as religion, schools, hospitals, welfare agencies, and neighborhood organizations in coping with life crises.

Familial Support Systems. In a recent study, Culler and Diaz-Guerrero (1982) employed a definition of support systems which was more inclusive than those which had been used in previous research. They referred to this expanded support network as the "webwork," indicating that it was composed not only of people but also of activities, objects, and events. Some of the activities included were "attending church," "singing Mexican songs," and "praying the rosary." Objects included were "medals and scapularies" as well as some more abstract ones like "Mexican poetry." The list of people, activities, objects, and events thought to contribute to moral and emotional support were presented to mothers and their adolescent children in Monterrey, Mexico and San Antonio, Texas (all San Antonio subjects were Mexican American). The subjects responded along a five-point scale from 0 (not at all) to 4 (very much) to the question: "Do you feel you have received moral or emotional support from [the item] which has been helpful in overcoming crises?" Both groups of mothers and adolescents rated the following items as very supportive: mother, father, grandmother, grandfather, brothers and sisters, relatives, and godfather and godmother.

Hispanic Perspectives in Family Therapy. The central role played by the family in the psychodynamics of mestizos has also been recognized by scholars who are developing innovative intervention approaches in mental health. Scopetta and Szapocznick (1980) have pioneered the development and use of culturally appropriate family therapy approaches with Cuban Americans in Miami, Florida. Preliminary ethnographic research by the investigators revealed that certain characteristics of Cuban Americans were important to the development of a culturally sensitive treatment model: (1) a preference for lineal relationships based on hierarchical, not vertical, structures; (2) a strong family influence; (3) an orientation for not interacting with the complex network of social systems in the host culture environment; and (4) a crisis-oriented approach to treatment and rehabilitation. In addition, the researchers observed that acculturation pressures resulted in disruption of the Cuban-American family (Scopetta and Szapocznik, 1980).

In response to the above findings, Scopetta and Szapocznik have developed a Brief Strategic Family Therapy at the Spanish Family Guidance Clinic in Miami, Florida. This approach focuses on acculturation-related dysfunctions with a therapeutic approach which facilitates the use of new and alternative modalities of transactions by affecting reorganization and restructuring within the family and with the extrafamilial milieu.

These investigators have also developed an intervention modality, for use in their family therapy, which seeks to enhance the bicultural adjustment of adolescents. This approach, entitled Bicultural Effectiveness Training (BET), consists of 12 lessons which are presented to the conjoint family composed of all family members above the age of seven who live with the problem adolescent. Each of the 12 lessons takes from one and one-half to two hours. The following are some of the topics covered in the BET approach: how do families relate to their environment; family change; family relationship styles; how is a family stressed; and what is biculturalism?

Another approach to psychotherapy with mestizos which utilizes family dynamics is being developed by Constantino (1981) in his work with Puerto Ricans in New York City. The approach, directed at children and their mothers, is based on the folklore of traditional Puerto Rican culture. The story-telling therapeutic procedures, TEMAS I and TEMAS II, incorporates three factors: (1) Puerto Rican heritage as manifested in folk stories or *cuentos*; (2) the mother as a pivotal figure in the Puerto Rican family; and (3) adaptive ego functions as reflected in the mainstream culture. Constantino assumed that folklore as a therapeutic modality possessed the capability of motivating attentional processes by presenting culturally familiar characters, by modeling the character's thoughts, beliefs, and behaviors with which children can identify, and by mediating a more functional relationship with the mother. Furthermore, in addition to the intrinsic cultural values present in *cuentos* that are repeated through the years, adapted or modified folk stories created by living within the Anglo culture provide a new synthesis for children in conflict between two cultures, thus enhancing ego functioning and promoting optimal mental health.

Importance of Cultural Identity

From the mestizo perspective, identification with the culture is a definite indicator of the person's stability and sense of meaning in life. However, the mestizo world view also recognizes that cultural change is a reality which all individuals must face. Thus, the research methodologies and instruments to be used with mestizos should reflect not only the salience of cultural and individual identity but also the important role which cultural change plays in identity development and personality dynamics in general.

Sociocultural Premises and Views of Life. Diaz-Guerrero has devoted much of his research career to the development of instruments for assessing the degree of identification with Mexican culture. His efforts have produced two instruments—Sociocultural Premises and Views of Life—described in chapter 3.

Mexican-American Family Values Inventory. Influenced by the works of Diaz-Guerrero, Ramirez (1969) developed an inventory of Mexican-American family values in order to assess the degree to which the Mexican-American adolescents and young adults were identified with the values of traditional Mexican-American culture. In later work, Ramirez, Taylor & Peterson (1971) developed a set of picture cards to which children and adolescents were asked to tell stories. This instrument, entitled School Situations Picture Stories Technique (SSPST), assessed the degree to which the adolescent experienced interpersonal conflicts related to cultural value differences between the school and home environments. The more closely identified the adolescent was with traditional Mexican-American culture, the more conflicts he/she experienced at school. On the other hand, the more identified he/she was with mainstream American culture, the greater the number of conflicts experienced at home.

Assessing Degree of Acculturation in Adults. Some investigators have focused on the effects of acculturation on the identity of mestizos. For example, Padilla (1980) and his colleagues have developed a model of acculturation for Mexican Americans. Data were collected by administering questionnaires which include two types of items—cultural awareness (CA) and ethnic loyalty (EL). After administering the questionnaire to 381 respondents in southern California and doing a factor analysis on the data, the investigators concluded that four factors were found to be related to the dimension of CA: the respondent's cultural heritage, the spouse's cultural heritage and pride, the parents' cultural heritage and pride, and perceived discrimination. Similarly, four factors were found to be related to the dimensions of EL: language preference and use, cultural pride and affiliation, cultural identification, and social behavior orientation. From these data, Padilla and his colleagues constructed profiles of acculturation types. The following is an example of one of the profiles identified:

> An individual with low CA (according to the model) has a cultural orientation which reflects the mainstream "American" culture (as do the parents and the individual's spouse, if married). This is manifested by knowledge of, identification with, and preference for the United States' "American" culture and for English language as the language of preference. In all probability, this person will also score low on EL, which would indicate little pride in the culture or origin and affiliation with more Mexican oriented acquaintances. The person would also perceive little or no discrimination toward Mexicans at either the individual or group level. Finally, the social behavior of this particular individual would be non Mexican-oriented [p. 66].

Szapocznik, Scopetta, Kurtines, and Arnalde (1978) have developed two acculturation scales (self-reported behaviors and value dimensions). The scales have been used with subjects of differing generation, age, and socioeconomic levels in the Miami, Florida, area. Behavioral acculturation scale items tap language preference in various domains; they also include items of preferences in music, food, etc. The value acculturation scale consisted of 22 problem situations, reflective of Kluckhohn and Strodbeck's

(1961) theory of value orientations. Each of the problem situations was followed by three statements presenting three possible solutions to that problem. The data collected by the authors indicated that the behavioral scale was psychometrically superior to the value scale. The researchers also presented a model of Cuban-American acculturation which was suggested by their findings.

Cuellar and his colleagues (Cuellar, Harris, & Jasso, 1980) have also developed an acculturation scale for Mexican Americans. The scale was developed with both normals and psychiatric in-patients. The Acculturation Rating Scale for Mexican Americans (ARSMA) consists of 20 items which are scored on a five-point Likert scale ranging from Mexican/Spanish (1) to Anglo/English (5). The authors indicated that a primary concern in the development of their scale was that it should be applicable with disturbed patients, such as psychotic individuals whose self-report may not be very reliable. The scale is supposedly flexible enough that it can be scored on the basis of informant information, observational data, and on the rater's judgment scale. ARSMA may be administered in English, Spanish, or both, depending on the preference of the subject. Items on the scale represent four factors: (1) language familiarity, usage, and preference; (2) ethnic identity and generation; (3) reading, writing, and cultural exposure; and (4) ethnic interaction.

Importance of Generational Status

Research that has focused on generational status (Buriel, 1981) has produced data which indicates that acculturation is a complex process. Buriel collected data on first, second and third generation Mexican-American children and his findings indicated that although first generation children are the most "Mexicanized" in terms of their cultural identities, they are also the most bicultural. The investigator concludes,

> . . . the significant positive correlation between the two sets of identity ratings for first and second generation children indicates that for these Mexican American students identity with Anglo American culture tends to be greatest among those individuals having the strongest identity with their ancestral culture. . . . At least for first and second generation children whose early socialization is heavily influenced by Mexican American culture, embeddedness in the ancestral culture may provide rewarding personal experiences and feelings of self-worth and security. This in turn may encourage and facilitate explorations of new cultural avenues and the formation of a bicultural identity [pp. 10–11].

Importance of Pluralistic Identity

Most sociocultural milieus in which mestizos live are multicultural. Individuals find themselves in communities where they are expected to participate in more than one culture. This is particularly true of members of minority groups, regardless of whether they are Mexican Americans in the United States, Huichol Indians in Mexico, or people of French descent in Canada. As was mentioned in chapter 4, these pluralistic milieus offer unusual opportunities for development of identities which are pluralistic or multicultural and, indeed, many mestizos are multicultural. However, this fact has often been ignored in the development of research methodologies and instruments—since most of these assume that people are monocultural. Instruments and methodologies for studying culture change are, for the most part, focused on unidirectional change. That is, these instruments assess degree of assimilation to mainstream American culture. In the last ten years, however, research has begun to focus on biculturation/multiculturation processes in culture change. The Hispanic psychologist/educator George I. Sanchez had discussed the possibility of dual cultural orientation in his writings published in the 1930s, and Irving Child described conflicts associated with dual life orientations among young male Italian Americans living in the East Coast of the United States in 1939. In 1967, Ramirez developed an interview schedule to study adjustment in adolescent Mexican Americans. He discovered that several of them had identified positively with mainstream American and Mexican-American cultures and that they participated actively and effectively in both cultures. Valentine (1971) also identified bicultural orientations to life among black adolescents. McFee (1968), working with American Indians living in bicultural reservation communities, found that these people had expanded behavioral repertoires giving them greater flexibility of behavior and an ability to participate competently in both Indian and mainstream American cultures. He developed a grid of cultural skills which assessed the degree of ability to participate in activities of both cultures. Lambert and Tucker (1972) also found that some people in Canada developed a French-English dual cultural orientation in their lives and that bilingual programs in the schools supported the development of this orientation. As was mentioned earlier in the chapter, Ramirez and Castaneda (1974) identified elementary school children, both Mexican American and non-Mexican American, who participated actively and effectively in Mexican-American, mainstream, and other cultures represented in their classrooms. The investigators conceptualized biculturalism in terms of cognitive flexibility or bicognition—bicultural individuals were those who could switch back and forth between the field-sensitive and field-independent cognitive styles in performing school tasks and were able to combine elements from both styles in order to arrive at new coping and problem-solving strategies. As was mentioned in the previous section, Ramirez and Castaneda (1974) also developed an observation instrument for assessing the degree to which children are accepting of cultures other than their own and the degree to which they respect different cultural orientations.

Multicultural Identity in Adults. In recent research (Ramirez, Cox, & Castaneda, 1977; Ramirez, Cox, Garza, & Castaneda, 1978), a multiculturalism inventory and a psychohistory schedule for assessing multicultural orientation to life have been used with Mexican-American college students. The psychohistory technique (PSAM) was described earlier in the chapter. The Biculturalism/Multiculturalism Experience Inventory consists of three types of items: demographic, personal history, and multicultural participation. (The inventory is described in more detail in chapter 6.)

Importance of Political, Economic, Religious, and Historical Variables

In the context of the mestizo world view, the individual develops and functions in a political, historical, economic, and religious milieu from which he/she cannot be extricated. That is, the individual cannot be understood separate and apart from those forces which have shaped his/her life style and world view and which are having an influence on his/her present behavior and philosophy of life. As has already been noted in chapter 2, the Mexican philosophers and social scientists in the 1930s and 1940s, as well as some contemporary social scientists and psychiatrists in Latin America, Canada, and the United States, have recognized the important role which historical, political, economic, and religious variables play in psychodynamics.

John Dollard (1935) was one of the first social scientists in the Americas to emphasize the important and extensive role culture plays in personality development and functioning. For Dollard, culture was an all-encompassing concept in the life of the individual. Of all the culture-and-personality studies he reviewed, only one, Thomas and Znaniecki's *Polish Peasant in Europe and America* (1927), met his strict criteria for culture personality research. With respect to Dollard's praise for the work by Thomas and Znaniecki, Sarason (1974) observed:

> Even a cursory reading of the Thomas and Znaniecki volumes, or for that matter, any good anthropological account of particular people and locale, makes clear that a community is a highly differentiated and configurated set of relationships, things, functions, and symbols, grounded in implicit and explicit traditions which in turn reflect geographic, economic, religious, political, and educational factors. Dollard is quite correct in maintaining that when psychologists and psychiatrists use such words as "milieu" or "environment" or "social factors," they recognize the inextricable relationship between culture and personality at the same time that they expose their ignorance of the dimension by which the culture becomes comprehensible [pp. 101–102].

Focus on Religious Variables. One aspect of culture which most psychologists and psychiatrists have ignored has been religion. Because of the separation which occurred between science and religion in Europe (as discussed in chapter 1), most psychologists influenced by the European world view have not only ignored religion in the study of personality, but, as Sarason has observed, they have even rejected those psychologists who ventured to deal with this subject. Sarason (1974), for example, explained how Dewey was labeled a philosopher because he focused on the influence of religion on personality development:

> Dewey was, of course, a philosopher and proudly so, but one has only to sample the corpus of his later work to recognize how much of it is directly relevant to present-day psychology's problems as a social science—the nature of inquiry, the means and end of action, and the processes of social change. Dewey created his school at the University of Chicago in 1896, a time when psychology was winning its independence from philosophy and advancing into the laboratory to study the elements of human behavior, or that of some other animal, with the methodological trappings of science. The bold, freewheeling scientific spirit became a sacrifice to the worship of false gods. It is no wonder that for decades Dewey was viewed as an erstwhile psychologist who became an educator and philosopher [pp. 47–48].

Sarason further observed that William James was also labeled a philosopher because of his interest in religious phenomena:

> To a lesser extent William James suffered a fate similar to that of Dewey, as his interests and activities took him from the psychological laboratory to such areas as pragmatism and *religious phenomena*. From the standpoint of academic psychology, he too "became" a philosopher. What did pragmatism and religious phenomena have to do with psychological science? [pp. 48 and 49].

Fortunately, some contemporary researchers have had the courage to include the role of religion in the study of personality. The American psychiatrist, Robert Coles (1975), through the use of a modified life history approach, combined with the use of photographs, has not only demonstrated the important role of religion in personality, he has also shown that economic, political, and historical values play a central role. In his book, *The Old Ones of New Mexico* (1975), he described his approach to data collection:

> I have been visiting certain families, talking with them, trying to find out how they live and what they believe in. I make weekly, sometimes twice-weekly, calls, but have no standard questions in mind, no methodology to implement. I simply talk with my hosts at their leisure. Whatever comes up I am grateful to hear about. The men and women have spoken to me in both Spanish and English, often in one language for a spell, then in the other [p. xiv].

In addition to information obtained by way of his interviews, Coles also presented photographs (taken by colleague Alex Harris) of people from the mountains of northern New Mexico in the same area in which he did his interviews. The contribution made by these photographs in terms of placing his subjects in an economic, historical, and religious context is best described by Coles himself:

> The people he presents here are not the people whose words I present, but they might well have been, because they are very similar in appearance and life history, and in their faith. I cannot emphasize strongly enough my gratitude to this young and dedicated photographer-colleague of mine. If I have learned a lot from listening to the people about to have their say in this book's pages, I have also learned so very much from looking at Alex Harris's photographs and talking with him about what he had seen and heard. This book is our joint effort to set down some of our observations [p. xv].

Coles' observations emphasized the important role which photographs can play in placing subjects in the broad context of their sociocultural environment. The following quotations from Coles' interviews serve to give a flavor for the historical, political, economic, and religious context in which his subjects lived:

> Sometime after church Domingo and I walk through the cemetery. It is a lovely place, small and familiar. We pay our respects to our parents, to our aunts and uncles, to our children. A family is a river; some of it has passed on and more is to come, and nothing is still, because we all move along, day by day, toward our destination. We both feel joy in our hearts when we kneel on the grass before the stones and say a prayer. At the edge of the cemetery near the gate is a statue of the Virgin Mary, larger than all the other stones. She is kneeling and on her shoulder is the Cross. She is carrying it—the burden of her Son's death. She is sad, but she has not given up. We know that she has never lost faith. It is a lesson to keep in mind [p. 50].

> My great-uncle was very proud of our blood; he would argue with my grandfather right in front of us, and we would sit and watch them and forget everything else—and that does not happen often with young children! My grandfather would insist that we are American, even if we speak Spanish and came originally from Spain. My great-uncle would say that nations have empires, even when they lose the land that went to make up the empire: so long as the people are scattered all over, there is the empire. "We are the Spanish empire," he would say [p. 60].

> You bend with the wind. And Anglo people are a strong wind. They want their own way; they can be like a tornado, out to pass over everyone as they go somewhere. I don't mean to talk out of turn. There are Anglos who don't fit my words. But we are outsiders in a land that is ours. We are part of an Anglo country and that will not change. I had to teach the facts of life to my four sons, and in doing so I learned my own lesson well [p. 22].

As part of their webwork research described above, Culler and Diaz-Guerrero (1982) identified the following religious persons, symbols, and activities Mexican-American and Mexican mothers and adolescents had rated as supportive (both morally and emotionally) in overcoming life crises: Our Lady of Guadalupe, Jesus Christ, religion, special saints, prayer, receiving communion, going to church, attending mass, praying the rosary, parish priest, religious festival, confession, and medals and scapularies.

Focus on Political Variables. Two researchers from Venezuela have done pioneer work with mestizos regarding the effects of political factors on personality development. Montero (1980) has constructed an instrument to assess degree of political socialization in Venezuelan adolescents. Salazar (1975), on the other hand, has assessed attitudes concerning nationalism and patriotism in Venezuelan children and their parents.

In a study that focused on the effects of social power on the behavior of Mexican-American and Anglo school children, Ramirez (1977) found that the social influence of an Anglo authority figure was greater than that of a Mexican-American authority figure. The investigator concluded that the results reflect the fact that both Mexican-American and Anglo students have little exposure to a Mexican American occupying a power position.

Focus on Economic Variables. The impact of economic factors on personality development is strongly represented in the community psychology which is evolving in Latin America. Escovar (1981) describes this developmental trend as follows:

> Community psychology constitutes the last trend of Latin American social psychology. It emerges directly from the previous trend and the efforts of social psychologists to develop a discipline more consonant with economic development effects. Within this trend there are two tendencies: one that can be called Community Social Psychology and the other Community Psychology. The former comes closer to being an applied social psychology in the "community"; whereas the latter focuses on the relationship between the individual and his environment and his control or lack of control over contingencies to that environment. Both the emphasis on economic and political variables are evident in the definition of Community Psychology given by Montero (1980), that branch of Psychology which has as the main objective the study of those psychosocial factors important in the development and maintenance of an individual's control and power over his personal and social environment; control and power that are exercised for the solution of common problems and to obtain changes in those environments and in the social structure.

In conclusion, the new methodologies, instruments, and training programs being developed in the Americas are making it possible for psychologists and psychiatrists to be less dependent on European world view-based theories and conceptual frameworks such as psychoanalysis and psychological differentiation. Furthermore, these innovative development efforts are helping to make researchers less dependent on instruments and tests, leading them to focus more on behavior, on what Dollard (1935) identified as the "organic reality of the person."

ASSESSING THE DEGREE TO WHICH THE METHODOLOGY OF RESEARCH AND INTERVENTION PROJECTS IS CONSONANT WITH MESTIZO WORLD VIEW

It has already been mentioned that the future of mestizo psychology is closely linked with the research methodology and the instruments for collection of data used in the psychological research done with mestizos in the Americas. At present, European-influenced psychology (with its emphasis on the laboratory method, control and manipulation of variables, and its beliefs in universal concepts, theories and instruments for collecting data) has a powerful hold on training programs in psychiatry, psychology and the social sciences in general. In addition, European world view perspectives are supported by members of editorial boards of major journals and publishers of textbooks and monographs. Quite often, the innovative ideas of researchers and program developers, vis-à-vis the tenets of the mestizo world view, are discouraged or criticized by the European world view-based establishment in the social sciences. Even the views of some of the leading scholars in cross-cultural research are often misleading. The philosophical position of some of these scholars often appears to be supportive of the tenets of mestizo psychology; however, their methodology, choice of instruments, and their theoretical orientations often leave much to be desired. As Koivukari (1977) has pointed out, what appears to be emic is often merely European etic in disguise. Thus, we need a model for cutting through the rhetoric and for examining methodology in research and intervention/research projects. We need guidelines for determining the degree to which the researcher has been responsive to tenets of the mestizo world view in psychology and psychiatry. We need to focus on certain critical questions that can help us to determine if the study or program in question meets the standards of the mestizo world view:

1. Is the theoretical or conceptual framework being used by the researcher or intervener consonant with the world view of mestizo subjects or clients? That is, does the theoretical/conceptual framework on which the study or intervention is based reflect some of the tenets of the mestizo world

view? For example, a cursory examination of the psychoanalytic perspective used by Fromm and Maccoby (1970) reveals its inappropriateness for mestizo subjects and communities—the assumption of European cultural superiority is readily evident. In light of the foregoing question, the theory of psychological differentiation is also inappropriate for mestizos because this model assumes that people of traditional cultures are psychologically unsophisticated and underdeveloped.

2. Is the research methodology consonant with the culture and world view of mestizo subjects? To answer this question it is necessary to focus on several issues:
   - *Selection of subjects.* Does the procedure for selection of subjects reflect the fact that there is a great intercultural and intracultural variability among mestizos? It is erroneous to speak of Mexicans, Canadians, Puerto Ricans, or Cuban Americans. Selection procedures should recognize the salience of generational status, region of origin, degree of multiculturalism and bilingualism, and socioeconomic status in populations being studied.
   - *Group comparisons.* If two groups were compared, were the samples comparable? As Campbell (1961, 1972) has noted, it is virtually impossible to obtain samples from more than one society which are truly comparable.
   - *Characteristics of instruments used for collecting the data.* Were instruments used merely translations of instruments, techniques, and tests developed in another culture or for a non-mestizo group? Are the content and structure of the instruments consonant with the tenets of the mestizo world view and with mestizo psychodynamics? Are the demands that the instruments make of the subjects appropriate to their roles in the context of their cultures (i.e., many adult mestizos with traditional orientations view instruments such as the Draw-a-Person Test, the Embedded Figures Test, and the Semantic Differential as child-like, meaningless tasks)?
3. Were the data collected in historical-social-economic-political-cultural and religious context? (Flagrant violations of this principle involve the use of games which simulate reality or the exclusive use of paper and pencil measures.)
4. Were interpretations of the data made in historical-social-economic-political-cultural and religious context? As was discussed in chapter 3, some of the works of Oscar Lewis (1961, 1965) interpreted the data in the context of psychoanalytic theory and largely ignored the socio-cultural context in which they were collected

Table 5.1 provides a set of questions (related to the mestizo appraisal standards presented above) which can be used to evaluate the design, methodology and philosophical underpinnings of studies and programs which focus on mestizo populations:

TABLE 5.1. How Well Does the Study or Program Meet the Mestizo Standards?

The Standards	Not at All Characteristic 1	2	3	4	Very Characteristic 5
Theory or conceptual framework					
1. Degree to which the theory or conceptual framework is consonant with mestizo world view.					
Subjects					
2. Degree to which subjects reflect intracultural diversity of target group or groups.					
3. Degree to which SES, linguistic, generational status and acculturation/biculturation information were taken into consideration in subject selection.					
4. If two or more groups were compared—degree to which groups are comparable.					
Instruments					
5. Degree to which contents of the instruments were reflective of the mestizo view.					
6. Degree to which structure of the instruments was reflective of the mestizo view.					
7. Degree to which demands that the instruments made on subjects were consonant with the mestizo view.					

The Standards	Not at All Characteristic 1	2	3	4	Very Characteristic 5
Data collection and interpretation					
8. Degree to which data were collected in a historical, social, economic, political, cultural and religious context.					
9. Degree to which data were interpreted in a historical, social, economic, political, cultural and religious context.					

In summary, we must be cognizant of the fact that most of the research methods, instruments, and techniques in psychiatry and the social sciences are biased toward the European world view. In addition, we should also recognize that most training programs in psychology and psychiatry are based on the tenets of the European world view as described in chapter 1. In particular, we must be cautious of European etic disguised as emic—although several cross-cultural researchers reflect the mestizo world view in their rhetoric, their bias toward the European world view is evident in their choice of methodology and instruments. Some years ago, Price-Williams (1975) provided a warning which we would all do well to consider in evaluating our own work as well as that of others: "Our own categories of explanation and definition, embedded in our psychological theories, may not be appropriate when projected on some other culture [p. 23]."

SUMMARY

The choice of research methodologies and instruments for collection of data in research and intervention programs with mestizo subjects is very important to the future of mestizo psychology. It is important to recognize that the European world view dominates most of the thinking, the training programs, and the research and intervention technologies of psychology and psychiatry throughout the world. European theories and conceptual frameworks such as psychoanalysis and psychological differentiation have produced distorted and inaccurate pictures of mestizos and of their communities and cultures. These inaccurate conceptualizations have, in turn, supported an assimilationist perspective in intervention with mestizo subjects and communities. In order to truly understand mestizo psychodynamics, there is need to develop methodologies and instruments based on the mestizo world view. In addition, we need to use a mestizo evaluation framework to select appropriate methodologies and instruments for data collection and to properly evaluate the validity of research and intervention programs implemented in mestizo communities.

REFERENCES

Buriel, R. Acculturation and biculturalism among three generations of Mexican American and Anglo American school children. Unpublished paper, Pomona College, 1981.

Campbell, D. T. The mutual methodological relevance of anthropology and psychology. In F. L. K. Hsu (Ed.), *Psychological anthropology*. Homewood, Ill.: Dorsey Press, 1961.

Campbell, D. T., & Naroll, R. The mutual methodological relevance of anthropology and psychology. In F. L. K. Hsu (Ed.), *Psychological anthropology*. (Rev. ed.) Cambridge, Mass.: Schenkman, 1972.

Child, I. L. *Italian or American? The second generation in conflict*. New Haven: Yale University Press, 1943.

Cole, M., & Scribner, S. *Culture and thought*. New York: Wiley, 1974.

Coles, R. *The old ones of New Mexico*. Garden City, N.Y.: Anchor Books, 1975.

Constantino, G., Malgady, R. G., & Vazquez, C. A comparison of the Murray-TAT and a new thematic apperception test for urban Hispanic children. *Hispanic Journal of Behavioral Sciences*, 1981, *3*, 291–300.

Cuellar, I., Harris, L. C., & Jasso, R. An acculturation scale for Mexican American normal and clinical populations. *Hispanic Journal of Behavioral Sciences*, 1980, *2*, 199–217.

Culler, R. & Diaz-Guerrero, R. The webwork: A new approach in describing individual support networks. Unpublished manuscript, 1982.

Dershowitz, A. Jewish subcultural patterns and psychological differentiation. *International Journal of Psychology*, 1971, *6*, 223–231.

Diaz-Guerrero, R. Mexican psychology. *American Psychologist*, 1977, *33*, 934–944.

Dollard, J. *Criteria for the life history with analyses of six notable documents*. New Haven: Yale University Press, 1935.

Escovar, L. A. *Design for a course on social psychology* in Latin America. Miami, Fla.: Latin American and Caribbean Center, Florida International University, 1980.

Fromm, E., & Maccoby, M. *Social character in a Mexican village: A socio-psychoanalytic study*. Englewood Cliffs, N.J.: Prentice-Hall, 1970.

Garza, R. T. Personal control and fatalism in Chicanos and Anglos: Conceptual and methodological issues. In J. L. Martinez *Chicano psychology*. New York: Academic Press, 1977.

Holtzman, W. H. Culture, personality development, and mental health in the Americas. *Interamerican Journal of Psychology*, 1979, *13*, 27–49.

Holtzman, W. H., Diaz-Guerrero, R., & Swartz, J. D. *Personality development in two cultures*. Austin, Tex.: University of Texas Press, 1975.

Kluckhohn, F. R., & Strodbeck, R. *Variations in value orientations*. New York: Row Peterson, 1961.

Koivukari, M. Fundamental issues of the cross-cultural approach and its methodology in psychology. Reports for the Department of Psychology: University of Jyvaskyla, Finland, 1977.

Lambert, W. E., & Tucker, G. R. *Bilingual education of children: The St. Lambert experiment*. Rowley, Mass.: Newbury House, 1972.

Lewis, O. *Life in a Mexican village: Tepoztlan restudied*. Champaign-Urbana: The University of Illinois Press, 1951.

Lewis, O. *Five families: Mexican case studies in the culture of poverty*. New York: Basic Books, 1959.

Lewis, O. *The children of Sanchez: Autobiography of a Mexican family*. New York: Random House, 1961.

Lewis, O. *La vida: A Puerto Rican family of the culture of poverty—San Juan and New York*. New York: Random House, 1965.

McFee, M. The 150% man, a product of Blackfeet acculturation. *American Anthropologist*, 1968, *70*, 1096–1103.

Montero, M. Fundamentos teoricos de la psicologia comunitaria. Unpublished manuscript, 1980.

Padilla, A. M. The role of cultural awareness and ethnic loyalty in acculturation. In A. M. Padilla (Ed.), *Acculturation: Theories, models and some new findings*. Boulder, Colo.: Westview Press, 1980.

Pike, K. Language in relation to a unified theory of structure of human behavior (Part 1). Glendale, California: Summer Institute of Linguistics, 1954.

Price-Williams, D. R. *Explorations in cross-cultural psychology*. San Francisco: Chandler & Sharp, 1975.

Ramirez, A. Chicano power and interracial group relations. In J. L. Martinez (Ed.), *Chicano psychology*. New York: Academic Press, 1972

Ramirez, M. Identification with Mexican family values and authoritarianism in Mexican Americans. *The Journal of Social Psychology*, 1967, *73*, 3–11.

Ramirez, M. Identification with Mexican-American values and psychological adjustment in Mexican-American adolescents. *International Journal of Social Psychiatry*, 1969, *11*, 151–156.

Ramirez, M., Taylor, C., & Petersen, B. Mexican-American cultural membership and adjustment to school. *Developmental Psychology*, 1971, *4*, 141–148.

Ramirez, M., & Castaneda, A. *Cultural democracy, bicognitive development and education*. New York: Academic Press, 1974.

Ramirez, M., Cox, B. G., & Castaneda, A. The psychodynamics of biculturalism. Unpublished technical report to Office of Naval Research, Arlington, Virginia, 1977.

Ramirez, M., Cox, B. G., Garza, R. T., & Castaneda, A. Dimensions of biculturalism in Mexican-American college students. Unpublished technical report to Office of Naval Research, Arlington, Virginia, 1978.

Ramirez, M., Diaz-Guerrero, R., Hernandez, M., & Iscoe, I. Coping with life stress in families: A cross-cultural comparison. Unpublished manuscript, 1982.

Ramirez, M., & Price-Williams, D. R. Cognitive styles of children of three ethnic groups in the United States. *Journal of Cross-Cultural Psychology*, 1974, *5*, 212–219.

Rotter, J. B. Generalized expectation for internal vs. external control of reinforcement. *Psychological monographs*, 1966 *80* (1, Whole No. 609).

Salazar, J. Actitudes de estudiantes venezolanos de secundaria y de sus padres, hacia la patria, los simbolos nacionales y el estado. In G. Marin (Ed.), *La psicologia social en latinoamerica*. Mexico, D.F.: Editorial Trillas, 1975.

Sarason, S. B. *The psychological sense of community: Prospects for a community psychology*. San Francisco, Calif.: Josey Bass, 1974.

Scopetta, M. A., & Szapocznik, J. A comparison of brief strategic family therapy approaches in the treatment of Hispanic children. Spanish Family Guidance Clinic, University of Miami, School of Medicine. Unpublished manuscript, 1980.

Szapocznik, J., Scopetta, M. A., Kurtines, W., & Arnalde, M. A. Theory and measurement of acculturation. *Interamerican Journal of Psychology*, 1978, *12*, 113–130.

Szapocznik, J., Scopetta, M. A., & King, O. E. Theory and practice in matching treatment to the special characteristics and problems of Cuban immigrants. *Journal of Community Psychology*, 1978, *6*, 112–122.

Thomas, W. I., & Znaniecki, F. *Polish peasant in Europe and America*. Vol. 2. New York: Alfred A. Knopf, 1927.

Triandis, H. C., Vassiliou, V., Vassiliou, G., Tanaka, Y., & Shanmugam, A. *The analysis of subjective culture*. New York: Wiley, 1972.

Valentine, C. A. Deficit, difference, and bicultural models of Afro-American behavior. *Harvard Educational Review*, 1971, *41*, 131–157.

Witkin, H. A., Dyk, R. B., Faterson, H. F., Goodenough, D. R., & Karp, S. A. *Psychological differentiation*. New York: Wiley, 1962.

CHAPTER 6

Coping with Diversity in the Americas: The Need to Integrate Mestizo and European Research Approaches and Methodologies

Reason and intuition complement each other.

—Antonio Caso (1943)

As scientists we become so involved with our methodology that we perceive the world through one pair of methodological spectacles without even being aware that we are doing so.

—John W. Osborne (1982)

Perhaps there is an intrinsic connection between cognitive totalism and political totalitarianism: the mind that can only tolerate one approach to understanding reality is the same kind of mind that must impose one all-embracing structure of power if it ever gets into position of doing so.

—Peter Berger, Brigette Berger, and Hansfried Kellner (1973)

Problems related to diversity are undermining the stability of many nations in the Americas and also contributing to suspicion and misunderstanding among the nations of the hemisphere. This chapter focuses on the need to integrate mestizo and European research approaches and methodologies for the purpose of understanding and resolving problems related to diversity. In particular, this chapter focuses on the psychodynamics of biculturalism/multiculturalism—the skills and sensitivities of those persons who would make ideal leaders for a pluralistic world. The basic assumption on which this chapter is founded is that neither psychology as a science nor the nations of the Americas as political entities can afford to cope with problems of diversity by resorting to cognitive totalism or political totalitarianism.

NATURAL SCIENCE VS. PHENOMENOLOGICAL APPROACHES TO PSYCHOLOGICAL RESEARCH

Throughout much of its history, psychology has been struggling with controversies over the nature of the research methodology and the philosophy of science which it should adopt. On one side are those who would like to see the discipline modeled after the natural sciences; on the other, there are those who claim that the unique nature of the phenomena studied by psychologists demands an equally unique methodology and philosophy of science. A recent controversy between Professors Greeno (1982) and Osborne (1982) in the *American Psychologist* indicated that this issue is still very much alive. In a critique of a literature review on learning by Greeno, Osborne observed:

> Cognitive psychologists such as Greeno tend to conceptualize learning in terms of cognitive processes that result in overt behaviors, but humanistic psychologists conceptualize learning as a complex of organismic processes producing a change in world view, which leads to changes in overt behavior. . . . This approach to learning ties it to the learner's way of life as it embodies his or her philosophical and religious values and life experiences. . . . There is an urgent need to keep in touch with the fullness of human nature and not become so involved with one scientific perspective, natural science, that the real-life world of human beings becomes the natural scientific world [p. 331].

Greeno countered Osborne's criticism with the following observations:

> Cognitive psychology is "guilty as charged" of adopting an approach more consistent with natural science, in which the individual and the environment are viewed from a perspective external to both and the characteristics of cognition and experience are understood to be the outcome of an interaction of the individual's mind and the situation. Phenomenologists, in contrast, consider the central problem of psychology to be understanding how individuals construct meaning for situations. Historically, sciences have progressed significantly by overcoming egocentrism of that kind, although it has been defended on ideological grounds from the Ptolemaicists in astronomy to the vitalists in biology and now by the phenomenologists in psychology. History has repeatedly shown that approach to be unproductive [p. 333].

From the discussion in the preceding chapters, it could be concluded that the controversy between the European and mestizo world views in psychology and psychiatry is similar to that between the natural science and phenomenological approaches to research reflected in the dialogue between Greeno and Osborne. Another conclusion which can be drawn from discussions in the preceding chapters is that the bicultural/multicultural orientation of some of the mestizos in the Americas embodies an amalgamation of the native American and the European perspectives. Thus, both the European-mestizo and natural science-phenomenology controversies are central to the study of biculturalism/multiculturalism in the Americas. That is, bicultural/multicultural processes represent a combination of personality characteristics, thinking styles, and orientations to life which reflect both the European and mestizo world views, as well as the natural science and phenomenological perspectives on the study of psychological phenomena. To properly understand and conceptualize bicultural/multicultural processes, then, what is required are research perspectives and methodologies that are representative of both the European and mestizo world views. That is, neither a predominant natural science nor a phenomenological perspective would suffice. What is required, then, is a combination of the two approaches, a perspective reminiscent of the dualistic philosophy of Antonio Caso (1943) discussed in chapter 3. As the reader will recall, Caso argued that in order to understand the reality of Mexico and its mestizo peoples, both the approaches and perspectives of science and metaphysics are required. What is needed in psychology, then, is an acceptance of the philosophical perspectives presented by Caso, which is characterized by the quotation at the beginning of this chapter. In addition, psychology also needs to recognize the importance of bicultural/multicultural processes in personality development and functioning. Both psychology and psychiatry must acknowledge that bicultural/multicultural people are living proof that the natural science and the phenomenological, the mestizo and the European, can be brought together in harmony. Thus, to truly understand the phenomenon of pluralism and diversity in the Americas, we need to integrate and amalgamate what has for too long been perceived as separate.

DIVERSITY AND THE AMERICAS

Diversity represents both the greatest blessing and the greatest challenge for the nations of the Americas. Canada is faced with the demands of many of its French-speaking citizens who want independence for the province of Quebec; for several years Puerto Rico has been attempting to resolve the status of its relationship with the United States; and in the United States itself ethnic, racial, regional, and sex differences have been at the forefront of the public consciousness for many years as blacks, Latinos, Asians, Native Americans, and women have been seeking equality of opportunity and greater representation in both the political and the economic spheres of society. In addition, recent waves of immigrants from Cuba, Haiti and Asia are causing considerable controversy among members of the body politic. In South America, most problems of diversity are focused on class differences and, also, around the fact that many members of Indian groups are not participating fully in the political, social, and economic lives of their respective countries. Diversity, then, is at the core of many of the serious problems affecting social, economic, and political stability facing many of the countries in the Americas. One of the greatest dangers is that leaders and policymakers will come to the conclusion that diversity is incompatible with democracy. For example, an American sociologist (*Time*, 1979), commenting on the crisis of leadership in the United States, observed that democracy and leadership are incompatible and that the nation's plural interests threaten to turn our country into a set of internal Balkan states, into hostile tribes. Observations such as this could result in disasterous consequences: leaders of countries in the Americas may come to conclude that the only answer to problems created by diversity lies in establishment of totalitarian forms of government. But how can this unacceptable conclusion be circumvented? How can problems of diversity be understood and conceptualized? How can leaders who are sensitive to diversity and effective at leading groups that are diverse be identified and trained?

The dynamics of biculturalism/multiculturalism embodies solutions which are potentially important to controversies of scientific methodology in psychology and to those concerning political problems facing many of the nations of the Americas. The bicultural/multicultural perspective is the alternative to political totalitarianism. Bicultural/multicultural orientations to life reflect thinking styles, attitudes, and political solutions that represent more than one way of approaching reality, more than one approach to the solution of problems. Given this fact, however, it also stands to reason that the study of bicultural/multicultural orientations to life requires a multiplicity of research approaches and perspectives.

UNDERSTANDING THE PSYCHODYNAMICS OF BICULTURAL/MULTICULTURAL PEOPLE

The project to be described below represents four years of research on young bicultural/multicultural adults; focus was on the relationship of identity to flexibility in leadership behavior. The research methodology used represented an integration of mestizo and European world view perspectives. It combined ethnographic, life history, and laboratory methods in the research design. Although the study was primarily focused on the ethnic groups of the Americas, the methodology and the conclusions drawn from the findings are applicable to any group in the hemisphere. What follows are the principal questions addressed by the researchers during the different phases of development of the project and also a presentation of the research procedures and findings related to each of the questions posed.

How can people with multicultural orientations to life be identified? Some of the early speculation and research on biculturalism/multiculturalism had led to the conclusion that it was difficult, if not impossible, for people to develop pluralistic identities. For example, Stonequist (1964) referred to members of minority groups as "marginal," conceiving of the marginal man as "poised in psychological uncertainty between two (or more) social worlds, reflecting in his soul the discords and harmonies, repulsions and attractions of those worlds [p. 329]." According to Stonequist, the "life-cycle" of marginal men followed three stages: (a) positive feelings toward the host culture; (b) conscious experience of conflict; and (c) responses to the conflict which may be prolonged and more or less successful in terms of adjustment. Furthermore, the third stage may encourage the individual to adopt one of three roles: (a) nationalism—a collective movement to raise the group's status; (b) intermediation—promoting cultural accommodation; and (c) assimilation. Stonequist noted the possibility that some of these conditions might result in creativity, citing the case of the Jewish people; but, for the most part, his model focused on conflict and implied that the only "healthy" resolution was assimilation into the dominant culture. Irvin Child's research (1943) with young male second generation Italian Americans in New Haven, Connecticut, also led him to conclude that it was difficult to achieve a bicultural identity. Child concluded that there were three types of reactions indicative of identity development in bicultural situations: the rebel reaction—desire to achieve complete acceptance by the American majority group and to reject the Italian culture and associations; the in-group reaction—the desire to actively participate in and identify with the Italian group while rejecting American society; and the apathetic reaction—a retreat from conflict situations and avoidance of strong "rebel" or "in-group" identities. This apathetic reaction, according to Child, could be observed in individuals making a partial approach toward both cultures in an effort to find a compromise or combination as a solution to the conflict.

Madsen (1964), in explaining the behavior of young adult Mexican Americans living in bicultural environments, subscribed to a conflict model similar to that used by Child (1943). In his article entitled "The Alcoholic Agringado" (1964), Madsen described the traumas of cultural transfer experienced by Mexican-American males. Madsen depicted the Mexican American as standing alone between two conflicting cultural worlds and resorting to alcohol for anxiety relief. Research by anthropologist Celia Heller (1968) with Mexican-American adolescents also concluded that these young people were limited to two monocultural choices leading either to complete identity with Mexican-American culture (which resulted in delinquency) or to assimilated Anglo-American life styles (which resulted in educational and economic success). Ramirez (1969) conducted intensive interviews with Mexican-American adolescents. His findings showed that while some Mexican-American youth experienced problems of identity, many young people in Texas and California functioned effectively in Anglo and Mexican-American cultures and had established bicultural identities with minimum conflict and problems of adjustment. McFee (1968) also identified bicultural orientations to life among some members of the Blackfeet

Indian tribe living in a bicultural reservation community in the United States. McFee emphasized the relationship of the situational context to the development and expression of flexibility and adaptability of behavior. He hypothesized that, in the course of tribal acculturation in a bicultural reservation community, a bicultural social structure becomes established that provides both cultural models (Anglo and Indian). Through the availability of models who represent both sociocultural systems, the individual develops an expanded behavioral repertoire made up of skills and knowledge representative of both Anglo and Indian cultures. Thus, McFee labeled the bicultural person he had identified through his research as the 150 percent man.

Valentine's research (1971) with urban Black American youth in the United States also identified subjects with bicultural orientations to life. Valentine focused on the behavioral flexibility evident in his bicultural subjects:

> The collective behavior and social life of the Black community is bicultural in the sense that each Afro-American ethnic segment draws upon a distinctive repertoire of standardized Afro-American behavior and, simultaneously, patterns derived from mainstream cultural systems of Euro-American derivation [p. 143].

Research by Ramirez and Castaneda (1974) with Mexican-American and Anglo-American elementary school children who were bicultural indicated that these children could perform effectively and comfortably in both cultures and that they had established close friendships with peers of both groups. These children also exhibited considerable flexibility in their classroom behavior, performing effectively in situations and tasks demanding the use of widely different skills and problem-solving styles. These observations led Ramirez and Castaneda to conclude that bicultural children were bicognitive or cognitively flexible and that this flexibility had developed as a result of socialization in two cultures.

Combining the findings of their research with those obtained by McFee and Valentine, Ramirez and Castaneda arrived at a definition of biculturalism/multiculturalism which could be used in efforts to identify subjects with pluralistic orientations to life:

> A bicultural/multicultural person has had extensive socialization and life experiences in two or more cultures and participates actively in these cultures. That is, his/her day-to-day behaviors show active participation in two or more cultures and extensive interaction with members of those sociocultural groups. In addition, the behavior of the bicultural/multicultural person is flexible in the sense that he/she uses different problem solving, coping, human relational, communication, and incentive-motivational styles. In line with the aforemen-

> tioned skills, the bicultural/multicultural person is adaptable in behavior, being able to make adjustments to a variety of different environments and life demands.

The investigators presented this definition to two professors, two counselors, and two students who were well acquainted with the majority of Latino students on a small campus of a public university located on the west coast of the United States. Based on the definition provided, each judge was asked to identify four students who were high on multiculturalism and four whom they judged to have a monocultural orientation to life. Out of all the students selected, eight (four high and four low) who had been identified in the lists of at least four of the judges were selected for further study. The investigators conducted intensive interviews (from four to six hours) with these eight subjects.

In addition to the interviews, the eight subjects were observed unobtrusively over a period of a week—their behaviors were recorded in detail as they participated in class and campus activities. The information obtained with the interviews and observations generated a pool of items which was combined with items derived from information obtained from earlier investigations as well as with items from related instruments (Ramirez, 1967; Teske & Nelson, 1973). Two questionnaires were developed—the Bicognitive Orientation to Life Scale, and the Biculturalism/Multiculturalism Experience Inventory. The questionnaires were assembled, pilot-tested, reviewed by external consultants, and revised—the same procedure was repeated three times. The resulting questionnaire for bicultural/multicultural experience consisted of three parts: demographic-linguistic information, personal history, and bicultural participation. Among the dimensions included in the latter two areas were socialization and educational experiences, interpersonal interactions, and experiences in situations related to school, political, athletic, religious, family, and recreational spheres. The following sample items were taken from each of the three parts of the questionnaire:

1. Demographic-Linguistic Information
   What was the approximate ethnic composition of the high school you attended? (check one)
   - all Latinos
   - mostly Latinos
   - Latinos and Anglos, about evenly
   - mostly Anglos
   - all Anglos

2. Personal History
   In high school my close friends were

- all Latinos
- mostly Latinos
- Latinos and Anglos, about evenly
- mostly Anglos
- all Anglos

3. Multicultural Participation
   When I discuss personal problems or issues, I discuss them with
   - only Latinos
   - mostly Latinos
   - Latinos and Anglos, about evenly
   - mostly Anglos
   - only Anglos

The complete Biculturalism/Multiculturalism Experience Inventory (B/MEI), together with instructions for scoring, can be found in the Appendix.

The Bicognitive Orientation to Life Scale (BOLS) was developed to provide an indication of flexibility by asking respondents to register their concurrence or disagreement with statements indicative of either a field-sensitive or field-independent orientation to life. Scale items express a field-sensitive orientation in the areas of (1) interpersonal relationships, (2) leadership style, (3) learning style, (4) attitudes toward authority, and (5) interest in science versus interest in the humanities. Corresponding items express a field-independent (FI) and a field-sensitive (FS) orientation in the same areas of behavior. The following are examples of FS and FI items: FS—When I look at a photograph of someone, I am more aware of the total person than of specific details such as hair color, facial expression, or body type. FI—When I look at a mural or large painting, I see all the little pieces and then, gradually, I see how they all fit together to give a total message.

Subjects indicated their extent of agreement with each statement via a four-point Likert scale. Each of the 24 statements was subsequently scored on a scale from one to four with higher scores being indicative of greater concurrence with the statement. A separate field sensitivity and field independency score was obtained by summing across the appropriate item clusters. A "bicognitive" score was derived by summing across both field-sensitive and field-independent scales. Subjects who were identified as bicultural/multicultural were those who had obtained a high bicognitive score on the BOLS and who had scored high on biculturalism/multiculturalism experience on the B/MEI. A bicultural/multicultural index was obtained for each subject by summing his/her BOLS and B/MEI scores.

The BOLS and B/MEI were administered to 1,046 subjects with Spanish surnames in colleges and universities throughout Texas and California. From this population a sample of 129 subjects was selected to answer the

TABLE 6.1. Historical Development Patterns

N	Patterns	Defining Characteristics
18	Parallel	Extensive and continuous exposure to Latino (or to a Latino culture and other minority group cultures) and mainstream culture beginning in the preschool period and continuing for at least two more life periods
73	Early Latino/gradual mainstream	Extensive, almost total exposure to Latino (or to a Latino culture and other minority group cultures) throughout all life periods with gradually increasing exposure to mainstream culture with increasing age
23	Early Latino/abrupt mainstream	Extensive, almost total exposure to Latino (or to a Latino culture and other minority group cultures) in the first two or three periods of life followed by sudden immersion in mainstream culture
11	Early mainstream/ gradual Latino	Reverse of early Latino/gradual mainstream
4	Early mainstream/ abrupt Latino	Reverse of early Latino/abrupt mainstream

next major question posed by the investigators: How do bicultural/multicultural orientations to life develop?

In order to answer the second question, the investigators developed a semi-structured life history procedure which they entitled Psychohistory Schedule for Assessing Multiculturalism (PSAM). The interviews ranged from an hour and fifteen minutes to an hour and thirty minutes in length and focused on five different life periods: preschool, elementary school, middle school, high school, and college. Questions centered around the following themes: language learning and usage; family and community life; school experiences; peer relations; dating; political behavior; religious beliefs; life crisis experiences; identity crises; perceived advantages and disadvantages of Anglo- and Mexican-American cultures; degree of comfort experienced while participating in Anglo, Mexican, and Mexican-American cultures; preference for ethnic background of marriage partner; philosophy of life; career goals; and contemporary multicultural identity. The scoring system developed for the PSAM is described in chapter 5.

Examination of the data from the interviews revealed five historical development patterns (HDPs) or paths of development of multicultural orientations to life (and several variations within each of these). The 129 subjects varied considerably in terms of their HDPs as reflected by the content of their life histories, as can be seen in table 6.1.

LIFE HISTORIES

Parallel Histories

Parallel describes persons whose lives as children and adolescents were influenced by equally frequent and equally extensive associations with Latino (or a combination of Latino with another minority group culture) and with mainstream United States culture.

Paula H. and her family were farm laborers in the fields of the Central Valley in California so, during the years of Paula's childhood and adolescence, her family moved several times from one neighborhood to another in and around the Fresno area. The neighborhoods she lived in and the schools she attended brought her into extensive contact with mainstream Anglo-American and Mexican-American children. Paula formed close friendships with peers from both cultures and visited frequently in the homes of both groups where she interacted extensively with their parents and siblings. Paula's parents spoke Spanish at home, and she would speak Spanish with them, although she spoke to her siblings in English. Her parents had close friendships with both Anglo and Mexican-American adults. In jobs which Paula held as an adolescent and young adult, she was supervised by both Anglo- and Mexican-American adults and her coworkers were members of both the Anglo and Mexican-American groups. Most of her teachers prior to going to college were Anglo, but she established a close friendship with a Mexican-American woman who was her basketball coach and Spanish teacher in high school. In college, Paula maintained close friendships with Anglo- and Mexican-American students, and she participated extensively in activities sponsored by both groups. She also dated both Mexican- and Anglo-American men, and she belonged to clubs in which the memberships were predominantly either Mexican-American or Anglo.

Nick S. was born and reared in Phoenix, Arizona. His mother is Anglo (mainstream American) and his father is a member of a Spanish-American family who settled in New Mexico in the seventeenth century. Nick has been close to both his father's and his mother's families (both of whom live in the Phoenix area) throughout his life, and, thus, has been conscious of his dual ethnic origins since early childhood. Although the members of his mother's and father's families differ extensively from each other in terms of language, values, and life style, Nick has always enjoyed shuttling between these two worlds and he has become fluently bilingual in the process. His first experience with ethnic barriers took place in middle school. At the time, he was initially shunned by traditional Mexican-American students who felt that Nick was a traitor to their group, because of his close friendships with Anglo peers. His rejection by traditional Mexican Americans was short-lived, however, because Nick never ceased to try to befriend the members of this group. But the experience which finally earned his complete acceptance by traditional Mexican Americans occurred in the middle of his first year of middle school. At the time, Nick averted a major "rumble" between Anglos and Mexican Americans by serving as a mediator between them and by dispelling rumors. Nick was perceived as fair and impartial by both sides, and he managed to pull the student body of his school together by forming a United Nations club on campus. He held several positions of leadership, serving as president of his class throughout the four years he attended. In college, Nick was highly respected by Mexican Americans, Anglos, and blacks. He chaired several committees in student government and served as an effective spokesperson when students had complaints to present to the faculty and administration. The following excerpts from his life history testify to Nick's pluralistic philosophy of life:

> I find that all cultures, groups, and individuals have something unique and genuine to offer to me. I have learned that if I really listen everyone is trying to teach me something that I should know about myself. I don't think I shall ever stop learning although there have been several times in my life when I have thought that nothing will ever surprise me or challenge me again, but, sure enough, I meet someone new or I visit a new city or a country I have never been to before and new doors open up in my mind.

Early Latino/Abrupt Mainstream

The early Latino/abrupt mainstream category was typical of persons who experienced nearly exclusive associations or functioning in Latino culture relatively early in life and who were later thrust into extensive contact with Anglo mainstream culture.

Ricardo S. was born in Mexico and his family moved to El Paso when he was five years old. Initially, the family lived in a tenement located in a section of town where everyone was of Mexican descent. He spoke Spanish exclusively both at home and in the neighborhood; he had no associations with Anglos during his first three years in the United States. When he was eight years old, his parents moved to a small town in Indiana where they were the only Mexican-American family. Initially, Ricardo felt lost and alienated, but he gradually mastered English and eventually became very popular with his peers at school and in the new neighborhood. At home, his parents would speak to the children in Spanish, but Ricardo and his siblings started to speak English exclusively once they had learned the language. After graduating from high school, Ricardo went to live with his uncle and aunt in El Paso and attended the University of Texas at El Paso. Initially, the move from Indiana to Texas was a shock; and, once again in his life, he felt alienated and lonely. After his first year in college, he decided to go to a Spanish-language institute in Mexico City; this experience had a profound effect on his life. He returned from Mexico speaking fluent Spanish and with a great interest in Mexican culture, which, in turn, led to his decision to major in archaeology. Upon his return, he established close friendships with both Mexican-American and Anglo students. He assumed the role of mediator and spokesperson for Mexican-American students on campus, often negotiating their demands with members of the university administration.

Early Latino/Gradual Mainstream

The early Latino/gradual mainstream pattern describes the life styles of persons who experienced early familiarity with Latino culture and gradually gained increasing exposure to mainstream culture.

Robert M. was born in the United States in a small town situated in the Rio Grande Valley of Texas. In the years prior to going to school, he rarely had occasion to interact with Anglo peers or adults. Robert spoke Spanish exclusively at home and in his neighborhood. His only exposure to English prior to attending school was through television, books, and magazines. The school he attended during the first two years of his elementary education had an all Mexican-American student body, but the teaching staff was made up of both Anglo and Mexican Americans. His first sustained exposure to Anglo adults was in the first grade where his teacher was Anglo. Prior to starting the third grade, Robert's parents were able to purchase a home in a neighborhood which was made up of both Anglo and Mexican-American families; his first sustained exposure to Anglo peers was in the new neighborhood. He gradually developed close friendships with Anglo peers and, in late elementary school and junior high school, he started visiting extensively in Anglo homes. As he became better acquainted with Anglo culture, he continued to maintain close friendships with Mexican Americans. This pattern of interaction with both Anglo and Mexican-American peers and adults continued into his college years.

Early Latino-Native American/Gradual Mainstream

Richard Z. was born in an Indian pueblo near Albuquerque, New Mexico. His father is a Latino and his mother is Hopi. During most of his childhood and early adolescence, Richard was seeped in both Latino and Hopi cultures. His grandfather was a medicine man in the pueblo, and Richard was very close to him and learned a lot about healing in the Indian tradition. His early years in school were spent in the company of Latinos and Indians. He was gradually introduced to mainstream culture through television, movies, and books and also by his acquaintances with Anglo teachers. He gradually came to meet more Anglo friends in his middle school years and developed many friendships with Anglos in his high school years. He was particularly fond of his track coach, who was Anglo-Cherokee; it was this man who helped him to gradually overcome a distrust which he had always had toward Anglo adults. In college, Richard was deeply involved in activities—both academic and social—with Latinos, blacks, American Indians, Asian Americans, and mainstream Americans. He was a student assistant in the financial aids office and was well known among the students for his sincere concern and empathy for all students experiencing economic crises. His philosophy of life, as stated in his interview, was reflective of his multiculturalism:

> I can truly say that I am now able to look at the uniqueness of the persons who I meet and not get hung up on superficial things like physical appearance, accent, clothing, etc. This was a real challenge to me, because of my initial distrust of White people and because I had never been around many Blacks. I feel that I am now able to make a special effort to find out who the people I interact with really are, who they really are behind the masks that we all use. I also want to know how they have overcome obstacles in their lives. To me that's what its all about—meeting the challenges of life and learning from them.

Early Mainstream/Abrupt Latino

Persons categorized under the early mainstream/abrupt Latino pattern had almost exclusive contact with Anglo culture during the first few years of their lives, and then experienced sudden emersion in Latino culture.

Maria J. was born in a small town in Iowa, and her nuclear family and a few relatives were the only Mexican-American residents of the town. Her parents and siblings rarely spoke Spanish, but about twice a year they would journey to a town in another part of the state where a number of Mexican-American families would get together for a day-long reunion. At these gatherings, she heard adults speaking in Spanish and telling stories about Mexico and the southwestern United States. Throughout elementary and middle school, Maria's close friends were all Anglos; and, other than her parents and some relatives, she did not have very much experience interacting with Mexican-American adults. Prior to the start of her first year in high school, Maria's family moved to a small town on the central coast of California. Maria experienced a great shock because, at the school she attended, it was rare for Anglos and Mexican Americans to interact with each other. In fact, it was not uncommon for the two groups to exchange insults and to have occasional fights. The Mexican Americans rejected her because she did not speak Spanish and the Anglos would not accept her because she was Mexican American. Initially, she joined a group of males and females who were rebels from both groups; but gradually, by her persistence and her ability to make friends with administrators and faculty, she gained the respect of both Anglos and Mexican Americans. In her junior year, she was elected to a position on the student council and in her senior year became class president. While in college, she continued to hold positions of leadership and responsibility and often mediated between Mexican-American and Anglo groups, preventing conflict between them.

Early Mainstream/Gradual Latino

Early mainstream/gradual Latino describes a developmental trend in which the person's early life involves exclusive contact with Anglo culture followed by a gradual introduction to Latino culture.

James S. was born in an all-Anglo suburb of Houston, Texas. His parents spoke English at home and, for the first six years of his life, James had no contact with Mexican-American peers or authority figures other than his siblings and parents. His first exposure to Mexican-American peers was in his first year of elementary school, where he became acquainted with the few Latinos who attended his school. James had increasingly more contact with Mexican Americans in middle school and high school. He also formed close friendships with Mexican-American teachers in his middle and high school years. James was well accepted by both Mexican-American and Anglo groups in his last two years of high school. He held various positions of leadership in high school, and he continued to be a leader in college.

The data collected through the life history interviews revealed that the identities of subjects interviewed varied from almost exclusively Latino or mainstream Anglo to indications of a strong identity with both cultural groups and, on occasion, with other groups as well. These components emerged as important determinants of the contemporary multicultural identity (CMIs) of the subjects: (1) functionalism, (2) commitment, and (3) transcendence. Functionalism refers to the ability of persons to participate effectively in two or more cultural groups.

Fitzgerald's (1971) description of the bicultural behavior of Maori university graduates in New Zealand provided examples of functionalistic behavior. He described his subjects as "shuttling" between two cultures but without making any corresponding changes in their cultural identities. He concluded from this that the Maoris could assume any number of social identities (i.e., certain learned roles expected of an individual outside his first culture) without assuming a corresponding cultural identity (i.e., the individual retains his identity with his first culture).

The second important component of the CMI—the degree of commitment to the cultural groups in which the person participates—concerns the willingness of the person to invest energy and time in those groups in order to improve the culture, vis-à-vis the well-being of the members of those groups. That is, the person exhibits a commitment to improving the lives of people in the groups in which he/she participates and, furthermore, the person commits himself/herself to improving the cultures of those groups. In addition, by playing the roles of cultural ambassador and mediator, the person also demonstrates a commitment to improving relationships and understanding between the several groups in which he/she participates. In connection with commitment, Adler (1974) stated:

> Multicultural man is the person who is intellectually and emotionally committed to the fundamental unity of all human beings while at the same time he recognizes, legitimizes, accepts, and appreciates the fundamental differences that lie between people of different cultures [p. 25].

Transcension, the third characteristic of CMIs, refers to the dynamics of identity formation. Adler described a person who is transcendent as follows:

> The parameters of his identity are neither fixed nor predictable, being responsive instead to temporary form and openness to change. . . . He is able, however,

TABLE 6.2. Contemporary Multicultural Identities

N	Contemporary Multicultural Identities	Defining Characteristics
39	Synthesized multicultural	Positive attitudes toward several cultures; competent functioning in more than one culture; feels accepted by members of more than one culture; feels committed to more than one culture as expressed through philosophy of life and life goals
22	Functional multicultural/ mainstream orientation	Functions competently in both Latino and mainstream cultures; more comfortable and self-assured in mainstream culture; greater commitment to mainstream culture expressed through philosophy of life and life goals
49	Functional multicultural/ Latino orientation	Functions competently in both Latino and mainstream cultures; more comfortable and self-assured in Latino culture; greater commitment to Latino culture expressed through philosophy of life and life goals
19	Monocultural	

> to look at his own original culture from an outsider's perspective. This tension gives rise to a dynamic, passionate, and critical posture in the face of totalistic ideologies, systems, and movements. . . . Intentionally or accidentally, multicultural persons undergo shifts in their psychocultural posture, their religion, personality, behavior, occupation, nationality, outlook, political persuasion, and values may in part or completely reformulate in the face of new examples [pp. 30–31].

Adler also concluded that the transcendent person has the ability to be a part of and also to stand apart from the different groups in which he participates.

The several CMI categories identified along with the definitions suggested by the life histories collected are presented in table 6.2. The distribution of the 129 subjects among the different categories is also presented in this table.

Synthesized Multicultural

Persons identified as synthesized biculturals/multiculturals exhibited the following personality characteristics: positive attitudes toward Latino and mainstream cultures; competent functioning in both Latino, mainstream, and other cultures with an ability to "shuttle" between the cultures; evidence of close interpersonal relationships with members of different age, sex, and socioeconomic groups from different cultures; behaviors demonstrating a commitment to assisting in the continued development of the cultures they participate in; and a transcendent philosophy of life.

Laura C.-S. was born in New York City. Her mother is Puerto Rican and her father is Jewish. Her early years were spent among Puerto Rican, Jewish, and mainstream American peers. Laura spoke three languages—Yiddish, Spanish, and English—and enjoyed participating in the multicultural environment of New York City. When she was twelve years old, her father accepted a job in Puerto Rico and the family moved to the island. Initially, the move was difficult for Laura; she was not completely fluent in Spanish, so was ostracized by her classmates. However, she was able to gain acceptance because of her interest in drama and dancing. She became very active in the theatre and developed an intellectual interest in the use of drama and dance to enhance intercultural understanding. During her senior year, she became a volunteer in the elementary schools, where she worked with Puerto Rican children who were experiencing problems of adjustment because their families had returned to the island after living for several years on the United States mainland. In college, Laura was majoring in ethnomusicology, and she founded a theatre and dance group. The members of both these groups were from very diverse ethnic, racial, and socioeconomic backgrounds. Her philosophy of life expresses her interests in encouraging intercultural understanding through the arts:

> Much of culture is expressed in dance, theatre, and painting. You don't need languages to percieve the heart and soul of a culture and a people. I am also very excited about the respect and understanding that is created by participating in or observing multicultural dancing and theatre. This is where the future of multicultural understanding lies; if we did diplomacy through art, all peoples would truly understand each other and we could achieve world peace.

Ray A. was born in San Antonio, Texas, and lived there for the first few years of his life while his father was stationed at one of the air bases in that city. When he was five years old, his family moved to Europe where they lived in several countries in neighborhoods both on and off the base. In early adolescence, his family moved to Japan, and they stayed there until the end of his sophomore year in high school. Ray had established close friendships with peers from all the different countries and cities in which he had lived; he could also speak different languages fluently. He and his family returned to the United States, to a city in northern California where Ray finished his last two years of high school. In his last two years of school, he excelled in sports, was a member of the debate team, and was president of the student council and of the United Nations club. In college, Ray was viewed as a leader by both Mexican Americans and Anglos. He led a fight to keep militant Mexican-American students from preventing the nomination of a bilingual/bicultural Anglo student for the office of president of the Mexican-American student club on campus. His transcendent philosophy of life was reflected in his commitment to assisting members of all ethnic groups at his university.

Functional Bicultural/Mainstream Orientation

Although functional bicultural/mainstream people are functionally multicultural with positive attitudes toward both Anglo and Mexican-American cultures, they have greater acceptance from Anglos and they are more comfortable in Anglo cultural settings and evidence a greater commitment to the goals of Anglo culture. They show no evidence of having a transcendent identity—that is, they see other people and themselves as being culture bound.

Ramiro J. was born and reared in Dallas, Texas. His family was well off economically, so he had lived in integrated neighborhoods and attended some of the best schools in the city. He was fluently bilingual and he had close friends who were both Mexican Americans and Anglos. He attended social and intellectual functions sponsored by members of both groups.

However, Ramiro admitted to feeling more comfortable with Anglos and when participating in Anglo cultural activities. In particular, he avoided interacting with what he referred to as the "rural, very Mexican" type. He said,

> The extreme Mexican types don't like me because they feel that I'm too stuck up, that I think I'm better than they are. I just can't deal with them, and I won't try because they just don't accept my values and interests. I just feel that the Mexican type has to learn that the world is not the way they would like it to be and they have to learn to change or they are just not going to make it.

Functional Bicultural/Latino Orientation

The definition for Functional Bicultural/Latino CMI category is very similar to that of the previous category with the exception that the person is more committed to Mexican Americans and feels more comfortable when participating in Mexican-American culture.

Andrea W. was born and grew up in a rural town in the Central Valley of California. Her family lived on a ranch/farm several miles from the town in which she attended school. Thus, during early childhood, her closest friends were her siblings and cousins. During the first six years of her life, her parents spoke Spanish exclusively, but when Andrea turned seven her parents converted from Catholicism to a Protestant religion. The majority of members of the church she attended were Anglos. From this time forward, Andrea had extensive contact with Anglos, going to Sunday school and to church retreats and attending many social functions sponsored through the church. Andrea also developed close friendships with the other Latino families who were members of her church. Throughout elementary, middle, and high school, she had close friends who were Latinos and Anglos and attended functions sponsored by both groups; however, she would always feel more comfortable with Latinos. This same pattern held during her college years even though she participated actively in many Anglo functions and had many Anglo friends; she always felt more comfortable when she was around Latinos. She explained her feelings in this way:

> Mexican-Americans and other Spanish-speaking peoples feel like members of my family to me. I guess Spanish makes me more comfortable. I feel it is a language of friendship and intimacy. Somehow, I can't seem to get too close to people who can't speak Spanish. Perhaps this will change in the future, but I don't think so.

A few of the subjects who had been identified as bicultural by the B/MEI and the BOLS turned out to be predominantly monocultural, and they were, therefore, classified as either Predominantly Latino or Predominantly Anglo.

That is, although they exhibited some competencies and had some experiences in a second culture, they would generally prefer not to participate in other cultures if given a choice. Fitzgerald (1971) also identified this phenomenon in his work with the Maori college graduates. While all his subjects knew how to participate in European functions, they occasionally chose not to do so. Fitzgerald observed:

> The element of individual choice then, becomes highly significant in such accultarative settings. Identification must involve such a complicated process of decision-making in face of multiple social and cultural situations [p. 49].

Thus, in these cases, there is no question that persons not only refused to participate in activities which were not part of their first culture, but also refused to consider developing an identity with another culture. Many of these monocultural people had at some time in their lives participated in another culture, but for one reason or another they had made the decision not to make a commitment to that culture. The component of commitment, therefore, plays a very important role in contemporary multicultural identity.

In general, our overall findings were strongly indicative of the fact that the process of development of multicultural orientations to life is an organic, dynamic process. The life history data highlighted the fact that people are always acquiring new sociocultural skills and perspectives—identified as personality building elements or resources in chapter 4. In addition, our subjects were constantly in the process of rearranging and combining these personality-building elements and resources. (For a more complete description of the model of identity development which emerged from our research, the reader is referred back to chapter 4.)

The third and fourth questions posed by the investigators were as follows: Are multicultural persons more effective than monocultural persons as leaders of groups that are culturally diverse? If multicultural people are more effective as leaders in these mixed ethnic group situations, what is it that makes them more effective?

To answer these questions, the investigators again employed a combination of mestizo and European approaches to research and data collection. They devised a simulated situation which made use of the laboratory method for studying small groups—reflective of the European world view—and they collected their data by employing observational and interview techniques—in line with a mestizo world view.

LEADERSHIP IN MIXED ETHNIC GROUPS

The subjects were 36 male Latino college students between the ages of 18 and 23 from university campuses in both California and Texas (half from each state). The subjects included in the study were tested with the M/BEI and the BOLS and identified as either multicultural or monocultural. They were asked to participate in an ethnically mixed discussion group composed of four males—the subject plus three confederates who had been pre-instructed to promote a certain point of view. For the purposes of the study, confederates were introduced to the real subject as fellow subjects and their true roles were not uncovered. In order to establish an ethnically mixed group, the three confederates were selected to represent three distinct populations: Anglo, Black, and Latino. Confederates were selected who visibly represented their ethnic group with respect to considerations such as regional accent and physical appearance.

When the subject and the three confederates arrived for the scheduled session, the two experimenters, both male, introduced themselves and asked the group members to sit in chairs arranged in a circle. The first experimenter told the group that the purpose of the research was to study decision-making processes in mixed ethnic groups and that they would be given 20 minutes to discuss a controversial problem concerning the preservation of the cultural integrity of a hypothetical, non-industrialized society: contact has been made with a traditional society (located in a remote mountainous region in Central America) in which mortality rates and malnutrition are high, but the people have a very supportive and cohesive family life and religion. Should we intervene, offering technological knowledge with respect to food production and health care or leave them alone? Prior to providing further details about the issue, the first experimenter informed the group that a group coordinator (leader) was needed. By means of a controlled lottery, the real subject was invariably selected to be the group leader. Immediately following the "selection," the first experimenter took the group coordinator (the subject) into an adjoining room for five minutes to give him further instructions on his task as group leader: he was to attempt to achieve group consensus in the ensuing discussion and to refrain from expressing his own opinion.

Meanwhile, the second experimenter assigned each confederate his role for that particular session, counterbalancing so that the Black, Anglo, and Latino would adopt either a pro-intervention, anti-intervention, or an undecided position an equal number of times. As part of the training and pilot testing phase, the three confederates had been trained at length in delivering convincing arguments for each of the three roles. While there were different confederates at the two sites, all used the same arguments and care was taken to maximize similarity of physical appearance and accent.

After the briefing, the subject and first experimenter returned to the session room and the four group members were each provided with a "fact sheet" to consult, as needed, during the session. The fact sheet consisted of a few paragraphs describing benefits and drawbacks of daily life in a recently discovered "traditional" society. The written description included sufficient information to justify either the intervention or nonintervention position. All members were then asked to write on a slip of paper their position (intervention or nonintervention) regarding the problem and these were collected prior to the start of the actual discussion.

Present in the room and introduced at this time was a trained observer who remained in a corner to record the coordinator's behavior during the session using a modified Bales (1950) behavior observation scale. The same trained observer was used at both the California and the Texas field sites in order to achieve greater reliability. Although interrater reliability for five raters was established during the pilot testing phase, all group discussions were tape recorded to verify the accuracy of the behavioral observations. The audio recordings were also used to ensure that the three confederates maintained high constancy of behavior (e.g., made the same arguments) across all sessions. The ratings of two independent judges revealed great consistency in both the content and intensity of the confederate statements, thus precluding the possibility that variations in leader behavior were caused by variations in confederate behavior. The rating also showed high accuracy of the Bales observer.

The coordinator was reminded that the group had 20 minutes for discussion and his attention was directed to a timer which was clearly visible to all group members. Upon completion of all preliminary instructions, the first experimenter told the group to begin the discussion as soon as he left the room, and then he left. The second experimenter remained in the room to officially start and time the discussion and to issue five- and two-minute-remaining time warnings.

The means and standard deviations on the different leadership behaviors for the two classifications—monocultural and multicultural—are presented in table 6.3.

The findings yielded five dimensions of group leader behaviors which subjects with a greater degree of multicultural experience used more frequently than subjects with less multicultural experience:

1. taking charge (quicker to assume leader role; being assertive, and active; assessing group process);
2. effectiveness of communication (asking for opinions, evaluations, and feelings; clarifying statements of members; clarifying issue being discussed);
3. attempting to reduce interpersonal conflict (mediating, seeking compromise solutions);
4. social sensitivity and personableness (acknowledging contributions made by members; addressing members by name);
5. coping with stress (fewer visible indicators of tension and absence of inappropriate behaviors).

TABLE 6.3. Comparison of Multicultural and Monocultural Leaders on Leadership Behaviors

Leadership Behavior	Means			
	Monoculturals ($N = 19$)	Multiculturals ($N = 17$)	F	p
1. Time in seconds to assume leadership	5.166	3.667	3.22	.08
2. Active and assertive	3.412	5.417	3.41	.07
3. Asks members for opinions, evaluations and feelings				
Total	9.47	15.00	13.49	.0008
Anglo	2.33	4.83	5.33	.03
Black	2.25	3.33	2.73	.11
Mexican-American	3.25	4.41	6.96	.01
4. Acknowledges contributions of members				
Total	.667	1.917	3.20	.08
Anglo	.083	.333	1.71	.20
Black	.500	1.083	2.97	.10
Mexican-American	1.667	1.066	3.01	.08
5. Clarifies issue under discussion	1.890	3.000	4.70	.04
6. Assesses group progress	.750	1.667	1.87	.18
7. Mediates between members in conflict	.916	2.167	2.05	.17
8. Seeks compromises or intermediate solutions	1.162	2.014	1.99	.17
9. Addresses members by first name	.261	2.251	5.13	.03
10. Shows tension and inappropriate behavior	1.21	.120	3.41	.07

Ratings on global leadership style indicated that high multicultural subjects were more flexible, that is, these subjects tended to be less autocratic and more democratic. High multicultural subjects were active and assertive, but they combined these behaviors with tactfulness and personableness. Low multicultural subjects, on the other hand, tended to behave in an authoritarian fashion, rudely interrupting the members of their group by shouting them down, or they would assume a very passive and laissez-faire management style allowing time to be wasted in unproductive arguments among the group members.

Results of the post-group interviews conducted with the group leaders showed that leaders of high multicultural experience were more accurate in reporting what actually transpired in their groups; in the actual group process, 59 percent of the high multiculturals were accurate, whereas only 37 percent of the low multiculturals were accurate. When asked to speculate as to why their group had failed to achieve consensus in the allotted time, the high multicultural subjects stated that they would most certainly succeed if given a second chance, and 53 percent of these subjects gave self-responsibility attributions for their perceived failure—that is, they made statements such as "I should have concentrated more on the person who couldn't make up his mind" or "I should have asked the two people who were doing most of the arguing to try to step into each others' shoes." In contrast to this, 69 percent of the low multicultural leaders gave other directed responsibility attributions; they made statements such as "Those two guys are too stubborn and narrow-minded to ever agree with each other" or "The members of my group just can't get along with each other."

In general, high multicultural leaders appeared to have more behavioral and perspective repertoires or resources available to them. They also made more effort to communicate with the Anglo and the Black group members; they made sure that all members in their group expressed their opinions and that they all understood each others' points of view. In contrast to this, monocultural leaders would tend to communicate more with the Latino group members, often ignoring the Anglo and Black members. Monocultural leaders were also less concerned with ensuring that points of view expressed by individual members were understood by others in their group.

The greater accuracy of reports made by multicultural leaders during the post-group interviews indicated that they were more understanding of the dynamics of their groups. This latter finding also indicates that they were more sensitive to the group process and to the interpersonal dynamics which transpired in their groups; they were also more open to their experiences; that is, they were less defensive (less likely to distort what actually transpired and to try to avoid blame for the group's "failure" to achieve consensus).

The multicultural leadership behaviors and skills identified above are essential to effective leadership in the diverse environments of the Americas. Also essential is the combination of European and mestizo world view-based approaches to research and intervention on the one hand and the phenomenological and natural science perspectives in psychology on the other to better understand and solve the problems that are contributing to conflict and distrust in the hemisphere. A leadership training program based on some of the findings reviewed above is presented in chapter 8.

As psychologists and psychiatrists, it is our responsibility to bring to the awareness of the body politic and of the scientific community the incisive observation by Berger et al. (1973) which was quoted at the beginning of this chapter:

> Perhaps there is an intrinsic connection between cognitive totalism and political totalitarianism: the mind that can only tolerate one approach to understanding reality is the same kind of mind that must impose one all-embracing structure of power if it ever gets into the position of doing so [p. 235].

SUMMARY

The nations of the Americas face serious problems which are related to intranational and international diversity. In order to ensure that these problems do not lead to continued conflict, separatism, misunderstanding, and distrust, we need to understand the psychodynamics of multiculturalism—how it develops and how it is manifested in behavior in cross-cultural situations. In order to accomplish this goal, we need to confront a long-standing but still important controversy in psychology: as scientists, should psychologists adopt the methodology of the natural sciences or should they use the more phenomenologically oriented humanistic approaches? The answer offered here is that if we are to truly understand diversity we need approaches to research which are in themselves reflective of diversity; we need both the mestizo (more representative of phenomenology) and the European (more representative of the natural sciences) approaches and perspectives to scientific investigation. These two perspectives and approaches were combined in a research project which (1) identified multicultural leaders and (2) compared the behaviors of these leaders with those of monocultural leaders in mixed ethnic groups under conditions of conflict. The approach succeeded in identifying leadership behaviors which reduce conflict in mixed ethnic group situations.

REFERENCES

Adler, P. S. Beyond cultural identity: Reflections on cultural and multicultural man. In R. Brislin (Ed.), *Topics in culture learning*. Vol. 2. University of Hawaii, East-West Culture Learning Institute, 1974.

Bales, R. F. Interaction process analysis: A method for the study of small groups. Cambridge, Mass.: Addison-Wesley, 1950.

Berger, P., Berger, B., & Kellner, H. *The homeless mind: Modernization and consciousness*. New York: Vintage, 1973.

Caso, A. *La existencia como economia y como caridad: Ensayo sobre la esencia del cristianismo*. Mexico, D.F.: Secretaria de Educacion Publica, 1943.

Child, I. L. *Italian or American? The second generation in conflict*. New Haven: Yale University Press, 1943.

Fitzgerald, T. K. Education and identity—A reconsideration of some models of acculturation and identity. *New Zealand Council of Educational Studies*, 1971, 45–47.

Greeno, J. C. Response to "The hegemony of natural scientific conceptions of learning." *American Psychologist*, 1982, *37*, 332–334.

Heller, C. S. *Mexican-American youth: Forgotten youth at the crossroads*. New York: Random House, 1968.

Madsen, W. The alcoholic agringado. *American Anthropologist*, 1964, *66*, 355–361.

McFee, M. The 150% man, a product of Blackfeet acculturation. *American Anthropologist*, 1968, *70*, 1096–1103.

Osborne, J. The hegemony of natural scientific conceptions of learning. *American Psychologist*, 1982, *37*, 330–332.

Ramirez, M. Identification with Mexican family values and authoritarianism in Mexican Americans. *The Journal of Social Psychology*, 1967, *73*, 3–11.

Ramirez, M. Identification with Mexican-American values and psychological adjustment in Mexican-American adolescents. *International Journal of Social Psychiatry*, 1969, *15*, 151–156.

Ramirez, M., & Castaneda, A. *Cultural democracy, bicognitive development and education*. New York: Academic Press, 1974.

Stonequist, E. V. The marginal man: A study in personality and culture conflict. E. Burgess & D. J. Bogue (Ed.), *Contributions to urban sociology*. Chicago: University of Chicago Press, 1964.

Teske, R., & Nelson, B. H. Two scales for the measurement of Mexican American identity. *International Review of Modern Sociology*, 1973, *3*, 192–203.

A cry for leadership, *Time*, August 6, 1979, *114* (6), 24–28.

Valentine, C. A. Deficit, difference, and bicultural models of Afro-American behavior. *Harvard Educational Review*, 1971, *41*, 131–157.

Witkin, H. A., Dyk, R. B., Faterson, H. F., Goodenough, D. R., & Karp, S. A. *Psychological differentiation*. New York: Wiley, 1962.

CHAPTER 7
The Mestizo World View and Mental Health in the Americas

It seems reasonable to think of man as existing in a "bio-psycho-social" field. This depicts an open transactional system that allows uninterrupted bidirectional flow of information and energy transactions extending from the deepest and most minute recesses of the body (intracellular metabolic processes) to the social field, encompassing cultural forces, even historical forces that contributed to shaping the culture.

—Morton F. Reiser (1975)

When I fell off my horse and broke my leg, I was taken to the hospital and the doctors and nurses took care of me, but I did not feel completely well again until I went to see the medicine man; he made me feel like my body was whole again.

—a member of the Navajo nation
(from *Innovation*, Winter 1976)

My eye caught sight of a cloud. It was darker than the rest. It was alone. It was coming my way. The hand of God, I was sure of it! So that is how one dies. All my life, in the spare moments a person has, I wondered how I would go. Now I knew. Now I was ready. I thought I would soon be taken up to the cloud and across the sky I would go, and soon it was no longer above me, but beyond me; and I was still on my land, so dear to me, so familiar after all these years. I can't be dead, I thought to myself, I am here and the cloud is way over there, and getting further each second. Maybe the next cloud, but by then I had decided God had other things to do. Perhaps my name had come up, but He had decided to call others before me, and get around to me later. Who could ever know his reasons?

—an Hispanic American from New Mexico
(from Robert Coles' *The Old Ones of New Mexico*, 1975)

The three perspectives on health and illness, life and death, presented above are reflective of the mestizo world view. There are three major characteristics of this belief system: (1) integration of mind and body—a holistic view; (2) the quality of the relationship between the person and the physical and social environments; and (3) the quality of the relationship between the person and the supernatural. This chapter examines each of these components in detail. In addition, the roles of the indigenous healers will be examined and their various approaches to healing will be identified. The final section of the chapter reviews current attempts at integrating mestizo, native American, and European perspectives and approaches to develop intervention and primary prevention programs.

HOLISTIC VIEWS OF HEALTH AND MALADJUSTMENT

> Mental goes by the spirit of the body. The mind is governed by the spirit of the body. If the body feels something the mind is affected [A Curandero, from A. Kiev, *Curanderismo*, 1968].

> Body and mind are conjoined, the core essence of a person, responding to and regulating his various activities [Fabrega & Manning, 1973].

> Health is defined as a harmonious balance between a person's physical, psychological, and spiritual entities, illness can manifest itself as disruption in a person's social, physical, or psychological life [Chavira & Trotter, 1978]

In the mestizo world view of mental illness and health, the body and the mind are believed to be conjoined. Within the context of this perspective, the entire domain of human behavior is believed to be influenced by both biological and sociocultural events and forces. Thus, changes in the body are believed to have profound effects on the personality style. For example, Fabrega and Manning (1973) have observed that mestizos in the Chiapos highlands of Mexico believe that gaining weight makes the person less energetic, slower, lazier, and more cautious and restrained. They also point out that, among this group of mestizos, emotions play an important role in causation of illness:

> Inspection of the list of emotions that are described as pathogenic indicates that pleasantness or unpleasantness are not critical factors. Rather, their amount and persistence in the individual across time appears to be critical. Emotions and feelings are seen as inevitable, but when present they should be discouraged (in actions, talk, or thought) or neutralized (as with alcohol) so that the body at no time or during any one interval carries an excessive load [p. 228].

These investigators also found that interpersonal relationships are also believed to have a direct bearing on health, "Arguments, separations, envious coveting, love triangles, intensely satisfying exchanges, etc. all have medical relevance precisely because they give rise to excessive feeling [p. 228]."

The holistic view of health/illness characteristic of the mestizo world view has resulted in development of theories of disease and of health care systems which are very different from those of Western European cultures. For example, in the context of the mestizo world view, disease is viewed as being closely related to everyday life and considered to be intimately connected to the quality of family and community relationships as well as relationships with the supernatural. Health care systems, thus, are seen as part of the broad context of culture. As Kleinman (1980) observed in the context of a holistic perspective of illness and health, health care is a system that is social and cultural in origin, structure, function, and significance. In figure 7.3, the complexity of health care systems which are based on holistic perspectives of health and illness can be discerned.

GOOD RELATIONS WITH THE PHYSICAL AND SOCIAL ENVIRONMENTS

In the mestizo world view, health and illness are associated with the quality of the relationship between the person and his/her physical and social environments. As was discussed in chapter 2, in many of the religions of the native peoples of the Americas, man is considered to be part of the natural order of things in the cosmos. Some North and South American Indian groups share a common view—all things in the cosmos are interrelated, and harmony and balance between all elements of the universe plays a central role in illness and in health.

In many of the Native American and mestizo groups in Latin America, the quality of the person's relationship with his/her social environment figures importantly in the beliefs regarding illness and health. As was discussed in chapter 4, the mestizo cultures of Latin America emphasize the importance of developing and maintaining good interpersonal relationships with others, particularly with members of the nuclear and extended families. Illness in these societies is often viewed as a consequence of conflicts with or separation from important others. Feelings of guilt are often associated with illness and maladjustment. For example, guilt over not living up to the expectations and wishes of parents and other family members is believed to result in poor health. Envy is also believed to play an important role in causes of illness associated with the interpersonal domain. Rubel (1966), through his research with Mexican Americans in South Texas, identified the central role of envy in the causation of illness or maladjustment. That is, if a person is envied by another, he/she might experience symptoms of illness or maladjustment. One of the most common illnesses in Latino cultures, *mal-de-ojo*, is believed to be caused by a form of envy. If a person's physical features (usually the face) are admired by another (usually a much older person) and the admirer does not touch the admired person (by lightly running the palm of the hand over the face), the admired person can become ill. The symptoms—fever and a general feeling of malaise—can only be relieved by contacting the person who admired the patient and asking him/her to carry out the appropriate caress.

Many illnesses and problems of adjustment in mestizo cultures are believed to be caused by feelings of alienation from the family group, the community, or the culture of origin. For example, in young people, illness is often associated with the acculturation process. For children and adolescents in particular, illness and maladjustment are believed to be associated with alienation from parents, grandparents, and siblings as a result of adoption of life styles and value systems which differ from those of the home culture. Madsen (1964) documented several cases of acculturation alienation among young adult Mexican Americas in rural South Texas. These people had become assimilated into Anglo mainstream culture and in the process had rejected their home culture. Madsen observed that these individuals experienced considerable feelings of guilt over having abandoned their original culture and that they developed a dependency on alcohol in their attempts to alleviate anxiety; he, thus, referred to these people as "alcoholic agringados." Fried (1959) also documented cases in which adults had become ill as a result of having become separated from their community and culture of origin. Indians in Peru who had migrated from their villages in the mountains to urban areas in the lowlands, and who were forced to adopt the life styles of city dwellers, tended to develop physiological and emotional symptoms. Acculturation has also been identified as one of the causes of physical and emotional illness among members of North American Indian groups (Hallowell, 1951; Spindler, 1952).

Disruption of good relations with the physical environment is given a central role in the explanation of causes of illness and psychological maladjustment among many of the cultures of the Indian groups in North America. The person who does not perform the proper ritual of atonement for killing an animal, for uprooting a plant, or for taking the fruit of a tree or a bush can become ill or experience unhappiness and lack of harmony in his/her life. Wyman and Kluckhohn (1938), for example, identified etiological factors which the Navajos believe can produce sickness: natural phenomena such as lightning, winds, thunder, and sometimes the earth, sun, or moon; and some species of animals, including bear, deer, coyote, porcupine, snakes, eagles, and fish. Kaplan and Johnson (1967), in their research on Navajo psychopathology, discovered that illness was believed to result from possession by certain aspects of dangerous animals, natural phenomena, witches, or ghosts.

RELIGION, SPIRITUALISM, AND HEALTH: GOOD RELATIONS WITH THE SUPERNATURAL

> To Western man, illness is an impersonal event brought about by neutral, non-emotional natural agents such as germs, while for the Mexican American illness

> relates to the individual's life, his community, his interpersonal relationships and, *above all to his God*. Disease is defined not only in naturalistic, empirical symptomatic terms, but also in *magical and religious terms* [Kiev, 1968, p. 77].

One of the most important goals sought through the religious practices and rituals of the indigenous cultures of the Americas is that of developing and maintaining good relations with the supernatural. For example, Leon-Portilla (1968) explained that the Mayas developed an elaborate system for measuring time, because this allowed them to predict the arrivals of the time-bearing dieties, and, in turn, permitted them to situate themselves under the influence of those dieties whose burdens were favorable. The people followed the advice of the wise men and the priests who knew the intricacies of the calendars, and they relied on these shamans to help them maintain good relations with the supernatural. Lamphere (1969) explained that the Navajos developed various chants or "sings," with each chant being a system of ritual procedures designed to prevent the development of "ugly conditions" associated with the disruption of good relations with the supernatural. The belief reflected in these rituals is that the creators of the present world emerged from the "lower worlds" and taught the ancestors of the Navajos the ceremonial knowledge necessary to perform the chants. For example, the myth of the Male Shooting Way tells of two heroes (Holy Young Man and Holy Boy) who experience a series of trials and misfortunes. Various supernaturals aid the heroes by teaching them a ceremony which counteracts their troubles.

In the beliefs of the indigenous and mestizo peoples of the Americas, the status of a person's relations to the supernatural figures importantly in considerations of illness or maladjustment. Maladjustment or illness is believed to be a direct result of a breakdown of the good relations which must exist between the person and the supernatural. In the Latino cultures, a breakdown of good relations with the supernatural is believed to occur when the person commits a transgression against God or his/her family. In many of the native cultures of North America, it is believed that disruption of good relations with the supernatural can occur as a result of contact with "ugly things"—anger, weapons, and even the instanding-one (associated with natural phenomena, witches, and ghosts) which have entered the body. Alienation of the individual from the supernatural can occur as a result of contact with witchcraft or by the action of snakes, bears, lightning, etc.

Treatment for illness and psychological maladjustment associated with the native and mestizo religions of the Americas usually involves the reestablishment of good relations between the patient and the supernatural. The treatment itself is usually carried out by those persons who are believed to have access to the supernatural. For example, in Latino culture the native curer uses prayer and encourages the patient to do penance. In addition, the patient is usually encouraged to reestablish good relations with his/her family. Among the Navajo, the singer engages in specific actions during the course of the chant which exemplify the theme of "taking in" or "applying to." The objective of these actions is to identify the patient with the supernatural and make him/her sacred. To further this effect, sacred objects derived from the spiritual world are put into contact with the patient's body to sanctify him/her.

The process of mestizoization in the Americas (as mentioned in chapters 1 and 2) resulted in the amalgamation of the beliefs and rituals of the native religions with those of the European religions. Thus, much of the supernatural power which had been associated with a pantheistic deity in the native religions was transferred to God, Christ, the Virgin, or the saints, or even members of the clergy. However, some of the supernatural power and the "routes" of access to that power remained outside the realm of official religion and the clergy. Thus, certain individuals in the native cultures—*curanderos*(as), shamans, spiritists, medicine men, magicians, and witches—who are believed to have access to supernatural power play a central role in the treatment of illness and prevention of disease.

CURANDEROS(AS), ESPIRITISTAS, AND MEDICINE MEN: MEDIATING BETWEEN THE PERSON AND THE SUPERNATURAL

The person who is experiencing symptoms of psychological maladjustment and/or physical symptoms of illness seeks the help of someone in the community who is believed to have supernatural power or to have access to such power. The cure is done either directly by the curer or by the curer's intercession with the supernatural. In the Americas, there are three major types of curers—*curanderos*(as), *espiritistas*, and medicine men. The rituals and paraphernalia of these practitioners are quite diverse, but in general their curative activities fall into four major categories:

1. Confession, atonement, and absolution;
2. Restoration of balance, wholeness, and harmony through self-control;
3. Involvement of the family and community in the treatment; and
4. Communication with the supernatural.

Confession, Atonement, and Absolution

The practices of most of the native healers of the Americas are closely associated with religion because, in the mestizo world view, religion and science (and, thus, religion and healing) are seen as belonging to the same domain. Jerome Frank (1961) identified the unity of religion and healing in non-Western cultures as the major determinant of differences observed between Western and non-Western healing, "In the West psychiatry and religion are distinct enemies. In many other cultures the therapist may also be the religious agent, and use of the techniques of confession, atonement, and absolution follow naturally [p. 121]."

Since sin and guilt are among the principal causes of illness and maladjustment in the native and mestizo cultures of the Americas, confession, atonement, and absolution are frequent rituals used in treatment. In some cases, atonement is accomplished through prayer or penance; in others, it may involve the necessity of cleansing the body, accomplished by brushing the body with the branches of a rosemary bush or by sprinkling with holy water. The Puerto Rican *espiritista* is likely to make use of seances and role playing to rid the ailing individual of evil spirits as well as to call on the person's protective spirits for help in the cure. North American Indian medicine men, on the other hand, are more likely to use chanting, storytelling, and body rubs.

Restoration of Balance, Wholeness, and Harmony through Self-control

In many of the native and mestizo cultures, illness and maladjustment are seen as end products of lack of self-control on the part of the individual. The person allows his/her feelings, emotions, or desires to run unchecked, hurting the self and others in the process. Thus, the person who is in need of help is perceived as being out of balance and harmony, and his/her spirit is believed to be fragmented. An important aspect of treatment, then, is to teach the person self-control. This is best exemplified in the treatment rituals used by the Navajo medicine men. The ceremonies usually involve a religious tale about something going wrong, and how, when supernatural figures are called upon, they are able to cure or correct the problem. Medicine men reenact the stories and, through song and chanting, take on the characteristics of the supernatural being in order to cure the patient. For example, there is a series of stories involving Coyote, who is famous for his excesses—greed, lust, envy, and trickery—often hurting himself and others through his actions. These stories help to identify human weaknesses; they show how a person can become like Coyote and indulge in excesses of lust, alcohol, drugs, etc. After the medicine men perform the curing ceremony, they continue to counsel the patient, helping him to control his excessive behavior by reminding him of Coyote.

Self-control was also given great importance by the Nahua peoples of Mexico (see chapter 2). There were specific scripts provided for parents so that they might give advice to their young children regarding the importance of self-control. The schools to which these children were sent later in life also made self-control one of the most important educational goals.

Restoration of balance, wholeness, and harmony in the person who is ill or maladjusted is also achieved through exorcising negative elements or spirits and protecting the person from evil forces and bad spirits. As was mentioned earlier in this chapter, illness or maladjustment is also believed to result from the casting of spells or from contact with "ugly things" or dangerous elements of one kind or another. Thus, curative rituals often involve ridding the person's body of these negative elements or confronting the evil spirit who has possessed the person or has taken temporary hold of his/her soul. These procedures are best exemplified in the work of North American Indian medicine men and Puerto Rican *espiritistas*. The following description of the treatment of a 15-year-old girl by a Puerto Rican *espiritista* was taken from *Innovations* (1976). The girl's presenting problem was violent arguments with her father, to which she would react by leaving the house and wandering the streets without being aware of her identity or of the surroundings. The patient was taken to a seance led by an *espiritista*.

> This girl was allowed to abreact in the seance while in trance possession, screaming unintelligible words, fainting, having convulsion-like movements of a sexual nature. The medium and two women of the group saw that she did not hurt herself and assisted her to make the ritual movements of hands warding off the spirits. After she came out of the trance, an assistant medium in turn entered into a trance and confronted her with a "good spirit," who said: "Do you think that you are a big girl? Even though you are well developed, you are still young. Don't you know what could happen to a girl like you in the streets?" Members supported the medium saying: "Yes, something evil could happen to you on the streets."
>
> The girl was not impressed by these admonitions, and the medium entered into a deeper trance, breathing more quickly and speaking in another pitch of voice reflecting his changed trance state, speaking this time as a "bad spirit": "I am your bad spirit, I am going to get you in trouble. I like what happens on the streets, you are not going to get rid of me. I go where you go." The group echoed his remarks. The girl panicked, seemingly became aware of the possible consequences of her own impulses, and said: "Leave me alone, leave me, become spirits of light and progress." The group joined in, reciting the Lord's Prayer to reinforce the influence of the "good spirit" [p. 10].

Involvement of Family and Community in the Treatment

Restoration of good relations between the person who needs help and his/her social environment is believed to be so important that, in some cultures, treatment is not believed to be effective unless family and community members are involved. While family and community participation is more common in the treatment procedures and rituals of the North American Indians, it is also used by *curanderas* and *espiritistas* in Latino cultures. In some cases, the patient is treated at home in the context of his/her family, but more usually family members and close friends accompany the patient to the place where the treatment is carried out— a *centro*, a *hogan* or the *curandero's* home. Involvement of members of the family and the community in treatment serves to reestablish good relations between these people and the person who is ill or maladjusted. Thus, wholeness and harmony with family, community, and culture are restored. A very important by-product of involvement of family and community in treatment is that the participants usually make a commitment to support the patient and to assume responsibility for his/her gradual reintegration into family and culture. An example of the important role family and community members can play in the treatment program of the medicine men is described in a case history in *Innovations* (1976):

> Edward Yazzi is a Vietnam veteran, and like many of his buddies, had trouble adjusting to civilian life when he returned home. He gained weight, had frequent nightmares about killing and being killed, and complained that his "mind was messed up." The medicine man Yazzi consulted recommended a three-day ritual which is one of the ceremonies traditionally included in the rubric of the "Enemy Way." A major ceremony such as that of the Enemy Way involves the gathering of many friends and relatives. They share in the prayers of blessing for the restoration of the patient and receive blessings from the ceremony themselves. Emphasis is on the unity of experience. To be sick is to be fragmented. To be healed is to become whole and to be whole one must be in harmony with family, friends, and nature. Navajo healing rituals involve family, friends, and nature. They usually take place in a hogan, a simple, eight-sided earthen dwelling which has religious significance as a kind of microcosm of the Navajo spiritual world. In the hogan prayers are chanted with ritual objects that are taken from the natural world of the reservation: juniper branches, bird feathers, dyes from berries and barks. Every ceremony involves a religious tale about something going wrong, and how, when supernatural figures were called upon, they were able to cure or correct the problem. The medicine man re-enacts the story, and through song and chanting, becomes the supernatural being in order to cure the patient. There is a strong aesthetic component in the ritual ceremonies. A catharsis, purging, or removal of a symptom does not seem to arise from anything like the Christian confessional or talking therapies, but rather out of a highly stylized, ritualized art form in which the patient participates as a protagonist, often with his family and friends. For Edward Yazzi, the troubled veteran, for example, a three-day "squaw dance" was prescribed. This is one of the ceremonies traditionally included in the rubric of the "Enemy Way." Instead of striving for insight, the medicine man may ritualistically confront an "evil one" who took the mind of the person he wants to help. He will say, "I want

the mind that you stole." The medicine man, by identifying with the holy person, takes on special powers, and through the supernatural figure in the religious tale is believed to be able to cure the ailing patient [p. 15].

Communication with the Supernatural

One of the most important skills or abilities—and one which is believed to set the native healer apart from other members of his/her sociocultural group—is the ability to communicate with the supernatural. The healer is either believed to be able to communicate with the spirit world directly or to facilitate communication between the person who needs help and the supernatural world. People who have this mediumship ability have been given the name of *shaman* by social scientists. Harner (1973) provided a definition of a shaman:

> A shaman may be defined as a man or woman who is in direct contact with the spirit world through a trance state and has one or more spirits at his command to carry out his bidding for good or evil. Typically, shamans bewitch persons with the aid of spirits or cure persons made ill by other spirits [p. 85].

Treatment activities related to contact with the spirit world are based on the belief in the concept of soul, that is, a belief that all living things have souls which are immortal. The belief is that the soul retains the personality, knowledge, and motivations of the individual or living thing to which it belonged in life. Under the proper conditions, these souls can contact and affect persons living in the physical world. The activities of the souls are similar to the activities of the living beings to which they belonged on earth; therefore, spirits are believed to be both good and evil. They can either heal or create illness.

Through his investigations of Puerto Rican spiritism, Harwood (1977) has identified a spirit hierarchy. Spirits are ranked according to their moral perfection; those occupying different moral ranks are also believed to reside on separate spatial planes. He described this spiritual hierarchical arrangement as follows:

> The lowest level of the spirit hierarchy, which is conceived as starting only a few inches above the earth, is inhabited by spirits that departed from bodies in an unsettled state (*espiritus intranquilos*). These spirits may be bound to earth through a special attachment to the living which grows either out of inordinate love or an unmet obligation (e.g., an unpaid debt). Spirits may also occupy this lowest rank because they have failed to fulfill their spiritual potential in life. People who have died prematurely (especially through suicide, or fatal accident, or violent crime) fall into this category, as do those who have devoted their lives to material pursuits. To enable these "little elevated" spirits (*espiritus*

> *poco elevados*) to quit the earthly ambience and ascend to the next spiritual rank, incarnate spirits (i.e., the living) must perform certain services in their behalf. These services, which include reciting prayers, lighting candles, and offering flowers, are spoken of as "giving the spirit light" (*darle la luz al espiritu*). If not "given light," these restless spirits may become subjugated to earthly malefactors (*brujos*—"sorcerers"), who use them in harming enemies [pp. 72–73].

Figure 7.1 is a diagrammatic representation of the spirit hierarchy as presented by Harwood.

Healers who communicate directly with the supernatural engage in both diagnostic and treatment activities. During the initial consultation, the healer usually has two objectives: to determine the identities of the patient's protective spirits and to pinpoint the client's problems and diagnose their causes. A frequent practice in diagnosing a client's condition involves the medium calling upon his/her spiritual guide to make contact with other spirits who are influencing the client. The spirits contact the client through his/her dreams or through the healer. Diagnoses of both physical and spiritual

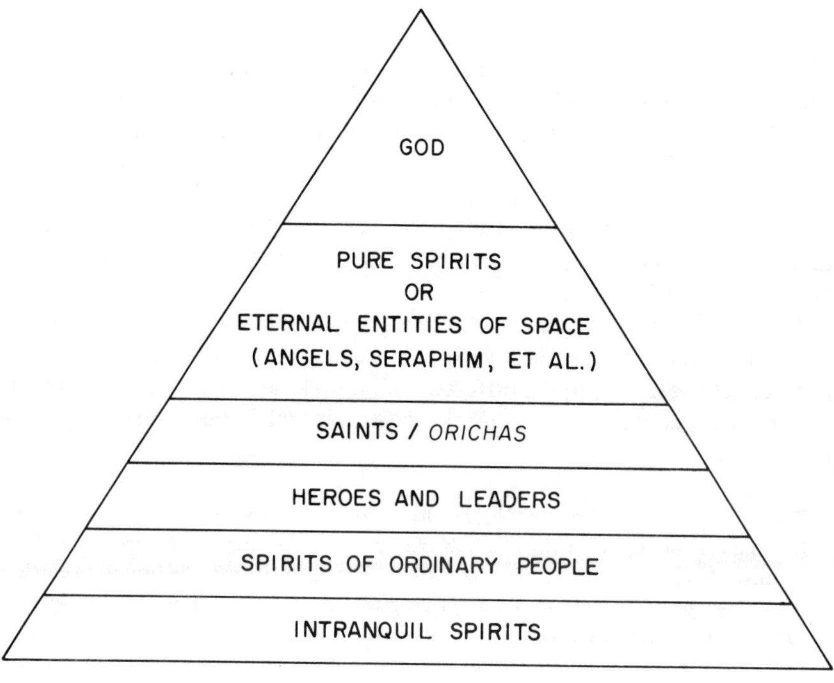

Fig. 7.1. The spirit hierarchy.

etiology are quite frequent, and conjoint treatment involving physician and healer may result.

The treatment procedures followed by many Puerto Rican spiritists or mediums include the following.

Exorcism is part of most *espiritista* sessions. It is done to remove harmful spiritual influences which clients may have brought with them to the meeting or which they may take away with them when they leave. The ritual is performed by fumigating the client with cigar smoke or sprinkling him/her with holy water.

Working the cause is done by the medium interrogating the spiritual agent until he or she admits responsibility for the client's problems and begs the victim's forgiveness.

Giving the spirit light is done by the medium giving the client a program of rituals designed to elevate the offending spirit (to a higher level in the hierarchy) and, thus, permanently remove its harmful effects. The program usually consists of reciting a particular prayer several times during the day or performing other tasks which are believed helpful in elevating the spirit from the lowest rung on the hierarchy, e.g., offering flowers, candles, or other ritual paraphernalia. Sometimes the client must restore disrupted relationships with his/her family in order to succeed in elevating the offending spirit.

MODELS FOR UNDERSTANDING AND PROMOTING MENTAL HEALTH IN THE AMERICAS

In summarizing the material covered in this chapter up to this point, it can be concluded that, in order to properly represent the mestizo world view, a holistic health/illness model is needed. That is, an integrated model which views the mind and body as conjoined and which conceives of health and illness as being affected by biological, sociocultural, and supernatural factors and forces. Fabrega and Manning (1973) have observed that an integrated/holistic model of this type is consistent with the most recent knowledge derived from research on psychosomatic medicine. Holistic/integrated models have also been found to be consonant with recent developments in behavioral health (Matarazzo, 1982). Reiser's (1975) review of neurobiological research is also supportive of an holistic/integrated model of health/illness. In fact, Reiser proposed a model which is reflective of the fact that people live in a biopsychosocial field. Figure 7.2 is based on a diagram presented by Reiser but it includes modification made by the author in order to include the supernatural realm.

A holistic/integrated model such as that described above demands development of health care models for intervention and primary prevention

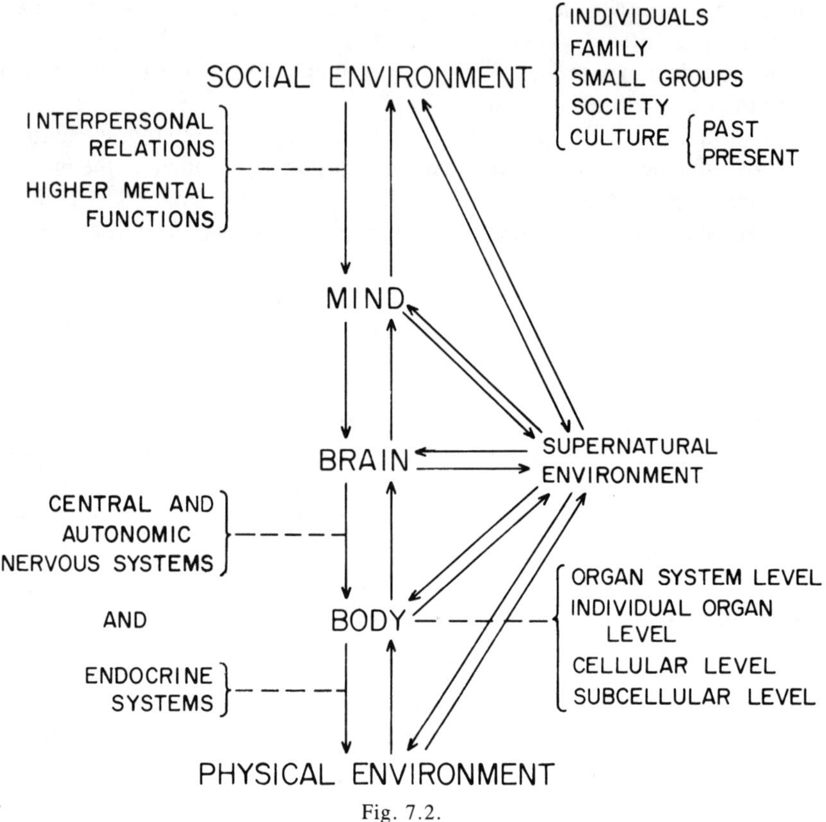

Fig. 7.2.

which are themselves integrated and holistic. Such a health care model must incorporate the different domains which are part of the mestizo view of illness and health. Figure 7.3 was taken from Kleinman (1980) and modified by the author in order to include the supernatural domain.

In recent years, several efforts have been made to develop procedures for the health care of mestizo peoples in the Americas which are based on the model presented in Figure 7.4. Most of these efforts have attempted to integrate native American, mestizo, and European approaches to treatment and diagnosis. The philosophical framework for these integrative approaches was provided in part by the writings of E. Fuller Torrey (1973), whose work led to the recognition of the importance of shared world view in diagnosis and treatment. With respect to the therapist's being able to name what is wrong with the patient, Fuller Torrey stated,

> The very act of naming it has a therapeutic effect. The patient's anxiety is decreased by the knowledge that a respected and trusted therapist understands

> what is wrong. The identification of the offending agent (childhood experience, violation of taboo) may also activate a series of associated ideas in the patient's mind, producing confession, abreaction, and general catharsis. This is the principle of Rumpelstiltskin. Based upon personality studies of the Brothers Grimm in the early nineteenth century, the principle illustrates the magic of the right word [p. 16].

Some of the most important attempts to integrate mestizo and European approaches in diagnostic and intervention strategies involve training professional mental health practitioners to use some of the diagnostic and healing procedures employed by *curanders*, *espiritistas*, and medicine men. Kreisman (1975) described treatment of Mexican-American patient schizophrenics at the Denver General Hospital where conventional therapy was adapted to the model of *curanderismo*. In the late 1970s the White Cloud Center at the University of Oregon Medical School sponsored a project (personal communication from Spero M. Manson) which encouraged physicians and medicine men to share knowledge and work together to integrate approaches for treating North American Indian patients. In another project, at the New Jersey College of Medicine and Dentistry, attempts are being made to encourage health and mental health professionals to employ some of the procedures of the Puerto Rican *espiritistas*.

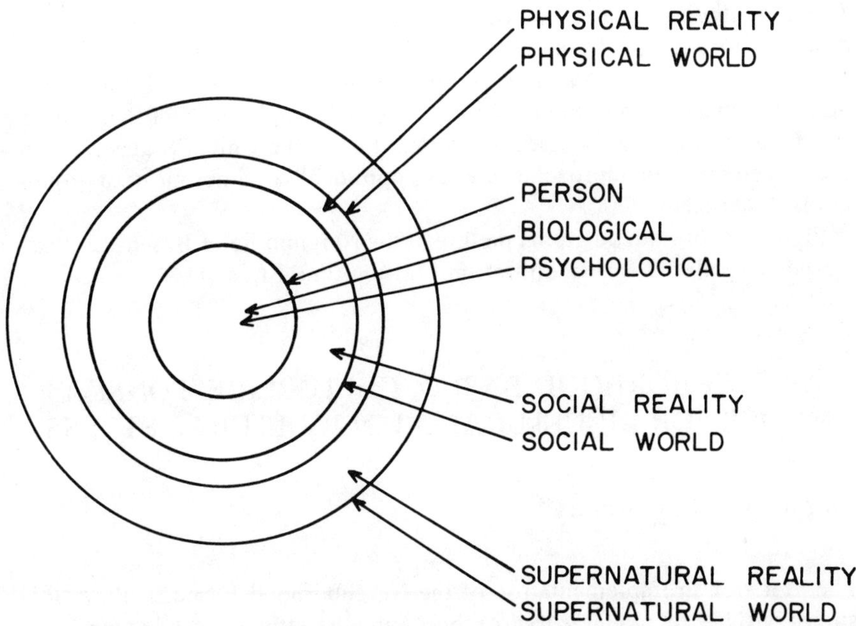

Fig. 7.3. Types of reality that are important to a mestizo health care system.

Vivian Garrison (1979), an anthropologist who has worked closely as a consultant and co-therapist with mental health professionals and paraprofessionals recommended, "interventions might be more acceptable [to the Puerto Rican patient] if they resemble some of the spiritualist diagnostic process in which a series of questions are stated to be affirmed or denied." She also listed other kinds of approaches that might be in keeping with Puerto Rican expectations that would probably contribute to more effective therapy for them: (1) a walk-in service with a short-term treatment pattern; (2) extensive use of paratherapeutic techniques such as home visits and environmental intervention; (3) the use of paraprofessionals; (4) the "helper" therapy principle involving someone in the care and treatment of others who has himself been helped; (5) role-playing and "acting out" rather than "talking out" techniques; (6) and limitation of goals of therapy to more immediate relief of symptoms and problem solving rather than long-term personality reconstruction.

The efforts described above have provided a good beginning in the development of health care models for mestizos in the Americas, but we need models that are more comprehensive—models that show how the mestizo world view can be integrated with some of the procedures, techniques, and concepts of the European world view to arrive at effective programs for treatment and primary prevention. One such model which focuses on adjustment problems related to identity has been proposed by Ramirez (1981). This neighborhood-based, culture-responsive model (NCBR) is primarily designed to address the adjustment problems of adolescents, but it also provides intervention and prevention benefits for parents, siblings, and other members of the client's community. Although the NCBR has been specifically designed for Latino communities in the United States most of the procedures and approaches are also applicable to other mestizo groups in the Americas.

Figure 7.4 provides a global picture of the Neighborhood-Based, Culture-Responsive Model for Biculturation/Multicultural Stress.

A NEIGHBORHOOD-BASED, CULTURE-RESPONSIVE MODEL FOR BICULTURAL/MUTLICULTURAL STRESS

Step One: Ethnography

The first step in implementation of the Neighborhood-Based, Culture Responsive (NBCR) model is to do a thorough ethnography of the community in which it is going to be used. The specific goals of the ethnography follow.

ADJUSTMENT PROBLEMS OF CHILDREN AND ADOLESCENTS
RELATED TO BICULTURATION STRESS

(IDENTITY CONFUSION; CONFLICTS WITH PARENTS, AUTHORITIES, AND PEERS; DRUG AND ALCOHOL ABUSE; TEENAGE PREGNANCIES; SCHOOL DROP-OUT; OBESITY; DIABETES; HEART DISEASE, ETC.)

↓

ASSESSMENT OF PSYCHOLOGICAL AND HEALTH PROBLEMS
AND DEGREE OF MULTICULTURALISM IN LIFE ORIENTATION

1. MULTICULTURALISM / BICULTURALISM EXPERIENCE INVENTORY
2. BICOGNITIVE ORIENTATION IN LIFE SCALE
3. SCHOOL SITUATIONS PICTURE STORIES TEST
4. BEHAVIORAL HEALTH INVENTORY

IDENTIFICATION OF RESOURCES IN FAMILY, COMMUNITY, AND CULTURE

↓

ETHNOGRAPHIC APPROACHES

PUBLIC HEALTH | NATIVE HEALERS | CULTURAL/COMMUNITY SUPPORT GROUPS | FAMILY | SCHOOL | RELIGION

INTERVENTION AND PRIMARY PREVENTION

1. ESTABLISHMENT OF COMMUNITY SUPPORT AND REFERRAL NETWORKS USING RESOURCES IDENTIFIED ABOVE
2. THERAPY
   A. FAMILY / COMMUNITY GROUPS
   B. PEER GROUPS
3. SUPPORTING AGENCIES WHICH ARE ALREADY PROVIDING SUPPORT AND REFERRAL SERVICES
4. FORMER CLIENTS AND THEIR FRIENDS AND FAMILY MEMBERS

↓

GOALS

1. GREATER ADAPTABILITY AND FLEXIBILITY THROUGH BICOGNITIVE FUNCTIONING
2. MULTICULTURAL IDENTITY
3. POSITIVE BEHAVIORAL HEALTH PRACTICES

Fig. 7.4. A neighborhood-based, culture-responsive mental health model for children and adolescents.

Assessment. The degree of the politics of conflict, vis-à-vis the different value systems, belief systems, and life styles in the community must be assessed. Castaneda (1977) has observed that politics of conflict in communities can interfere with the development of bicultural/multicultural orientations to life. In particular, Castaneda argued that it is the acculturating individual's perception of the politics of the conflict that is the important determinant of the extent to which the person is willing to accept values, beliefs, and life styles different from those of his/her group of origin. Bicultural stress is greatest in those communities in which there is considerable separation and conflict between the different ethnic groups. The politics of conflict in a community make it difficult for its residents to develop multicultural orientations to life; this is particularly the case for adolescents who are in constant interaction with peers and adults of different groups.

Resources. Cultural, community, and familial resources which can be used in the intervention and prevention model need to be identified. As was discussed earlier in the chapter, the family, community, and culture play an important role in mestizo approaches to healing. Therefore, it is important to identify and use existing support systems in community, family, and culture.

Support and Referral Networks. Information which can help to establish support and referral networks must be obtained. That is, ethnographic information can lead to identification of needed relationships between the agencies and support sources which already exist in the family, community, and culture. Informal ties can be formalized for greater effectiveness; new ties can be developed by encouraging better communication links between different sources of support and by eliminating barriers and misunderstandings which discourage cooperation. This component of the ethnography is critical because the referral network is seen as the major source of client referrals as well as a source of support services which can help in implementation of the model. Agencies, institutions, organizations, and individuals in the referral and support network will also help to identify and train the people who will be primarily responsible for implementing the model.

Leader Models. The bicultural paraprofessional leader-models must be identified. Actual implementation of the intervention component of the program will be effected by people who are native to the community and who are themselves bicultural/multicultural. These persons have experienced and resolved biculturation stress problems similar to those which the clients and their families are struggling with. These people will lead intervention groups for clients, do client assessment, encourage maintenance of the referral and support networks, and serve as bicultural/multicultural models for clients in the community.

Variables Related to Successful Outcomes. The attitudes, perceptions, coping strategies, or orientations to life which determine successful bicultural/ multicultural adjustments in the community can be revealed through the ethnography. What are the characteristics of bicultural/multicultural individuals in the community? Which behaviors and values are associated with flexibility of behavior? What are the characteristics of the families and peer groups who cope well with politics of conflict and the diversity of the community? The answers to these critically important questions are derived from the ethnography.

TABLE 7.1. Family/Community Network Sessions

Goals	Activities Directed by Group Leader
1. Values clarification for young person and parents	Analysis of SSPST stories; discussion of members' perceived advantages and disadvantages of Latino and mainstream cultures; parents' perceptions of school; adolescent's perception of school
2. Role clarification for adolescent and parents	Same as above; also discussion of each member's description of the ideal son/daughter, parent, teacher, student
3. Improved communications between parents and young person	Description of family structure and transactional patterns from group leader's observations; assignment to community members to serve as *padrinos* (cultural brokers or facilitators) in relationships between adolescent and parents, adolescent and the school and other institutions and between parents and the school and other institutions; group leader's facilitation of communication between parents and adolescent in the sessions
4. Development of bicultural skills in adolescent and parent	Setting of behavioral goals by adolescent for more extensive participation in mainstream and Latino traditional cultures; assignment of community members to serve as *padrinos* (cultural brokers or facilitators)
5. Development of positive behavioral health orientations	Group leader initiates discussion regarding individual and family health. Discussion focuses on belief systems and values regarding health (illness in Hispanic and mainstream cultures and on how family conflicts and biculturation stress can affect health); establishment of health goals

Step Two: Client Assessment

The second step in implementation of the Neighborhood-Based, Culture-Responsive (NBCR) Model is a complete assessment of the clients who are referred for intervention. This involves development of a bicultural/multicultural personality and behavior health profile. To arrive at this profile, there are four instruments administered to the prospective client: the Multiculturalism/Biculturalism Experience Inventory; the Bicognitive Orientation to Life Scale; the School Situations Picture Stories Technique;[1] and the Behavioral Health Inventory.[2] The results of the profile permit the client and leader/model to plan an individualized intervention program and to identify the goals to be accomplished through the program.

Step Three: Implementation and Assessment

The third step involves implementation and assessment of the intervention program; the intervention program is a mixture of procedures and techniques derived from both the mestizo and European world views. The description which follows summarizes the major goals and the procedures used by the leader-model to accomplish these. Intervention is done in both family/community and peer group (same sex and mixed sex group sessions).

Family/Community Network Sessions. The activities of the family/community network sessions are designed to achieve clarification of values and roles in the young person's home and community life. Activities and procedures also help to identify value differences which may be associated with specific intrapersonal and interpersonal conflicts (identified through the School Situations Picture Stories Test—SSPST). Participants in these sessions should include all available family members and four people (two of whom are invited by the parents and two by the young person) who are not part of the immediate family. Parents and client are free to invite anyone in the community, including members of the extended family, native healers, clergy, school personnel, boy or girl friends, etc. Some of the objectives and activities of the family/community network sessions are presented in table 7.1.

Peer Group Sessions. Peer group sessions are conducted with eight participants of the same sex or with four male and four female participants. The peer group sessions, like the family network sessions, are designed to achieve values and role clarification, to develop perspectives for understanding values reflected by institutions, and for developing bicultural interpersonal and institutional skills. The sessions also seek to improve relationships with peers and to establish a sense of community among the subjects.

The Same-Sex Peer Group sessions will include eight intervention group subjects and group leaders (of the same sex as the subjects). Language(s) in which the session will be conducted will depend on the preferences of the members (see table 7.2).

Four male and four female subjects and one male and one female group leader will comprise the Mixed-Sex Peer Group Session. Language(s) in which sessions are conducted will depend on the preferences of the members (see table 7.3).

Assessment of client's progress. To assess the degree of progress being made by the child or adolescent client in the intervention component of the

TABLE 7.2. Same-Sex Peer Group Sessions

Goals	Activities Directed by Group Leader
1. Values clarification	Analysis of SPSST stories; discussion of group leader's and members' personal experiences with conflict; role playing of conflict situations which have meaning to group members
2. Role clarification	Same as above; discussion of ideal son/daughter, Latino, Anglo-American, father, mother, teacher, employer, employee
3. Understanding values reflected by institutions	Same as above with addition of discussion of ideal school, family, and community; group leader initiates discussion of how to identify values reflected by institutions such as the schools; members establish individual goals for understanding institutions in which they have experienced conflict and with the help of the group they devise plans to achieve their goals; assignment of community *padrinos*; reports of degree of success or failure in achieving goals; development of new plans with help of group members
4. Development of bicultural interpersonal and institutional behavior	Group leader describes personal experiences in developing a bicultural orientation to life; members examine own bicultural profiles and establish goals and implement plans to improve their bicultural skills in relating to institutions and individuals; group members serve as *padrinos* for each other and as consultants to each other
5. Development of positive behavioral health orientations	Group leader initiates discussion concerning behavioral health practices which are associated with good health and psychological adjustment; focus is on development of bicultural skills to take advantage of services offered by public health institutions and agencies as well as other health resources available in the community; setting of health goals

model, the SSPST as well as Biculturalism/Multiculturalism Experience and the Behavioral Health inventories are readministered at various times during the course of implementation of the program. Progress is measured by the resolution of value and life style conflicts, degree of development of positive behavioral health practices, and by the degree to which there is participation in the cultures represented in the community (as determined by information obtained from Step 1).

TABLE 7.3. Mixed-Sex Peer Group Sessions

Goals	Activities Directed by Group Leader
1. Development of an understanding of how value conflicts can create interpersonal conflict with members of the opposite sex in the same ethnic group	Analysis of SSPST stories: group leader's analysis and discussion of members' personal experience; role playing of actual conflict situations; discussion of male's perceptions of ideal female and female's perceptions of ideal male
2. Development of an understanding of how value conflict can create interpersonal conflict with members of the opposite sex in other ethnic groups	Same as above; also discussion of perceptions of male and female roles in other cultures
3. Role clarification	Analysis of SSPST stories; members' perceived differences in male and female roles in the several cultures in question; discussion of courting behavior in the different cultures; discussion of androgyny; discussion of differences in the family values of the cultures in question
4. Development of positive behavioral health orientation in interpersonal relationships	Discussion of ways in which relationships with others can affect health and psychological adjustment

Client Follow-Up

The fourth and final step involves encouragement of former clients to assist in implementation of the intervention and prevention programs. That is, clients who have benefited from the model are encouraged to serve as apprentices to group leader-models and to receive training in doing consultation with peer groups and with the referral-support networks.

SUMMARY

The mestizo world view, vis-à-vis illness/health and health care, is characterized by being integrated or holistic in contrast to dualistic. In the context of the mestizo world view, health/illness are related to the quality of the person's relationship to the social and physical environments as well as to the quality of his/her relationship with the supernatural. Native healers and shamans are believed to have access to the supernatural and their activities are directed at restoring holism; identification with the supernatural; protection from the supernatural; and reintegration of the client or patient with the family, culture, and community.

Recent advances and knowledge in psychosomatic medicine and behavioral health are based on mestizo models of health/illness and health care. Models for delivery of mental health services to mestizos in the Americas need to be congruent with the holistic/integrative view of health and illness. In the context of this holistic view, the use of a combination of European and mestizo approaches and techniques can lead to effective treatment practices and to encouragement of development of pluralistic identities in people who live in multicultural environments.

NOTES

1. The School Situations Picture Stories Test (SSPST). The subjects are tested individually with a series of eight line drawings of a person or persons in settings related to education. Subjects are presented with these cards, one at a time, in the following order: (1) student and teacher; (2) student and mother; (3) student and father; (4) two students of the same ethnic group; (5) two students—one Mexican American and one non-Mexican American; (6) student, parents, and principal; (7) student studying alone; and (8) student standing outside a school. The student is asked to tell a story about each picture and to make it as dramatic as she/he possibly can. A total conflict score is obtained by adding the number of interpersonal conflicts (related to value differences between people or between people and institutions) in the stories given by the subject.

2. The Bicultural Behavioral Health Inventory (BHL). The items of this paper and pencil test assess the client's typical diet, exercise regimen, sleeping habits, and use of coping techniques to stay in good health. The inventory also assesses the client's use of alcohol, cigarettes, drugs, and inhalants and also determines the client's knowledge of practices and issues related to prevention of illness and psychological maladjustment.

REFERENCES

Castaneda, A. Traditionalism, modernism, and ethnicity. In J. L. Martinez (Ed.), *Chicano psychology*. New York: Academic Press, 1974.

Chavira, J. A., & Trotter, R. T. The gift of healing. Edinburg, Tex.: Pan American University (unpublished monograph).

Coles, R. *The old ones of New Mexico*. Garden City, N.Y.: Anchor Books, 1975.

Fabrega, H., & Manning, P. K. An integrated theory of disease in the Chiapas Highlands. *Psychosomatic Medicine*, 1973, *35*, 223–239.

Field, M. G. The concept of the "health system" at the macro-sociological level. *Social Science and Medicine*, 1973, *7*, 763–785.

Frank, J. D. *Persuasion and healing*. Baltimore: Johns Hopkins Press, 1961.

Fried, J. Acculturation and mental health among Indian migrants in Peru. In M. K. Opler (Ed.), *Culture and mental health*. New York: The Macmillan Co., 1959.

Garrison, V. E. *Inner-city support systems project*. (Project No. MH28467). Bethesda, Md.: National Institute of Mental Health, 1979.

Hallowell, A. I. The use of projective techniques in the study of the sociopsychological aspects of acculturation. *Journal of Projective Techniques*, 1951, *15*, 27–44.

Harner, M. J. *Hallucinogens and shamanism*. New York: Oxford University Press, 1973.

Harwood, A. Puerto Rican spiritism: Description and analysis of an alternative psychotherapeutic approach. *Culture, Medicine and Psychiatry*, 1977, *1*, 135–154.

Innovations, Winter 1976, *3* (1), 12–18.

Kaplan, B., & Johnson, D. The social meaning of Navajo psychotherapy. In A. Kiev (Ed.), *Magic, faith, and healing*. New York: Free Press, 1967.

Kiev, A. *Curanderismo*. New York: Free Press, 1968.

Kleinman, A. *Patients and healers in the context of culture*. Berkeley, Calif.: University of California Press, 1980.

Kreisman, J. J. The curanderos's apprentice: A therapeutic integration of folk and medical healing. *American Journal of Psychiatry*, 1975, *132*, 81–83.

Lamphere, L. Symbolic elements in Navajo ritual. *Southwestern Journal of Anthropology*, 1969, *2* (5), 279–305.

Leon-Portilla, M. *Time and reality in the thought of the Maya*. Boston: Beacon Press, 1973.

Madsen, W. The alcoholic agringado. *American Anthropologist*, 1964, *66*, 355–361.

Matarazzo, J. D. Behavioral health's challenge to academic, scientific, and professional psychology. *American Psychologist*, 1982, *37*, 1–14.

Ramirez, M. Neighborhood-based mental health services for Mexican Americans. Unpublished manuscript, 1981.

Reiser, M. F. Changing theoretical concepts in psychosomatic medicine. In S. Arieti (Ed.), *American handbook of psychiatry*. Vol. 4. (2nd ed.) New York: Basic Books, 1975.

Rubel, A. *Across the tracks: Mexican Americans in a Texas city*. Austin: University of Texas Press, 1966.

Spindler, G. D. Personality and peyotism in Menomini Indian acculturation. *Psychiatry*, 1952, *15*, 151–159.

Torrey, E. F. *The mind game: Witchdoctors and psychiatrists*. New York: Bantam Books, 1973.

Wyman, L. C., & Kluckhohn, C. Navajo classifications of their song ceremonials. *Memoirs of the American Anthropological Association*, No. 50, 1938.

CHAPTER 8

Coping with Change and Improving Intergroup and International Relations in the Americas: Applications of Mestizo Psychology

> The fact that this continent is divided among Anglo-Saxons and Latins should be looked upon then as a blessing; because we all long for a higher, richer spiritual world, and it is only through the work of singularly gifted groups of people that a true all-comprehending type of civilization may come to life.
>
> —Jose Vasconcellos (1925)

> A new type of person whose orientation and view of the world profoundly transcends his indigenous culture is developing from the complex of social, political, economic, and educational interactions of our time. Whatever the terminology, the definitions and metaphors allude to a person whose essential identity is inclusive of life patterns different from his own and who has psychologically and socially come to grips with a multiplicity of realities. We can call this new type of person multicultural because he embodies a core process of self verification that is grounded in both the universality of the human condition and in the diversity of man's actual forms.
>
> —Peter Adler (1974)

At this time in history, the peoples and nations in the American hemisphere find themselves at a critical juncture in their destinies. Problems and conflicts arising from political and economic differences threaten to destroy the stability of nations and to undermine positive relations between nations and peoples in the hemisphere. Democracy or communism, capitalism or socialism, totalitarianism or individual rights are all critical questions which are dividing the people and countries of the Americas.

Still another major disruptive force for the individuals, groups, and nations of the Americas is change; many people in the hemisphere are currently experiencing radical changes in life styles, values, and belief systems. People are changing nationalities, roles, and identities; they are leaving their "roots" and finding it difficult to cope with the psychological consequences of change as well as with the new sociocultural systems and life styles which they are adopting.

In chapter 6 it was argued that, in order to solve the crisis of diversity in the Americas, we need multicultural leaders; this chapter goes a step further: it identifies the conceptual frameworks, intervention models, and skills which those leaders will need to help ensure successful adjustment to rapid change and to help create harmony in interethnic and international relations.

CHANGE AND ADJUSTMENT IN THE AMERICAS

Many people in the Americas live in conditions of severe poverty and have little or no economic or political power; they experience hunger, live in substandard housing, and their educational opportunities are either limited or nonexistent. Many of these people are also having to cope with extensive cultural and individual changes in their lives. The following are examples of some of the major changes which are being experienced by many people in the Americas.

Changes in Life Style as a Result of Intranational and International Migration

In many of the countries of Latin America and the Caribbean, large numbers of people are migrating from rural communities to urban centers either within the same country or to other countries in the hemisphere. On the other hand, in the United States, most of the recent migration has been from urban centers on the east coast and the midwest to cities in the west, southeast, and southwest. Migration usually involves the abandonment of "roots" established over many years and even over generations. In most cases, migration involves separation from family, close friends, and community, often resulting in extensive changes in the person's self-image. In almost all cases, including those in which migration occurs within the same country, the move requires changes in values and life styles (Pacheco, Wapner, and Lucca, 1980). The research of Alberto Seguin (1956) and Jacob Fried (1959) has documented the negative effects which drastic changes in values and life styles can have on physical and mental health. Maris (1975) likened the experience of adaptation to a new environment to the emotional experience of bereavement:

> When a student joins a university community, or a villager comes to a modern African city, their self-confidence is threatened by the unfamiliarity of the relationships in which they become involved. They may suffer no more than a brief embarrassment while they still respond awkwardly or get things wrong. But their sense of their own identity may be more profoundly disturbed, if they feel that adaptation requires them to betray their earlier attachments. The university, perhaps, seems to impose an upper middle-class or white suburban

culture which denies their nature; the city seems to denegrate the newco. background. In such situations, a conflict arises between the yearning to retu. to the reassuring predictability of the past, and a contradictory impulse to become the creature of circumstance, abandoning the past as if it belonged to another, now repudiated, being. Both impulses are self-destructive in themselves, but their interplay generates the process of reformulation by which the thread of continuity is retrieved. This reformulation of the essential meaning of one's experience of life is a unique reassertion of identity, which takes time to work out. In this it resembles grief: for though the circumstances are not tragic, and the gains may outweigh the losses, the threat of disintegration is similar [pp. 88–89].

Change in Ethnic Identity

In many countries in Latin America, in the Caribbean, and in many regions of the United States and Canada, a move from one country to another or from one region to another usually involves a change in ethnic identity. Whether the change be from Indian to mestizo, Indian to Ladino, easterner to southerner, or monocultural to bicultural/multicultural, it demands a reorganization of ethnic identity which may be psychologically stressful. Research has shown that, if the changes are too rapid or too extreme or if the politics of conflict are too intense, then it is difficult to integrate values and life styles of different groups and cultures into the self-image—the result is stress and confusion.

Thus, change, whether it be in life style and values or in identity, is a major cause of maladjustment in the Americas. There are potential negative consequences not only for the individuals who are undergoing the change, but also for the agencies and institutions who are most likely to be involved with these individuals. To cope effectively with these problems, multicultural leaders will need a community psychology model which has both intervention and primary prevention components.

COMMUNITY PSYCHOLOGY, INTERVENTION, AND PRIMARY PREVENTION IN PROBLEMS OF ADJUSTMENT RELATED TO CULTURE CHANGE

In chapter 4, it was observed that some of the philosophy and approaches of community psychology are compatible with the mestizo world view. Specifically, the community psychology movement in American psychology has encouraged acknowledgment of individual and cultural differences and has demanded sensitivity on the part of psychologists and psychiatrists to the world view of the clients they serve. In the following quote, Rappaport

(1977) provides a very clear statement with respect to the mission and principle tenets of community psychology:

> Community psychology is at its best when it is responding to grass-roots groups who require not treatment, cure, or re-education, but support with political, social and psychological resources. The perspective of community psychology must be one of support for cultural relativity, diversity, and equitable distribution of resources. Community psychology must be based first on a social and ethical value system which recognizes the right to be different, on an ecological perspective which views all people and all cultures as worthwhile in their own right; and third, on a belief in equal access to material and psychological resources [p. 53].

Iscoe (1974) views community psychology as helping to encourage the development of greater access to knowledge, power and resources in communities:

> the concept of competent community implies that in order for a community to be effective in providing an atmosphere of positive mental health for its citizens it must have access to power and must have knowledge of a series of different approaches which can be used for achieving the goals of better quality of life for its residents [p. 607].

Thus, it is no accident that the community psychology movement has become so popular in Latin America and the Caribbean. An examination of the titles of presentations and symposia of the last three congresses of the Society for Interamerican Psychology gives evidence of the phenomenal growth which community psychology is enjoying in these areas.

Community psychology approaches will undoubtedly continue to play an important role in community development efforts in the Americas. Therefore, there is need for a model which can focus on the dynamics of change in the hemisphere. Such a mestizo model of community psychology should address two major goals: (1) make it possible to help individuals in coping with changes occurring in their lives and communities; and (2) help to make institutions, agencies, and governments more responsive to the people who are experiencing change. The model must not only give the people who are undergoing change a framework for understanding what they are experiencing, but it must also help them to achieve the coping techniques they need to obtain resources necessary to adjust to their new life styles and identities. Such a model must also encourage institutions and agencies who control resources to become aware of the needs of those who are experiencing the greatest degree of change.

A VALUES/BELIEF SYSTEMS-COGNITIVE STYLES MODEL

The values/belief systems-cognitive styles model is based on the assumption that belief systems, values, and cognitive styles are all important in understanding and coping with adjustment problems which result from radical and extensive changes. Problems experienced by people who are affected by cultural and identity changes are assumed to result from mismatches between the migrating individual's belief systems/values and preferred cognitive styles and those characteristic of the new jobs, roles, communities, and countries in the new environments.

People reared in traditional cultures, families, and communities have a world view based on traditional belief systems and values, and they are more likely to utilize coping techniques (communication; human relational; incentive-motivational; and thinking, learning, and problem-solving styles) which are predominantly field sensitive. Individuals migrating from traditional cultures, therefore, experience mismatch when they move to countries, cultures, or communities which are more modernistically oriented. For example, people who migrate from Mexico, Puerto Rico, Cuba, and Haiti to urban centers in the United States may find that their traditional world views and field-sensitive orientations to coping with life are incompatible with the modernistic world views and field-independent cognitive styles of the people and institutions in the new environments. The same holds for Indians who migrate from rural communities to urban centers in the United States, Canada, and Latin America. On the other hand, people moving from modern cultures, communities, and families have a world view reflective of modern belief systems and values, and they use coping techniques which are predominantly field independent. These predominantly modernistic/field-independent people experience mismatch when they move to countries, cultures, and communities which are predominantly traditional. Thus, for many persons migrating from urban centers in the midwest and the east coast of the United States to communities in the southeast, southwest, and west, the conflict is between the modernistic field-independent orientation of the "migrants" and the predominant traditionalistic values/belief systems and field-sensitive orientation of the native peoples and institutions.

To effect a better match between the person who is migrating and the people and institutions in the host communities, there is need to encourage development of flexibility in both the "migrant" and the peoples and institutions of the host communities.

More specifically, then, the goals of the values/belief systems-cognitive styles model are as follows: (1) to assist the "victims" or potential "victims" of change to understand the changes which are occurring in their lives and

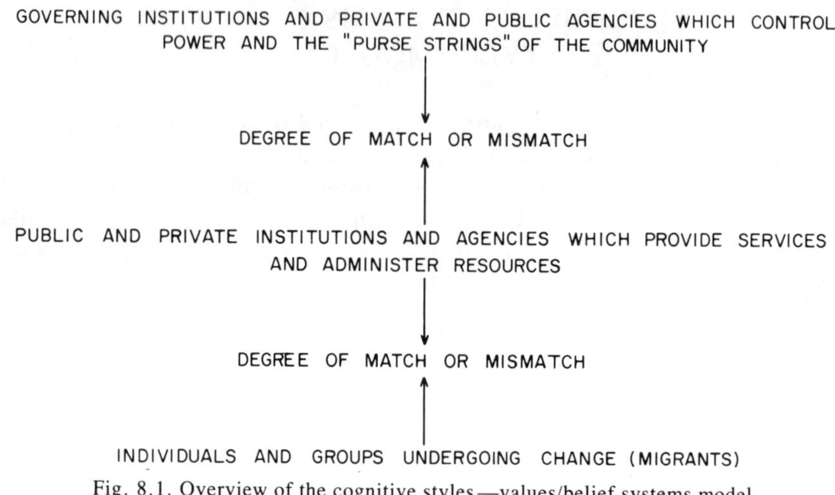

Fig. 8.1. Overview of the cognitive styles—values/belief systems model.

identities; (2) to give these "victims" or potential "victims" a framework for understanding how the new community and its institutions function and how they can use certain coping strategies and belief systems/values to match these communities and institutions in order to achieve success in the new setting and gain access to resources and services; (3) to provide communities and institutions with a framework which can make it possible for them to understand the diversity of their clientele and to be responsive to this diversity by providing services which are consonant with the belief systems and cognitive styles of the people they serve; (4) to provide institutions and agencies with a framework for understanding the forces which are creating changes in the lives of their clients and in the communities where their clients live; and (5) to provide community psychologists and psychiatrists with a framework for assessing the predominant styles of institutions, communities, and potential clients; and to provide psychologists and psychiatrists with guidelines for developing interventions with clients, institutions, and communities. The belief systems/cognitive styles model of community psychology is summarized in Figure 8.1. The model has assessment, intervention, and primary prevention components which are focused around individuals or groups on the one hand and around communities and their institutions on the other.

Individuals and Groups

Individuals and/or groups undergoing rapid culture change in a community are assessed with the following objectives in mind:

1. To identify the values/belief systems they are most identified with. Assessment is accomplished by administering the Traditionalism/Modernism Inventory (TMI) (Ramirez & Doell, 1982a). The following are sample items from TMI:

   Traditionalism Items:

   (a) I prefer to live in a rural community where everyone knows each other.
   (b) Traditional observances such as church services and graduation ceremonies add meaning to life.
   (c) We should not let concerns about time interfere with our interpersonal relationships.

   Modernism Items:
   (a) I prefer to live in a city that offers many cultural advantages.
   (b) Most traditional ceremonies are outmoded and wasteful of time and money.
   (c) If you are not careful, people can waste your time and you will never get anything done.

   The TMI yields a total traditionalism score, a total modernism score, and a flexibility score (degree of identification with both traditional and modern values/beliefs).
2. To assess their preferred cognitive styles. This is accomplished by administering the Bicognitive Orientation to Life Scale. See chapter 6 for a detailed description of this instrument.

In addition to administration of the two instruments, ethnographies and on-site behavior observations should also be done. In fact, in those cases where "migrants" are illiterate, behavior observations and ethnographies are used exclusively.

Once the assessment phase has been completed intervention proceeds as follows:

Step 1. Introductory presentation of model using slides of drawings/cartoons and vignettes describing the major assumptions of the model regarding match and mismatch. One of the vignettes used is a story told by Bettelheim (reported in Rappaport, 1977) about the time when he was a prisoner in a concentration camp in World War II. Bettelheim was in need of treatment for an infection in his hand, but he had observed how guards either dismissed or accepted prisoners' requests for medical treatment at whim. Particularly unsuccessful were attempts to win the guards' sympathy by pleading the discomforts experienced over illness (a traditional, field-sensitive approach). Bettelheim concluded that his type of approach was inconsistent with the values and thinking styles of the guards. To match their field-independent, modernistic style, he told the guards that the infection was preventing him from working efficiently and that the guards should decide what action was called for. Bettelheim was immediately referred to the hospital for treatment. Similar vignettes are presented which describe coping with different agencies, institutions, and supervisors.

Step 2. Introduction to the assessment and to assessment procedures and instruments of the model. There is extensive use made of exercises and role playing to acquaint participants with procedures and techniques for self-assessment, assessment of others, and for the assessment of institutions and agencies.

Step 3. Introduction to the behaviors and coping styles characteristic of the cognitive style which is unfamiliar to the participants. Participants are introduced (by way of drawings and cartoons presented on slides) to findings obtained from assessment of top- and mid-level institutions, agencies, organizations, and corporations (which are either the source of the culture change and/or which control services and resources which are necessary for effecting a good adjustment to change). Role playing, modeling, and simulation exercises are used to familiarize participants with new behaviors and coping styles to be used in an effective match program.

Primary prevention is another important goal of the model. The overall objectives of the primary prevention component are to identify "populations at risk" in communities and to determine how their adjustment is likely to be affected by cultural changes (given problems being experienced by present "victims"). For example, children of adults, and the younger siblings of adolescents presently experiencing adjustment problems related to culture change are likely to be populations at risk. Another objective is to introduce these at-risk populations to the model and to provide initial training in the use of both field-sensitive and field-independent (bicognitive) coping styles and traditional and modern belief systems. Ramirez and his colleagues have been doing this for several years through an educational model entitled Culturally Democratic Learning Environments, a learning program for children in grades kindergarten through third. The model has been implemented in California communities where adults and adolescents were experiencing problems of adjustment related to culture change. More recently, Ramirez and his colleagues have developed another educational model (Cox, Macaulay, & Ramirez, 1982) which is also aimed at primary prevention with elementary school children. The model, entitled *New Frontiers*, is being implemented in preschool and kindergarten classes in several communities in the southwestern United States.

Communities, Agencies, Institutions, and Corporations

Those organizations (and individuals in them who hold the power) to whom the "migrant" is attempting to adjust or which control resources and services needed by the "migrant" need to be assessed. As was the case with individuals and groups, assessment focuses on values/belief systems and cognitive style orientations. Assessment is done in two ways: (1) through analysis of documents (reports, policy statements, minutes of meetings, performance standards, etc.), on-site observation, and administration of the Traditionalism-Modernism and Bicognitive Orientation to Life Scales.

The intervention program is planned and implemented once the analysis of data collected in the assessment phase is complete. Prior to attempts at intervention, certain critical questions are addressed: Which people, groups of people, departments, and so forth should be the direct targets of the intervention program? (For example, in some agencies or corporations it would be better to intervene directly with the supervisors of the migrants while in others it would be better to work with administrators and policy-makers.) What is the best way to approach the targets of intervention? (Will they require a field-independent or field-sensitive approach to the teaching of bicognitive skills?)

Step 1. Introduction to the model. The level of sophistication of the presentation will vary from group to group. The initial focus is on how mismatch can occur in the day-to-day activities of the agency or institution and how these can result in frustration for both "migrants" and staff members.

Step 2. Introduction to the assessment component and procedures of the model. Exercises and role playing activities serve to acquaint the participants with self-assessment, assessment of others, and assessment of the institution, agency, corporation, or organization that the participants work for. Using a match/mismatch focus, a presentation is made of assessment results with "migrants," mid- and top-level agencies, corporations, and institutions in the community. A determination is made of how participants can become more effective with "migrants" and in their interactions with other organizations in the community.

Step 3. Learning behaviors and approaches for matching the styles of "migrants" and of other agencies in the community. Most of the focus in this phase of implementation is on role playing and simulation activities as well as on modeling.

Step 4. The final step focuses on primary prevention. Forces related to change in the community are identified and an outline of a primary prevention plan is developed for implementation with populations at risk.

Problems of adjustment related to rapid and radical change will continue to plague peoples and communities in the Americas. The model presented above is but one approach which can be derived from the mestizo psychology perspective. Other models and approaches must be developed and implemented to ensure that the challenges created by change will lead to positive results in the lives of both individuals and communities.

As was noted in the introduction to this chapter, a second major set of problems facing the Americas concerns conflicts and misunderstandings over political and economic issues. Here again mestizo psychology can make important contributions.

INTRANATIONAL AND INTERNATIONAL CONFLICT IN THE AMERICAS: POLITICS AND ECONOMICS

Conflict and misunderstanding over political and economic issues are threatening the well-being of peoples of several nations of the Americas and are also proving disruptive to harmonious relations between the nations of the hemisphere.

Political Issues

Struggles between supporters of democracy on the one hand and communism on the other are causing conflict and dissension both within many of the countries in Central America, South America, and the Caribbean Basin as well as between the governments of some of these countries. Both Chile and Nicaragua have experienced armed struggles between supporters of the left and the right; El Salvador is presently in the throes of such a conflict. Despite the fact that conflicts over political ideology are of long-standing in the Americas, the principal issues still remain clouded and confused by stereotypes, superficial impressions, and old clichés. The peoples of the Americas, leaders as well as average citizens, need conceptual frameworks which can help them to understand the cultural and individual differences reflected in the misunderstandings and conflicts related to issues of political and economic ideology. Specifically, they need conceptual frameworks which can help them to focus on the critical components of these issues.

Economic Issues

The wide gap which exists between the life styles of the well-to-do and the poor in many of the countries of the Americas is a constant source of resentment, suspicion, and misunderstanding. The people of most of the countries in the Americas are becoming increasingly more divided along class lines. In many of the countries of Central and South America and in the Caribbean, most of the wealth, natural resources, land, and political power are in the hands of a few. In the United States, widespread unemployment and reductions in social programs are accentuating feelings of separatism among members of different classes, races, and ethnic groups. In addition, international economic problems are becoming a major source of difficulties in international relations in the Americas. The recent economic crisis in Mexico, highlighted by two back-to-back devaluations of the peso and nationalization of the privately owned banks is but one case in point. Argentina, Chile, Bolivia, Venezuela, and Peru are also experiencing difficulty in meeting their commitments to foreign lenders. As international financial institutions such as the International Monetary Fund demand stringent measures in the economic policies of Latin American countries in need of more loans, the citizens and members of the governments of these countries become resentful over what they interpret as intervention in internal affairs and interruption in the attainment of national goals which they see as crucial to the continued development of their countries. Again, these conflicts and misunderstandings demand the implementation of conceptual frameworks which encourage sensitivity to cultural and individual differences. They also demand multicultural approaches and perspectives.

A TRAINING PROGRAM IN INTERETHNIC AND INTERNATIONAL RELATIONS

A training program which focuses on intergroup and international relations in the Americas is being developed (Ramirez & Doell, in progress) at the University of Texas at Austin. The program is based on the Flexibility Synthesis and Unity Model, described in chapter 4. That is, it is based on the assumption that, in order to be effective in interethnic and international settings (or even in settings where a person is negotiating with people of different socioeconomic, regional, racial, or religious backgrounds), a negotiator should exhibit the following characteristics: an openness to diversity—a willingness to learn from a variety of people and sociocultural environments; a desire to learn new ways of communicating, of relating to others, of thinking, of learning, of problem solving, and of teaching; and a willingness to integrate what he/she has learned from different people and sociocultural environments in order to arrive at multicultural sensitivities, copying styles, and perspectives. Thus, the principal objective of the program is to encourage the development of perceptual styles, behaviors, and skills which were observed in research with multicultural leaders (Ramirez et al., 1980).

The program is being designed for leaders who are involved in international or intergroup negotiations concerning conflicts related to political and economic issues. Some of the components of the program could also be useful for training people who work in business, in the media or members of the general citizenry who are interested in making informed decisions on political and economic issues. The basic components of the program and the instruments and procedures used in it can be applied to any country, culture, group, or in any international setting. In other words, the concepts and conceptual frameworks which make up the program are transcultural. The program can also be applied to any conflict or controversy by altering the content of some of the instruments and the scripts of the simulation and role playing exercises.

The components of the program were derived from the research of anthropologists, psychologists, and sociologists in the Americas. The following is a brief description of the concepts and conceptual frameworks which are part of the training program.

Cognitive Complexity in Perceptions of Individuals, Groups, and Nations

Negative stereotypes and other inaccurate perceptions of individuals, groups, and nations in the Americas interfere with cooperative efforts to resolve conflicts over political and economic issues. Research has shown that negative stereotypes are products of cognitive modes which are simple and concrete (Secord & Backman, 1964). Perceptions reflected in negative stereotypes are based on oversimplifications of the true characteristics of individuals or groups, and they ignore individual, group, and national differences (Bruner & Perlmutter, 1957; Hartley, 1946; Secord & Backman, 1964).

On the other hand, perceptions of individuals and groups which are more accurate tend to be reflective of complex perceptual modes; that is, they tend to be diverse and multidimensional and are often characterized by the integration of discrepant information. Harvey, Hunt, and Schroder (1961) characterized thinking styles in people in terms of concreteness/abstractness. The following are characteristic of the concrete style: (1) making exteme distinctions such as good/bad, right/wrong, and so forth; (2) intolerance for ambiguous situations; and (3) a low capacity to act "as if"—to take the role of the other person, to put the self in another's "shoes." In the realm of person perception, Bieri (1955) conceptualized abstract modes of thinking as cognitive complexity, that is, the use of several independent domains in describing others. Ramirez (1967) employed the concept of cognitive complexity to explain how students who were well liked or very disliked were perceived by classmates who had known them for a number of years. Fourth, fifth, and sixth grade children were asked to free associate (for a 10-second period) to names of their classmates who had been previously ranked very high or very low sociometrically. The findings showed that children with the highest sociometic rankings had received the greatest number of associations and that overall perceptions of them were more complex (the associations they received could be categorized into more domains, i.e., physical appearance, clothing, social characteristics, intellectual characteristics, etc.) than were those associations given to the names of children with the lowest sociometric rankings in the class. Similarly, more recent research (Ramirez, 1981) on stereotypes of nations and groups showed that, when stereotypes are negative, the associations which reflect them are lower in number, and they are more unidimensional; on the other hand, positive or mixed perceptions are reflected through more numerous associations which are multidimensional in content.

Traditional-Modern Belief Systems and Values

Many of the political and economic controversies in the Americas can be conceptualized in terms of the modernism-traditionalism conceptual framework introduced by Nisbet (1970). As Castaneda (1977) observed, "Modern and traditional define a different perception of reality and may be thought of as the genesis of diametrically opposed sets of values and goals." Castaneda noted that the life styles of traditional societies are focused around the following beliefs: (1) the universe was created by a supernatural force or forces; (2) the individual should be primarily identified with his/her family, tribe, religion, ethnic or racial group; and (3) institutions should be hierarchical in structure with the authority determined in terms of age, birth right, or position in the family or group. Modern societies, Castaneda indicated, are based on a different set of beliefs: (1) the universe was created by natural forces which can be rationally explained by science; (2) individual identity (individualism) is more important than loyalty to family, community, group, or religion; and (3) institutions should be based on principles of democracy and egalitarianism.

The traditional-modern conceptual framework is useful for understanding differences between Latin American and North American societies. Mexican philosophers and social scientists (Diaz-Guerrero, 1955; Paz, 1952) described most of Latin American society as traditional, whereas North American society has been described as largely modern in its orientation (Berger et al., 1973; Inkeles & Smith, 1974, 1973; Nisbet, 1970). This framework can also be applied to individual differences. The life styles and values of many people in the Americas reflect combinations of modern and traditional orientations to life because their socialization and life experiences have exposed them to both belief systems. For example, a person might be traditional in the familial or religious domains, but be quite modern in the worlds of work or entertainment.

Culture, Context, and Communication

Many misunderstandings between individuals, groups, and nations in the Americas are the result of an inability to communicate effectively. Research by the anthropologist Edward T. Hall (1977) provides a conceptual framework which can help individuals, groups, and nations to understand cultural and individual differences in communication styles. Hall hypothesized that one of the functions of culture is to provide a highly selective screen between man and the outside world. The purpose of the screen is to protect the individual's nervous system from information overload. The screen determines which cues from the outside world the individual pays attention to and which he/she ignores. High context groups or sociocultural systems require a high degree of personal interaction and involvement in the communication. Context is built up and developed through shared experiences, information, or ideas. The high context person focuses on people when he/she is involved in communication. Low context cultures, on the other hand, rely heavily on sophisticated information systems; their communication tends to be more technical, less dependent on personal ties, and more dependent on proper procedures for working the system. The low context person, therefore, is more focused on procedures than on the people with whom he is interacting.

Hall has concluded that Hispanic as well as Indian cultures tend to be high context while mainstream United States culture tends to be closer to the lower context end of the continuum. As is the case with traditionalism-modernism, however, many peoples in the Americas have been socialized in both high and low context sociocultural systems, so they operate in the high context style in certain life domains and in the low context style in others.

Cognitive Style, Flexibility, and Adaptability

Conflicts and misunderstandings in the Americas can be conceptualized in terms of differences evident in the personality styles of different individuals, groups, and nations. Socialization in high context, traditional cultures, groups, or families encourages development of a personality style which is quite different from that which develops in low context, modernistic settings. Another major key to conceptualizing conflict in the Americas is degree of flexibility and adaptability of individuals to different situations, individuals, groups, and sociocultural systems. Psychologists have long been interested in how individuals develop flexibility and adaptability. For example, it has been observed that some people can get along well with individuals of many different backgrounds and cultures and can feel at ease in different countries, communities, neighborhoods, and homes; however, others tend to be uncomfortable unless they are with people they know and in familiar surroundings (Ramirez et al., 1980). Crucial to the study of flexibility and adaptability to different environments and life styles is the knowledge that each individual has a unique personality style which is reflected in his/her preferred cognitive style. Personality/cognitive styles are reflected in the way people communicate and relate to others, the rewards which motivate them to work effectively, and the ways they learn new materials, solve problems, teach things to others, and negotiate with others. Three major cognitive styles have been identified through psychological research (Ramirez and Castaneda, 1974):

Field independent. Individuals who are predominantly field independent are characterized by task orientation in interpersonal relationships, a tendency to use an impersonal, formal style in communicating with others, a preference for non-social rewards, and a tendency to focus on details of ideas, problems, and documents.

Field sensitive. Predominantly field sensitive individuals are characterized by a strong social orientation in interpersonal relationships with a tendency to personalize communications, a preference for social rewards, and a tendency to focus on the global aspects of ideas, problems, and documents.

Bicognitive. Bicognitive individuals are characterized by the ability to use the field independent and field sensitive cognitive styles interchangeably, and by a tendency to combine elements of these two styles to arrive at new approaches to coping with life's problems and to problem solving. (Although most adults are bicognitive to some degree, they often exhibit a preference for either field sensitivity or for field independence.)

The Training Program

Participants in the training program are exposed to a wide variety of activities including short lectures, slide presentations, role playing, simulation situations, and experiences in using different assessment instruments (role playing and simulation are omitted if they are incompatible with the world view of participants). Participants become conscious of stereotypes which could interfere with interpersonal relationships and negotiations. They become familiar with how multicultural leadership styles, high and low context, modernism and traditionalism, and cognitive styles can be used to ensure effective functioning in intergroup and international settings. In addition, participants learn how to assess the context of cross-cultural situations, how to evaluate their own belief systems and those of others, and how to assess their preferred cognitive styles in various situations. Furthermore, they learn how to match their behaviors to the cognitive styles of those with whom they interact within cross-cultural settings. They learn how to encourage others to become more flexible in order to more effectively negotiate with them.

Assessment of participants is a critical component of the training program; it serves to pinpoint the particular skills and sensitivities which the participants need to develop, thus, making it possible for trainers to individualize training to ensure maximum benefit for each of the participants. A variety of assessment instruments are used as part of the training activities and procedures.

Free Association Technique. The participants are asked to free associate to certain stimulus words or names associated with the particular issue or issues being negotiated and to the names of particular groups or nations involved in negotiations.

Time and Context Instrument. This instrument, developed by Doell (1982), assesses the degree of experience with and knowledge of different modes of communication in high and low context sociocultural systems. In addition, the instrument indicates whether the person tends to operate according to polychronic or monochronic time (Hall, 1977).

Traditionalism-Modernism Instrument. This scale, developed by Ramirez and Doell (1982), assesses the degree of identification with traditional and modern values and belief systems. The instrument yields scores for modernism and traditionalism as well as for flexibility (the degree of identification with both sets of values and belief systems).

Bicognitive Orientation to Life Scale. This questionnaire assesses the preference for field independent or field sensitive cognitive styles as well as degree of bicognition (tendency to use both field independent and field sensitive styles).

Multicultural Leadership Scale. This instrument consists of vignettes requiring decisions by leaders working with groups in which the membership is diverse and in which there is conflict among the members. The subject is given a choice among three different approaches which could be used by the leader for each situation posed. One of the three choices is an approach used most often by multicultural leaders as identified through small group research (Ramirez, Garza & Cox, 1980).

Training Procedures and Activities

The components of the training program include negative stereotypes and cognitive complexity, cultural differences and similarities, match and mismatch of cognitive styles, and cognitive flexibility in negotiations, and multicultural leadership skills.

Negative stereotypes and cognitive complexity involves the use of the results of the free association procedure (Ramirez, 1967) to determine the nature of the stereotype(s)—if any—and the degree of cognitive complexity involved in perception. This component of the training program provides self-awareness to the participant. Role playing exercises are also used to encourage the development of greater cognitive complexity in perception of individuals, groups, and nations, and to attempt to modify both extreme positive or negative stereotypes.

The procedures and activities directed toward cultural differences and similarities include the administration of the Traditionalism-Modernism Inventory and the Sensitivity to Cultural Context and Communications Scale. Every participant scores his/her own set of items and, following this procedure, the scores are interpreted. Slides of drawings/cartoons are presented to show how traditional and/or modern belief systems and high and low context can explain differences in values and behavior among individuals, groups, and cultures. Role playing and simulation activities using the two conceptual frameworks in interpersonal relationships and on negotiation of issues relevant to the trainees are carried out.

To examine the role of match or mismatch of cognitive styles and cognitive flexibility in negotiations, the Bicognitive Orientation to Life Scale (BOLS) is administered, scored, and discussed with the participants. Discussion of how the BOLS is scored and interpreted makes it possible for participants to understand their individual bicognitive profiles. A slide show presentation on culture and individual differences in cognitive styles is accompanied by a lecture on this same subject. The participants perform exercises in flexibility and adaptability to learn how to match others. Simulation procedures train participants to facilitate negotiations and to mediate in situations where there is mismatch between individuals or groups.

The Multicultural Leadership Scale is administered to assess the degree of multicultural leadership skills evident in each participant. Behavior and strategies of multicultural leaders are the subject of a lecture and slide presentation. Role playing and simulation activities are focused on assisting participants to develop multicultural leadership skills.

Most of the components of this training program have been tested in a limited way with considerable success. Nevertheless, the training program presented here can only be considered an initial effort at dealing with a set of serious and complex problems. There is no question, however, that mestizo perspectives in psychiatry, psychology, and the social sciences in general can make a significant contribution to understanding the issues leading to separatism among people and nations of the hemisphere.

SUMMARY

The people and nations of the Americas are undergoing rapid and extensive changes in life style and identity. A community psychology type model of intervention and primary prevention can be used by psychologists and psychiatrists to assist individuals and groups in coping with the stresses of change and can help institutions, agencies, and governments to provide culturally responsive programs for those suffering from the negative effects of rapid change.

Another major threat to well-being and peace in the Americas concerns conflicts over political and economic issues. Here again, mestizo psychology can be of assistance by offering a conceptual model of leadership training which encourages more harmonious and effective negotiations in international and intergroup relations. Through this model, concepts and conceptual frameworks which have evolved from the research of social scientists of the Americas are being applied in the form of assessment and training procedures which help encourage development of multicultural sensitivities, skills, and perceptions.

REFERENCES

Adler, P. S. Beyond cultural identity: Reflections on cultural and multicultural man. In R. Brislin (Ed.) *Topics in culture learning* (Vol. 2) University of Hawaii East-West Culture Learning Institute, 1974.

Berger, P., Berger, B., & Kellner, H. *The homeless mind: Modernization and consciousness*. New York: Vintage, 1973.

Bieri, J. Cognitive complexity and predictive behavior. *Journal of Abnormal and Social Psychology*, 1955, *51*, 263–268.

Bruner, J. S., & Perlmutter, H. V. Compatriot and foreigner: A study of impression formation in three countries. *Journal of Abnormal and Social Psychology*, 1957, *55*, 253–260.

Castaneda, A. Traditionalism, modernism, and ethnicity. In J. L. Martinez (Ed.), *Chicano psychology*. New York: Academic Press, 1977.

Cox, B. G., Macaulay, J., & Ramirez, M. *New frontiers: A bilingual early learning program*. New York: Pergamon Press, 1982.

Diaz-Guerrero, R. Neurosis and the Mexican family structure. *American Journal of Psychiatry*, 1955, *112*, 411–417.

Doell, S. R. The time and context instrument. Unpublished manuscript, University of Texas at Austin, 1982.

Fried, J. Acculturation and mental health among Indian migrants in Peru. In M. K. Opler (Ed.), *Culture and mental health*. New York: Macmillan, 1959.

Hall, E. T. *Beyond culture*. Garden City, N.Y.: Anchor, 1977.

Hallowell, A. I. The use of projective techniques in the study of the sociopsychological aspects of acculturation. *Journal of Projective Techniques*, 1951, *15*, 27–44.

Hartley, E. L. *Problems in prejudice*. New York: King's Crown Press, 1946.

Harvey, O. J., Hunt, D. E., & Schroder, H. M. *Conceptual systems and personality organization*. New York: John Wiley & Sons, 1961.

Inkeles, A., & Smith, D. H. *Becoming modern*. Cambridge, Mass.: Harvard University Press, 1974.

Iscoe, I. Community psychology and the competent community. *American Psychologist*, 1974, *29*, 607–613.

Madsen, W. The alcoholic agringado. *American Anthropologist*, 1964, *66*, 355–361.

Maris, P. *Loss and change*. Garden City, N.Y.: Anchor, 1975.

Nisbet, R. A. *Tradition and revolt*. New York: Vintage, 1970.

Pacheco, A., Wapner, S., & Lucca, J. Migration as a critical person-in-environment transition: An organismic-developmental interpretation. *Revista de ciencias sociales*, 1980, *1*, 123–157.

Paz, O. *The labyrinth of solitude*. New York: Grove Press, 1961.

Ramirez, M. Effect of sociometric rank, meaningfulness, and distinctiveness of cues on paired-associate learning. *Proceedings of the American Psychological Association*, 1967, 3–4.

Ramirez, M. Stereotypes and inter-American relations. Unpublished manuscript, University of Texas at Austin, 1981.

Ramirez, M., & Castaneda, A. *Cultural democracy, bicognitive development and education*. New York: Academic Press, 1974.

Ramirez, M., & Doell, S. R. The traditionalism-modernism inventory. Unpublished manuscript, University of Texas at Austin, 1982.

Ramirez, M., & Doell, S. R. A training program for the improvement of inter-American relations. University of Texas, (in progress)

Ramirez, M., Garza, R. T., & Cox, B. G. Multicultural leader behavior in ethnically mixed task groups. Unpublished technical report to Organizational Effectiveness Research Programs, Office of Naval Research, Arlington, Virginia, 1980.

Rappaport, J. *Community psychology: Values, research, and action*. New York: Holt, Rinehart and Winston, 1977.

Secord, P. R., & Backman, C. W. *Social psychology*. New York: McGraw-Hill, 1964.

Seguin, C. A. Migration and psychosomatic disadaptation. *Psychosomatic Medicine*, 1956, *18*, 404–409.

Vasconcellos, J. *La raza cósmica: Misión de la raza iberoamericana*. Barcelona: Agencia Mundial de Libreria, 1925.

Chapter 9
Conclusion

This book has presented the tenets and assumptions of a psychology and psychiatry of the future—theories and approaches which differ in many respects from the European world view-based personality psychology and psychiatry of the past. Whereas the European world view is a product of a modernistic ideology of the industrial era, the mestizo/Americas world view is more reflective of the balance between traditionalism and modernism which we are achieving in the postindustrial age. Whereas the old psychology and psychiatry are divisive, separating mind from body and natural science from phenomenological approaches, the new Americas psychology and psychiatry are synergistic. Whereas the European world view-based psychology and psychiatry are assimilationistic, the mestizo world view-based theories and approaches celebrate diversity and emphasize multicultural orientations to life.

THE PSYCHOLOGY OF THE AMERICAS AND MEGATRENDS

In his book, *Megatrends* (1982), John Nasbitt observes that American society is in the process of moving from the old to the new, and he identifies ten forces (the megatrends) which are shaping the structure of the new society. Most of these growth forces will also facilitate the acceptance of the tenets and approaches of the psychology and psychiatry of the Americas. Those forces of change which are most influential in promoting the growth and acceptance of the new psychology and psychiatry are:

1. The change from an industrial society toward an information society;
2. The shift from hierarchies to networks;
3. The trend from national economies to hemispheric and world economies;
4. The population and economic growth shift from North to South; and
5. The trend from either/or to multiple options in our lives.

The most important megatrend vis-à-vis acceptance and growth of the psychology of the Americas is the recent shift in growth of population, wealth, and economic activity from the northern and eastern regions of the

United States to the southeast, southwest, and west. The influence of European culture and ideology which was most pervasive when the center of population and economic development was in the north and east is giving way to the impact of cultures and ideologies of the southeastern, southwestern, and western regions of the United States, as well as to those of the Caribbean Basin, Latin America, and Asia. The shift in ideological influence is making Leopoldo Zea's (1943) dream a reality—a culture and philosophy unique to the Americas is beginning to emerge. This change in regional and global influence is also having the effect of making the cultures and life styles of certain peoples and groups more influential and visible in the Americas—namely, those of Hispanics, Indians, Asians, and those of monocultural/monolingual "psychological mestizos" who were influenced by the counterculture and the civil rights movements. The key to the new ideology is the acceptance and appreciation of diversity.

THE PSYCHOLOGY OF THE AMERICAS AND DIVERSITY

The psychology of the Americas is a psychology of diversity and a true psychology of individual differences. This new psychology rejects notions of cultural superiority; its motto is "You can learn something from everyone."

As Nasbitt (1982) has pointed out, in the current post-industrial society, the emphasis is on individual differences, on personalizing, and on paying more attention to individual needs and interests. The increase in technological sophistication in the new era is encouraging the development of a balance between high tech and high touch. Nasbitt observes:

> Ahead of us for a long period is an emphasis on high touch and comfort to counterbalance a world going mad with high technology. Uniformity in style, whether it is traditional or modern, will give way to great eclectic mix [p. 48]. . . The great lesson we must learn from the principle of high tech/high touch is a modern version of the ancient Greek ideal: balance [p. 40].

THE PSYCHOLOGY OF THE AMERICAS AND THE FUTURE OF THE WORLD

As has been noted in this book, diversity represents both the greatest opportunity and the greatest challenge for the Americas. Indeed, in the Americas as well as in other parts of the world, diversity represents the greatest challenge to attaining peace and harmony. The magnitude of this challenge is as obvious today in the Americas as it is in the Middle East, Eastern Europe, and Southeast Asia. The major questions of the 1980s are: "Can we work for the common goals of peace, quality of life, and equality of opportunity despite our diverse backgrounds, interests, and needs?" and "Will we reject totalitarian solutions to our present dilemmas?" As has been argued in this book, the answer lies in multiculturalism. The psychology of the Americas is a psychology of multiculturalism; it is a psychology which stresses mediation, synthesis, and synergism. The future of the Americas and the world depends on the degree of success which psychology and psychiatry will have in encouraging the development of multicultural orientations to life. For the first time in the history of the world, social scientists and mental health professionals hold the key to peace and understanding. Will we respond to this challenge?

REFERENCES

Nasbitt, J. *Megatrends*. New York: Warner Books, 1982.

Zea, L. *En torno a una filosofia Americana*. Mexico, D.F.: El Colegio de Mexico, 1943.

Appendix

Biculturalism/Multiculturalism Experience Inventory

PART I

1. Name: ______________________________

2. Address: ______________ ______________
(number, street) (city, state, zip code)

3. Phone Numbers: *Day*: __________ *Evening*: __________

4. Sex (check one): __ male __ female

5. Age: __

6. Date of Birth: ______ ____ ____
month day year

7. Place of Birth: ____ ____ ____
city state country

8. Father's Place of Birth: ____ ____ ____
city state country

9. Mother's Place of Birth: ____ ____ ____
city state country

10. Please indicate the ethnic background of the following persons (check where applicable):

	yourself	*father*	*mother*
Mexican-American/Chicano(a)/Latino			
Black			
Anglo/White			
Asian-American			
Native-American			
Other (specify)			

11. What school do you now attend? ______

12. What is your major? ______

13. What is your class standing? (check one): __ freshman __ sophomore __ junior __ senior __ graduate

14. Even if your are not currently active, what is your religious background? (check one) __ Catholic __ Protestant __ Jewish __ other: ________ (specify)

15. How many years have you lived in the United States: __

16. Have you lived in a country other than the United States? (check): __ yes __ no
    16a. If yes, which country or countries: ______
    16b. For how many years? __

17. Are you a resident of the state in which you attend school? (check one): yes __ no
    17a. If yes, how many years have you been a resident? ______

18. Have you lived in a state other than the one in which you attend school? (check one): __ yes __ no
    18a. If yes, which state or states? ______
    18b. For how many years? __

19. Where did you spend the first 15 years of your life? (list all places):

    ____

    ____

20. Where do you consider home? ____________________
city, town, or community

20a. How would you describe this community? (check one):
__ rural __ semi-rural __ semi-urban __ urban

21. What language(s) does your father speak? ____________________

22. What language(s) does your mother speak? ____________________

23. What language(s) do you speak? ____________________

24. How well do you speak Spanish? (check one): __ very fluently __ somewhat fluently __ can communicate basic ideas __ can speak only some basic words and phrases __ no knowledge of Spanish

25. How well do you speak English (check one): __ very fluently __ somewhat fluently __ can communicate basic ideas __ can speak only some basic words and phrases __ no knowledge of English

26. What language(s) do your parents speak at home? ____________________

27. What language(s) do you speak at home? ____________________

28. How many of the following do you have? younger brothers: __ younger sisters: __ older brothers: __ older sisters: __

29. What is the highest level of education achieved by each of your parents? (check one in each column):

	Father	*Mother*
less than high school		
some high school		
high school graduate		
some college		
college graduate		
advanced degree (for example, Ph.D., M.D.)		

30. Parents' occupation: (If retired, deceased, or unemployed, indicate former occupation)
    30a. Father's occupation: ________________
    30b. Mother's occupation: ________________

31. What is your marital status? (check one): __ never married __ divorced __ married __ separated __ widowed
    31a. If you are (were) married, what is (was) the ethnic background of your spouse? (check one):
    __ Mexican-American/Chicano/Latino __ Black __ Asian-American __ Native-American __ Anglo/White
    __ Other: ________ (specify)

32. Do you have relations who live in Latin America or in the Caribbean area? __ yes __ no
    32a. If yes, in what country? ________________

33. Do you have close friends who live in Latin America or in the Caribbean area? (check one) __ yes __ no
    33a. If yes, in what country? ________________

PART II

(Check appropriate choices)

34. The approximate ethnic composition of the high school I attended was
    __ 1. All Mexican Americans and/or Latinos
    __ 2. Mostly Mexican Americans and/or Latinos
    __ 3. Mexican Americans and/or Latinos about evenly
    __ 4. Mostly Anglos
    __ 5. All Anglos
    __ 6. Other (specify) ______

35. The ethnic composition of the neighborhood in which I grew up was
    __ 1. All Mexican American and/or Latinos
    __ 2. Mostly Mexican American and/or Latinos
    __ 3. Mexican American and/or Latinos about evenly
    __ 4. Mostly Anglos
    __ 5. All Anglos
    __ 6. Other (specify) ______

36. The ethnic composition of the neighborhood in which I now live is
 __ 1. All Mexican Americans and/or Latinos
 __ 2. Mostly Mexican Americans and/or Latinos
 __ 3. Mexican Americans and/or Latinos about evenly
 __ 4. Mostly Anglos
 __ 5. All Anglos
 __ 6. Other (specify) ______

37. At present, my close friends are
 __ 1. All Mexican Americans and/or Latinos
 __ 2. Mostly Mexican Americans and/or Latinos
 __ 3. Mexican Americans and/or Latinos about evenly
 __ 4. Mostly Anglos
 __ 5. All Anglos
 __ 6. Other (specify) ______

38. In elementary school, my close friends were
 __ 1. All Mexican Americans and/or Latinos
 __ 2. Mostly Mexican American and/or Latinos
 __ 3. Mexican Americans and/or Latinos about evenly
 __ 4. Mostly Anglos
 __ 5. All Anglos
 __ 6. Other (specify) ______

39. In high school, my close friends were
 __ 1. All Mexican Americans and/or Latinos
 __ 2. Mostly Mexican Americans and/or Latinos
 __ 3. Mexican Americans and/or Latinos and Anglos, about evenly
 __ 4. Mostly Anglos
 __ 5. All Anglos
 __ 6. Other (specify) ______

40. The ethnic background of the people I have dated is
 __ 1. All Mexican Americans and/or Latinos
 __ 2. Mostly Mexican American and/or Latinos
 __ 3. Mexican Americans and/or Latinos and Anglos, about evenly
 __ 4. Mostly Anglos
 __ 5. All Anglos
 __ 6. Other (specify) ______

41. The people with whom I have established close and meaningful relationships have been
 __ 1. All Mexican Americans and/or Latinos

— 2. Mostly Mexican Americans and/or Latinos
— 3. Mexican Americans and/or Latinos and Anglos, about evenly
— 4. Mostly Anglos
— 5. All Anglos
— 6. Other (specify) ______

42. When I am with my friends, I usually attend functions where the people are
— 1. All Mexican Americans and/or Latinos
— 2. Mostly Mexican Americans and/or Latinos
— 3. Mexican Americans and/or Latinos and Anglos, about evenly
— 4. Mostly Anglos
— 5. All Anglos
— 6. Other (specify) ______

43. At most of the functions I attend with my parents, the people are
— 1. All Mexican Americans and/or Latinos
— 2. Mostly Mexican Americans and/or Latinos
— 3. Mexican Americans and/or Latinos and Anglos, about evenly
— 4. Mostly Anglos
— 5. All Anglos
— 6. Other (specify) ______

44. My parents' close friends are
— 1. All Mexican Americans and/or Latinos
— 2. Mostly Mexican Americans and/or Latinos
— 3. Mexican Americans and/or Latinos and Anglos, about evenly
— 4. Mostly Anglos
— 5. All Anglos
— 6. Other (specify) ______

45. In the service, my close friends were
— 1. All Mexican Americans and/or Latinos
— 2. Mostly Mexican Americans and/or Latinos
— 3. Mexican Americans and/or Latinos and Anglos, about evenly
— 4. Mostly Anglos
— 5. All Anglos
— 6. Other (specify) ______

46. My childhood friends who visited in my home and related well to my parents were
— 1. All Mexican Americans and/or Latinos
— 2. Mostly Mexican Americans and/or Latinos

__ 3. Mexican Americans and/or Latinos and Anglos, about evenly
__ 4. Mostly Anglos
__ 5. All Anglos
__ 6. Other (specify) ______

47. My close friends at work are
__ 1. All Mexican Americans and/or Latinos
__ 2. Mostly Mexican Americans and/or Latinos
__ 3. Mexican Americans and/or Latinos and Anglos, about evenly
__ 4. Mostly Anglos
__ 5. All Anglos
__ 6. Other (specify) ______

48. The people where I work are
__ 1. All Mexican Americans and/or Latinos
__ 2. Mostly Mexican Americans and/or Latinos
__ 3. Mexican Americans and/or Latinos and Anglos, about evenly
__ 4. Mostly Anglos
__ 5. All Anglos
__ 6. Other (specify) ______
__ 7. Not employed

49. I enjoy going to gatherings at which the people are
__ 1. All Mexican Americans and/or Latinos
__ 2. Mostly Mexican Americans and/or Latinos
__ 3. Mexican Americans and/or Latinos and Anglos, about evenly
__ 4. Mostly Anglos
__ 5. All Anglos
__ 6. Other (specify) ______

50. The people who have most influenced me in my education have been
__ 1. All Mexican Americans and/or Latinos
__ 2. Mostly Mexican Americans and/or Latinos
__ 3. Mexican Americans and/or Latinos and Anglos, about evenly
__ 4. Mostly Anglos
__ 5. All Anglos
__ 6. Other (specify) ______

51. When I study with others, I usually study with
__ 1. All Mexican Americans and/or Latinos
__ 2. Mostly Mexican Americans and/or Latinos
__ 3. Mexican Americans and/or Latinos and Anglos, about evenly
__ 4. Mostly Anglos

— 5. All Anglos
— 6. Other (specify) ______

52. In the job(s) I have had, my close friends have been
— 1. All Mexican Americans and/or Latinos
— 2. Mostly Mexican Americans and/or Latinos
— 3. Mexican Americans and/or Latinos and Anglos, about evenly
— 4. Mostly Anglos
— 5. All Anglos
— 6. Other (specify) ______

53. When I have attended churches, the pastor and church members have been
— 1. All Mexican Americans and/or Latinos
— 2. Mostly Mexican Americans and/or Latinos
— 3. Mexican Americans and/or Latinos and Anglos, about evenly
— 4. Mostly Anglos
— 5. All Anglos
— 6. Other (specify) ______

54. When I am involved in group discussions where I am expected to participate, I prefer a group made up of
— 1. All Mexican Americans and/or Latinos
— 2. Mostly Mexican Americans and/or Latinos
— 3. Mexican Americans and/or Latinos and Anglos, about evenly
— 4. Mostly Anglos
— 5. All Anglos
— 6. Other (specify) ______

55. The ethnic affiliation of the priests, ministers, nuns, or other clergymen who have influenced my life have been
— 1. All Mexican Americans and/or Latinos
— 2. Mostly Mexican Americans and/or Latinos
— 3. Mexican Americans and/or Latinos and Anglos, about evenly
— 4. Mostly Anglos
— 5. All Anglos
— 6. Other (specify) ______

56. The teachers and counselors with whom I have had the closest relationships have been
— 1. All Mexican Americans and/or Latinos
— 2. Mostly Mexican and/or Latinos
— 3. Mexican American and/or Latinos and Anglos, about evenly

__ 4. Mostly Anglos
__ 5. All Anglos
__ 6. Other (specify) ______

57. I have attended functions that are predominantly Anglo in nature
__ 1. Extensively
__ 2. Frequently
__ 3. Occasionally
__ 4. Seldom
__ 5. Never

58. In the community where I grew up, I interacted with Anglos
__ 1. Extensively
__ 2. Frequently
__ 3. Occasionally
__ 4. Seldom
__ 5. Never

59. In the community where I grew up, I interacted with Mexican Americans and/or Latinos
__ 1. Extensively
__ 2. Frequently
__ 3. Occasionally
__ 4. Seldom
__ 5. Never

60. I visit the homes of Anglos (not relatives)
__ 1. Very often
__ 2. Often
__ 3. Occasionally
__ 4. Seldom
__ 5. Never

61. I invite Anglos to my home (not relatives)
__ 1. Very often
__ 2. Often
__ 3. Occasionally
__ 4. Seldom
__ 5. Never

62. I visit the homes of Mexican Americans and/or Latinos (not relatives)
__ 1. Very often
__ 2. Often

— 3. Occasionally
— 4. Seldom
— 5. Never

63. I invite Mexican Americans and/or Latinos to my home (not relatives)
— 1. Very often
— 2. Often
— 3. Occasionally
— 4. Seldom
— 5. Never

64. At social gatherings, I speak Spanish
— 1. Always
— 2. Most of the time
— 3. Occasionally
— 4. Seldom
— 5. Never

65. When in public, I speak Spanish
— 1. Always
— 2. Most of the time
— 3. Occasionally
— 4. Seldom
— 5. Never

66. I visit in Latin America and/or the Caribbean Basin
— 1. Very often (about once a month)
— 2. Often (several times a year)
— 3. Occasionally (once or twice a year)
— 4. Seldom (less than once a year)
— 5. Never

67. I visit relatives and/or close friends in Latin America and/or the Caribbean Basin
— 1. Very often (about once a month)
— 2. Often (several times a year)
— 3. Occasionally (once or twice a year)
— 4. Seldom (less than once a year)
— 5. Never

68. Relatives and/or close friends from Latin America and/or the Caribbean Basin visit me
   __ 1. Very often (about once a month)
   __ 2. Often (several times a year)
   __ 3. Occasionally (once or twice a year)
   __ 4. Seldom (less than once a year)
   __ 5. Never

69. I have attended functions that are predominantly Mexican American and/or Latino in nature
   __ 1. Extensively
   __ 2. Frequently
   __ 3. Occasionally
   __ 4. Seldom
   __ 5. Never

Name Index*

* The Name Index has two types of page references; italicized references denote bibliographic references; those not italicized refer to references to that person.

Subject Index

About the Author

Manuel Ramirez, III received his Ph.D. in Clinical Psychology from the University of Texas at Austin in 1963. He has taught at California State University at Sacramento, Rice University, Pitzer College of the Claremont Colleges, the University of Puerto Rico, the University of California at Riverside and the University of California at Santa Cruz. Dr. Ramirez is presently Professor of Psychology, Associate Director of the Institute for Human Development and Family Studies and Special Campus Consultant to the Hogg Foundation for Mental Health at the University of Texas at Austin. Ramirez has done research and intervention work in Mexico and Puerto Rico and also with Latinos, Native Americans and Blacks in the United States. He has done pioneer work in the development of mestizo psychology and he sponsored the first conference on Hispanic psychology in the United States in 1972. Ramirez is known for his research on the relationship of culture to cognitive styles and for his work on the psychodynamics of biculturalism/multiculturalism. He recently completed a review of all research and intervention programs for Hispanics funded by The Alcohol, Drug Abuse and Mental Health Administration of the Department of Health and Human Services. He is co-author of *New Frontiers* a bilingual/multicultural program in early childhood education published by Pergamon Press and he is consulting editor of the *InterAmerican Journal of Psychology* and the *Hispanic Journal of Behavioral Sciences*.

Pergamon General Psychology Series

Editors: Arnold P. Goldstein, Syracuse University
Leonard Krasner, SUNY at Stony Brook

Vol. 1. WOLPE—*The Practice of Behavior Therapy, Third Edition*
Vol. 2. MAGOON *et al*--*Mental Health Counselors at Work*
Vol. 3. McDANIEL—*Physical Disability and Human Behavior, Second Edition*
Vol. 4. KAPLAN *et al*—*The Structural Approach in Psychological Testing*
Vol. 5. LaFAUCI & RICHTER—*Team Teaching at the College Level*
Vol. 6. PEPINSKY *et al*—*People and Information*
Vol. 7. SIEGMAN & POPE—*Studies in Dyadic Communication*
Vol. 8. JOHNSON—*Existential Man: The Challenge of Psychotherapy*
Vol. 9. TAYLOR—*Climate for Creativity*
Vol. 10. RICKARD—*Behavioral Intervention in Human Problems*
Vol. 14. GOLDSTEIN—*Psychotherapeutic Attraction*
Vol. 15. HALPERN—*Survival: Black/White*
Vol. 16. SALZINGER & FELDMAN—*Studies in Verbal Behavior: An Empirical Approach*
Vol. 17. ADAMS & BOARDMAN—*Advances in Experimental Clinical Psychology*
Vol. 18. ZILLER—*The Social Self*
Vol. 19. LIBERMAN—*A Guide to Behavioral Analysis and Therapy*
Vol. 22. PEPINSKY & PATTON—*The Psychological Experiment: A Practical Accomplishment*
Vol. 23. YOUNG—*New Sources of Self*
Vol. 24. WATSON—*Child Behavior Modification: A Manual for Teachers, Nurses, and Parents*
Vol. 25. NEWBOLD—*The Psychiatric Programming of People: Neo-Behavioral Orthomolecular Psychiatry*
Vol. 26. ROSSI—*Dreams and the Growth of Personality: Expanding Awareness in Psychotherapy*
Vol. 27. O'LEARY & O'LEARY—*Classroom Management: The Successful Use of Behavior Modification, Second Edition*
Vol. 28. FELDMAN—*College and Student: Selected Readings in the Social Psychology of Higher Education*
Vol. 29. ASHEM & POSER—*Adaptive Learning: Behavior Modification with Children*
Vol. 30. BURCK *et al*—*Counseling and Accountability: Methods and Critique*
Vol. 31. FREDERIKSEN *et al*—*Prediction of Organizational Behavior*
Vol. 32. CATTELL—*A New Morality from Science: Beyondism*
Vol. 33. WEINER—*Personality: The Human Potential*
Vol. 34. LIEBERT, SPRAFKIN & DAVIDSON—*The Early Window: Effects of Television on Children and Youth, Second Edition*
Vol. 35. COHEN *et al*—*Psych City: A Simulated Community*
Vol. 36. GRAZIANO—*Child Without Tomorrow*
Vol. 37. MORRIS—*Perspectives in Abnormal Behavior*
Vol. 38. BALLER—*Bed Wetting: Origins and Treatment*
Vol. 40. KAHN, CAMERON & GIFFEN—*Psychological Methods in Evaluation and Counseling*
Vol. 41. SEGALL—*Human Behavior and Public Policy: A Political Psychology*

Vol. 42. FAIRWEATHER *et al—Creating Change in Mental Health Organizations*
Vol. 43. KATZ & ZLUTNICK—*Behavior Therapy and Health Care: Principles and Applications*
Vol. 44. EVANS & CLAIBORN—*Mental Health Issues and the Urban Poor*
Vol. 45. HILLNER—*Psychology of Learning: A Conceptual Approach*
Vol. 46. BARBER, SPANOS & CHAVES—*Hypnosis, Imagination and Human Potentialities*
Vol. 47. POPE—*The Mental Health Interview*
Vol. 48. PELTON—*The Psychology of Nonviolence*
Vol. 49. COLBY—*Artificial Paranoia—A Computer Simulation of Paranoid Processes*
Vol. 50. GELFAND & HARTMANN—*Child Behavior Analysis and Therapy*
Vol. 51. WOLPE—*Theme and Variations: A Behavior Therapy Casebook*
Vol. 52. KANFER & GOLDSTEIN—*Helping People Change: A Textbook of Methods, Second Edition*
Vol. 53. DANZIGER—*Interpersonal Communication*
Vol. 54. KATZ—*Towards the Elimination of Racism*
Vol. 55. GOLDSTEIN & STEIN—*Prescriptive Psychotherapies*
Vol. 56. HERSEN & BARLOW—*Single-Case Experimental Designs: Strategies for Studying Behavior Changes*
Vol. 57. MONAHAN—*Community Mental Health and the Criminal Justice System*
Vol. 58. WAHLER, HOUSE & STAMBAUGH—*Ecological Assessment of Child Behavior: A Clinical Package for Home, School, and Institutional Settings*
Vol. 59. MAGARO—*The Construction of Madness—Emerging Conceptions and Interventions into the Psychotic Process*
Vol. 60. MILLER—*Behavioral Treatment of Alcoholism*
Vol. 61. FOREYT—*Behavioral Treatments of Obesity*
Vol. 62. WANDERSMAN, POPPEN & RICKS—*Humanism and Behaviorism: Dialogue and Growth*
Vol. 63. NIETZEL, WINETT, MACDONALD & DAVIDSON—*Behavioral Approaches to Community Psychology*
Vol. 64. FISHER & GOCHROS—*Handbook of Behavior Therapy with Sexual Problems. Vol. 1: General Procedures. Vol II: Approaches to Specific Problems*
Vol. 65. HERSEN & BELLACK—*Behavioral Assessment: A Practical Handbook, Second Edition*
Vol. 66. LEFKOWITZ, ERON, WALDER & HUESMANN—*Growing Up to Be Violent: A Longitudinal Study of the Development of Aggression*
Vol. 67. BARBER—*Pitfalls in Human Research: Ten Pivotal Points*
Vol. 68. SILVERMAN—*The Human Subject in the Psychological Laboratory*
Vol. 69. FAIRWEATHER & TORNATZKY—*Experimental Methods for Social Policy Research*
Vol. 70. GURMAN & RAZIN—*Effective Psychotherapy: A Handbook of Research*
Vol. 71. MOSES & BYHAM—*Applying the Assessment Center Method*
Vol. 72. GOLDSTEIN—*Prescriptions for Child Mental Health and Education*
Vol. 73. KEAT—*Multimodal Therapy with Children*
Vol. 74. SHERMAN—*Personality: Inquiry & Application*
Vol. 75. GATCHEL & PRICE—*Clinical Applications of Biofeedback: Appraisal and Status*

Vol. 76. CATALANO—*Health, Behavior and the Community: An Ecological Perspective*
Vol. 77. NIETZEL—*Crime and Its Modification: A Social Learning Perspective*
Vol. 78. GOLDSTEIN, HOYER & MONTI—*Police and the Elderly*
Vol. 79. MIRON & GOLDSTEIN—*Hostage*
Vol. 80. GOLDSTEIN *et al*—*Police Crisis Intervention*
Vol. 81. UPPER & CAUTELA—*Covert Conditioning*
Vol. 82. MORELL—*Program Evaluation in Social Research*
Vol. 83. TEGER—*Too Much Invested to Quit*
Vol. 84. MONJAN & GASSNER—*Critical Issues in Competency-Based Education*
Vol. 85. KRASNER—*Environmental Design and Human Behavior: A Psychology of the Individual in Society*
Vol. 86. TAMIR—*Communication and the Aging Process: Interaction Throughout the Life Cycle*
Vol. 87. WEBSTER, KONSTANTAREAS, OXMAN & MACK—*Autism: New Directions in Research and Education*
Vol. 88. TRIESCHMANN—*Spinal Cord Injuries: Psychological, Social and Vocational Adjustment*
Vol. 89. CARTLEDGE & MILBURN—*Teaching Social Skills to Children: Innovative Approaches*
Vol. 90. SARBIN & MANCUSO—*Schizophrenia—Medical Diagnosis or Moral Verdict?*
Vol. 91. RATHJEN & FOREYT—*Social Competence: Interventions for Children and Adults*
Vol. 92. VAN DE RIET, KORB & GORRELL—*Gestalt Therapy: An Introduction*
Vol. 93. MARSELLA & PEDERSEN—*Cross-Cultural Counseling and Psychotherapy*
Vol. 94. BRISLIN—*Cross-Cultural Encounters: Face-to-Face Interaction*
Vol. 95 SCHWARTZ & JOHNSON—*Psychopathology of Childhood: A Clinical-Experimental Approach*
Vol. 96. HEILBRUN—*Human Sex-Role Behavior*
Vol. 97. DAVIDSON, KOCH, LEWIS & WRESINSKI—*Evaluation Strategies in Criminal Justice*
Vol. 98. GOLDSTEIN, CARR, DAVIDSON, WEHR—*In Response to Aggression: Methods of Control and Prosocial Alternatives*
Vol. 99. GOLDSTEIN—*Psychological Skill Training: The Structured Learning Technique*
Vol. 100. WALKER—*Clinical Practice of Psychology: A Guide for Mental Health Professionals*
Vol. 101. ANCHIN & KIESLER—*Handbook of Interpersonal Psychotherapy*
Vol. 102. GELLER, WINETT, EVERETT—*Preserving the Environment: New Strategies for Behavior Change*
Vol. 103. JENKINS—*The Psychology of the Afro-American: A Humanistic Approach*
Vol. 104. APTER—*Troubled Children/Troubled Systems*
Vol. 105. BRENNER—*The Effective Psychotherapist: Conclusions from Practice and Research*
Vol. 106. KAROLY & KANFER—*Self-Management and Behavior Change: From Theory to Practice*
Vol. 107. O'BRIEN, DICKINSON, ROSOW—*Industrial Behavior Modification: A Management Handbook*

Vol. 108. AMABILE & STUBBS—*Psychological Research in the Classroom: Issues for Educators and Researchers*
Vol. 109. WARREN—*Auditory Perception: A New Synthesis*
Vol. 110. DiMATTEO & DiNICOLA—*Achieving Patient Compliance: The Psychology of the Medical Practitioner's Role*
Vol. 111. CONOLEY & CONOLEY—*School Consultation: A Guide to Practice and Training*
Vol. 112. PAPAJOHN—*Intensive Behavior Therapy: The Behavioral Treatment of Complex Emotional Disorders*
Vol. 113. KAROLY, STEFFEN, O'GRADY—*Child Health Psychology: Concepts and Issues*
Vol. 114. MORRIS & KRATOCHWILL—*Treating Children's Fears and Phobias: A Behavioral Approach*
Vol. 115. GOLDSTEIN & SEGALL—*Aggression in Global Perspective*
Vol. 116. LANDIS & BRISLIN—*Handbook of Intercultural Training*
Vol. 117. FARBER—*Stress and Burnout in the Human Service Professions*
Vol. 118. BEUTLER—*Eclectic Psychotherapy: A Systematic Approach*
Vol. 119. HARRIS—*Families of the Developmentally Disabled: A Guide to Behavioral Interventions*
Vol. 120. HERSEN, KAZDIN, BELLACK—*The Clinical Psychology Handbook*
Vol. 121. MATSON & MULICK—*Handbook of Mental Retardation*
Vol. 122. FELNER, JASON, MORITSUGU, FARBER—*Preventive Psychology: Theory, Research and Practice*
Vol. 123. CENTER FOR RESEARCH ON AGGRESSION—*Prevention and Control of Aggression*
Vol. 124. MORRIS & KRATOCHWILL—*The Practice of Child Therapy*
Vol. 125. VARNI—*Clinical Behavioral Pediatrics: An Interdisciplinary Biobehavioral Approach*
Vol. 126. RAMIREZ—*Psychology of the Americas: Mestizo Perspectives on Personality and Mental Health*
Vol. 127. LEWINSOHN & TERI—*Clinical Geropsychology: New Directions in Assessment and Treatment*
Vol. 128. BARLOW, HAYES, NELSON—*The Scientist Practitioner: Research and Accountability in Clinical and Educational Settings*
Vol. 129. OLLENDICK & HERSEN—*Child Behavioral Assessment: Priniciples and Procedures*

NATIONAL UNIVERSITY
LIBRARY

c2 099691

VISTA LIBRARY

BF
698.9
C8
R35
1983 c2

Ramírez, Manuel,
1937-

Psychology of the
Americas

	DATE DUE		
MAY 1	1988		
JUL 0	1990		
MAR 04	199		